[redacted]

[redacted]

GAY RIGHTS OR WRONGS

GAY RIGHTS OR WRONGS

A Christian's Guide to Homosexual Issues and Ministry

Michael Mazzalongo, Editor

COLLEGE PRESS
PUBLISHING COMPANY
Joplin, Missouri

Printed and Bound in the
United States of America

Library of Congress Cataloging-in-Publication Data

Gay rights or wrongs: a Christian's guide to homosexual issues and ministry / Michael Mazzalongo, editor.
p. cm.
Includes bibliographical references.
ISBN 0-89900-731-7
1. Homosexuality—Religious aspects—Christianity. 2. Gay rights—Religious aspects—Christianity. 3. Church work with gays. I. Mazzalongo, Michael, 1947–
BR115.H6G38 1995
261.8'35766—dc20 95-8743
CIP

Table of Contents

Preface - Michael Mazzalongo, Editor. 7

Acknowledgments 8

PART I - HISTORY AND POLITICS
Chapter 1 - Homosexuality in the Past 11
Dr. J. Estep

Chapter 2 - The Politics of Pleasure 33
Dr. F. LaGard Smith

PART II - CAUSES AND CHANGE
Chapter 3 - The Causes of Homosexual Behavior 51
Dr. J.D. Robertson

Chapter 4 - Can Homosexuals Change? 67
Dr. J.D. Robertson

PART III - AIDS
Chapter 5 - The AIDS Agenda 83
Dr. F. LaGard Smith

Chapter 6 - AIDS: There will Never be a Cure! 107
James Taylor

PART IV - HOMOSEXUALITY AND THE BIBLE
Chapter 7 - Gay Theology? 127
Dr. F. LaGard Smith

Chapter 8 - The Bible Does Have Something to Say about Homosexuality 147
Dr. Carl Bridges, Jr.

Chapter 9 - Answering Pro-Gay Theology 171
Joe Dallas

PART V - MINISTRY TO HOMOSEXUALS
Chapter 10 - The Dynamics of Change 189
Bob Davies and Lori Rentzel

Chapter 11 - Ministering to People With AIDS 205
Mike Hawkins

Chapter 12 - For the Church: Conflict, Conviction and Compassion 219
Joe Dallas

APPENDIXES - RESOURCES
Appendix A - Complete reading list of books dealing exclusively with Gay and sexual issues .241

Appendix B - Ministry Network information for U.S., Canada, Europe 247

Contributors 289

Preface

This book brings together teachers, psychologists, ministers and other qualified men and women who have studied (and for some experienced) homosexuality over a long period of time.

It is hoped that this work will generate the kind of understanding necessary to be able to deal compassionately with the people who struggle with homosexuality. It is also my aim to equip the members of the church with the confidence to respond intelligently to the false arguments being made for the homosexual lifestyle by Gays and their sympathizers.

Michael Mazzalongo
Oklahoma City, 1995

Acknowledgments

I would like to thank the following people who have helped bring this book to completion.

Dr. Philip Patterson, who graciously encouraged my initial involvement.

Jeff and Leslie Jones of First Stone Ministeries from whom I learned about ministry to homosexuals and lesbians.

Jimmy Shepherd who provided the computer support.

Laura Eckert who worked in reviewing the final version.

Of course, the contributors, without whose dedication and humble spirit this project would not exist.

And finally, our Lord Jesus Christ whose love is the substance of my hope.

Part One

HISTORY AND POLITICS

CHAPTER ONE

HOMOSEXUALITY IN THE PAST

Dr. James R. Estep

In this first chapter, Dr. Estep traces homosexual behavior in ancient cultures until modern times. Dr. Estep is assistant Professor of Christian Education at Great Lakes Christian College in Michigan.

A. HOMOSEXUALITY IN THE ANCIENT NEAR EAST

Homosexuality was practiced in various forms in many ancient civilizations. It is not possible to trace the roots of this behavior to every nation but there were obvious signs of its existence within the societies that neighbored the Israelites in Old Testament times. These societies are a good starting point to follow the development of homosexuality into the present age.

1. Homosexuality in Mesopotamia

Mesopotamia represents a diversity of perspectives and opinions on homosexual conduct. In early Mesopotamia, homosexual conduct apparently received little attention. The earliest legal code known to humanity, the Code of Hammurabi (second millennium B.C.), is from ancient Mesopotamia and makes no mention of homosexual practices. However, later Mesopotamian law is not silent on the subject.

• *Homosexuality in the City of Sumer*: Perhaps the most ancient reference to homosexual conduct is contained in Sumerian legal documents. According to Sumerian law, wives had narrow legal rights in the marriage relationship. For example, adultery could *only* be committed by the wife against the husband, not *vice versa*; similarly divorce could only be initiated by the husband (as was the practice of Roman law centuries later). *However*, one legal document *possibly* suggests that special provisions were made in the event that a woman's husband was found to be a homosexual. Under such circumstances, a wife was permitted to divorce her husband and receive full benefits.

• *Homosexuality in Assyria*: Homosexuality was indeed present in Assyrian society, but was curiously absent from all Babylonian legal codes.[1] Some ancient Assyrian texts contain prayers for divine blessing on homosexual relationships,[2] while others suggest that homosexual prostitution was permitted, possibly on a ritualistic basis, and homosexual prostitutes were regular participants in public processionals.[3] However, as will be demonstrated, homosexual conduct was not always respected in Assyrian culture, and was even considered criminal in some instances.

For example, one Assyrian law deals with the offense of committing homosexual acts with a neighbor. The text considers such an act an offense against the state, and further stipulates that "If he is formally convicted, [he is subjected] to a twofold penalty, namely to be treated in the same way as he has treated his *victim* and to be made a eunuch."[4]

---

[1] G. R. Driver and John C. Miles, *The Assyrian Laws* (Oxford: Clarendon Press, 1935), p. 71.

[2] Wenham, G. J. "The Old Testament Attitude to Homosexuality," *Expository Times* (September 1991), p. 360.

[3] Ibid.

[4] Driver and Miles, p. 71.

• *The "Dog" in Mesopotamian Ritualistic Culture:* Mesopotamian texts also use the word dog as a metaphor for male homosexual prostitution.[5] It similarly occurs in Akkadian, Phoenician, Ugaritic, Arabic, Aramaic, Syriac, and Ethiopic texts.[6] While some have argued that the term applies to sacred *heterosexual* prostitution,[7] most scholars (including those who support Christian homosexuality) completely reject this interpretation.[8]

This particular element of Near East culture has direct relevance to the biblical text. Deuteronomy 23:18 (RSV) warns the Israelites not to the pay "the wages of a dog (כֶּלֶב, *kelebh*)," a phrase which is considered to be a euphemism for a sacred male prostitute,[9] which the immediate context would support.[10] This understanding is reflected in several other ancient cultures.

Summary of Mesopotamian Homosexuality

Bottero and Peschow, preeminent Assyriologists who did the first serious study of homosexuality in Assyrian legal codes, conclude as follows:

> Homosexuality in itself is thus nowhere condemned . . . Anyone could practice it freely, just as anyone could visit a prostitute, provided it was done without violence and without compulsion, and preferably as far as taking the passive role was concerned, with specialists.[11]

---

[5] Wenham, p. 362. Cf. Revelation 22:15 for possible reference.

[6] D. Winton Thomas, "*Kelebh* 'Dog': Its Origin and Some Usages of it in the Old Testament," *Vestus Testamentum* (1960), p. 410.

[7] Cf. Robin Scroggs, *The New Testament and Homosexuality* (Philadelphia: Fortress Press, 1983), p. 86; Bailey, pp. 52-53.

[8] Tom Horner, *Jonathan Loved David* (Philadelphia: Westminster Press, 1978), p. 66; John J. McNeil, *The Church and the Homosexual* (Kansas City: Sheed, Andrews, and McMeel, 1976), p. 57.

[9] Cf. P. C. Craige, *The Book of Deuteronomy (NICOT)* (Grand Rapids: Eerdman Publishing Company, 1976), p. 302; S. R. Driver, *Deuteronomy* (ICC) (Edinburgh: T & T Clark, 1902), pp. 264-265.

[10] G. Ernest Wright, "Deuteronomy," *Interpreter's Bible* (Nashville: Abingdon Press, 1953), p. 473.

[11] Bottero and Petschow, "Homosexualitat," *Reallexicon der Assyriologie*, 4.462 as cited in Wenham, p. 360.

However, this conclusion fails to note one significant factor: While it may have been *legal* in some cases, it was never fully accepted by Assyrian society. For example, D.S. Bailey comments: "Passive sodomy was evidently regarded as reprehensible, no less than criminal."[12] Regardless of the scholars' debates, two conclusions are obvious: (1) Homosexuality was a concern of the Mesopotamian cultures, and (2) Homosexual conduct carried with it a negative social stigma, to some degree, since it was considered slander to falsely accuse someone of committing passive homosexual acts.

2. Homosexuality in Egypt

Homosexual conduct was indeed present in ancient Egypt, as demonstrated by a variety of sources. Gravestones of old friends contain references that seem to indicate homosexual relationships, and their desire for it to continue in the afterlife.[13] Unlike the Greco-Roman culture, the pictographic evidence of homosexuality in Egypt is scant and vague; hence we must rely on the literary sources.[14] Herodotus, the Greek historian, noted what he considered to be strange sexual practices in Egypt, including necrophilia and bestiality, but made no mention of homosexuality.[15] However, literary evidence does attest to the practice of both male and female homosexuality in Egypt, particularly in military and religious contexts.

• *Homosexuality in Military Contexts*: In Egypt, homosexual intercourse was considered a sign of defeat and humiliation, and was often used to demonstrate superiority over a fallen enemy.[16] It was almost expected that the victorious armies

---

[12] Bailey, p. 34.

[13] Wenham, p. 361.

[14] Lise Mannichie, *Sexual Life in Ancient Egypt* (New York: KPI, 1987), p. 22.

[15] Herodotus, *Histories*, 2.46.89.

[16] Vern L. Bullough, "Homosexuality as Submissive Behavior: Example from Mythology," *The Journal of Sex Research* (November 1973),pp. 283-288.

would commit homosexual rape on their vanquished enemy as a means of humiliation, since homosexual conduct was regarded as an indignity.[17] For example, a death spell of the fifth and sixth dynasty Pharaohs commanded: "Go forth, plant thyself on him [the enemy] that he may not copulate with thee."[18] The passive partner was always viewed as being powerless or conquered.[19] However, this is not to imply that homosexuality was an acceptable practice in *all* military contexts. For example, Pharaoh Neferkare was disgraced by spending the night with his generals, possibly due to unequal social status, but definitely due to his sexual exploits with them.[20]

• *Homosexuality in Religious Contexts*: Homosexuality in Egyptian religion can be attributed to the gods Seth and Horus. Their legendary sexual encounter had a significant influence on the social customs of the Egyptians, since it supplied a religious impetus for homosexual activity.[21] In the mythological account of the conflict (first created in 1900 B.C.) between Seth and his younger brother Horus, Seth commits a homosexual act with his archrival Horus, and later demands the office of ruler claiming he had "performed doughty deeds of war" against Horus.[22] The intercourse was obviously anal, given the description in "*The Contendings of Horus and Seth.*"[23] It is for this reason that in Egyptian literature the god Seth is always associated with abnormal sexual acts, including homosexuality.[24]

A second aspect of homosexuality in the religious life of

---

[17] Horner, p. 21; Bailey, p. 31.

[18] *Utterance* p. 371 (652a).

[19] Ronald M. Springett, *Homosexuality in History and the Scriptures* (Washington D.C.: Biblical Research Institute, 1988), p. 36.

[20] Wenham, p. 361.

[21] Springett, p. 39.

[22] Bailey, p. 31.

[23] Bullough, pp. 285-286.

[24] Springett, p. 37.

ancient Egypt exists. *The Book of the Dead* (1550-950 B.C.) records a confessional formula for righteousness which contains two clear references to male homosexual practices:

> "I have not had sexual relations with a boy."[25]

> "O His-Face-Behind-Him, who comes forth from *Tep-het-djat*, I have not *been perverted*; I have not had sexual relations with a boy."[26]

Obviously the pleas for righteousness are referring to the abstaining from pederasty, i.e., homosexual relationship with a minor. Some view these denials of homosexual behavior as being simply magical or ritual formulas; but some Egyptian cities did in fact have local prohibitions on such activities.[27]

Similarly, two references are made to lesbian sexual relations in Egyptian literature, being made in a similar context to those mentioned above, and reflecting the same negative sentiments:

> "I [a female] have not had intercourse with any woman in the sacred places of my city god."

> "If she dreams that a woman has intercourse with her, she will come to a bad end."[28]

The first citations may possibly be referring to ritualistic prostitution, but nonetheless given negative connotations. The second indeed does demonstrate a negative social connotation to one having homosexual thoughts or fantasies.

Summary of Egyptian Homosexuality

Homosexual practices, both male and female, seem to have carried a negative connotation in ancient Egypt, and in

---

[25] "Book of the Dead," A20 in James B. Pritchard, *Ancient Near Eastern Texts* (Princeton: Princeton University Press, 1969) p. 34.

[26] "Book of the Dead," B27 in Pritchard, p. 35 [emphasis added].

[27] Mannichie, p. 22.

[28] Ibid.

fact, based on our discussion of *The Book of the Dead* confessionals, threatened their afterlife. Even D. S. Bailey concluded: "The ancient Egyptians regarded homosexual practices as in some degree morally objectionable and personally degrading."[29] Egypt's attitude toward homosexual conduct was indeed dissenting.

3. Homosexuality in Canaanite and Hittite Cultures

Due to the absence of significant literary or pictographic materials from Palestine and Asia Minor, little is known about the perceptions of homosexuality by their inhabitants. Even the literary discoveries from the ancient city of Ugarit make *no* mention of homosexual conduct. The Old Testament itself seems to indicate the immoral sexual preferences of the Canaanites in the Mosaic Law, "and if the story of Sodom (Gen 19) is supposed to illustrate Canaanite practices, the insinuation is even clearer."[30] Hence, the attitudes and legal codes regarding homosexuality in ancient Canaanite and Hittite cultures seem to reflect that of their Egyptian and Mesopotamian neighbors.

Hittite laws seem to reflect the same posturing as the Assyrian legal codes. They did not categorically forbid homosexual relations. Rather, they sought to place limitations on them, e.g., homosexual practices were prohibited between a father and a son or between close relatives. Hittite Tablet 2.189 reads: "If a man sins [i.e., has sexual relations] with a son, [it is] an abomination."[31] However, this prohibition may primarily be due to *the incestuous* relationship, and not the homosexuality.[32]

Summary of Canaanite/Hittite Homosexuality

In both Canaanite and Hittite cultures, homosexuality

---

[29] Bailey, p. 33.

[30] Wenham, p. 361.

[31] Ibid; Springett, p. 46 and fn. 54.

[32] H. A. Hoffner, "Incest, Sodomy, and Bestiality in the Ancient Near East," *Orient and Occident* (Neukirchen: Neukirchen Verlag, 1973), p. 83.

was connected to religion and fertility, which were frequently equated. "Homosexual activity and bestiality were considered ways of having intercourse with the gods and thus affecting the course of nature."[33] Occasionally, men would commit sexual acts with other men dressed as women, supposedly to simulate fertility.[34] Hence, the Canaanite and Hittite cultures contain the sacred aspect of homosexual conduct similar to that of the Egyptians, but without the negative connotations associated with it.

B. HOMOSEXUAL CONDUCT IN THE GRECO-ROMAN CULTURE

Never has homosexual behavior been so tolerated, accepted, and even institutionalized in Western civilization as it was during the Greco-Roman period (4th century B.C. to 5th century A.D.). In fact, even before the establishment of the Hellenistic world by Alexander the Great in 333 B.C., homosexual activities "had a relatively prominent place in Greek social life" by the sixth century B.C.[35] Homosexual practices ranged from pederasty (male homosexual intercourse with a male adolescent), adult homosexual conduct, pederastic and adult homosexual prostitution, homosexual religious rituals, lesbianism, homosexual rape, and simply practicing homosexual behavior for sexual pleasure.[36]

A predominant feature of homosexual conduct in the Greco-Roman world was the incredible openness at which it was done and the public acceptance of it.[37] John Boswell, a

---

[33] Springett, p. 48.

[34] Ibid, p. 47-48.

[35] Victor Paul Furnish, *the Moral Teaching of Paul: Selected Issues* (Nashville: Abingdon Press, 1985), p. 58.

[36] Cf. Ronald M. Springett, *Homosexuality in History and the Scriptures* (Washington D.C.: Biblical Research Institute, 1988), p. 104.

[37] William Durant, *Life of Greece* (New York: Simon and Schuster, 1944), pp. 301-302.

history professor at Yale University and self-avowed homosexual, comments:

> Gay people were in a strict sense a minority, but neither they nor their contemporaries regarded their inclinations as harmful, bizarre, immoral, or threatening, and they were fully integrated into Roman life and culture at every level.[38]

1. Forms of Homosexual Practice in Greco-Roman Culture

As in contemporary American culture, homosexual conduct was not limited to any one fashion or another, but was practiced in a variety of forms. The three most prevalent forms, which will be discussed in this section, are (1) Lesbianism, i.e., female homosexual practices, (2) Pederasty, i.e., homosexual acts with a male minor/adolescent, and (3) Adult homosexual activities.

• *Lesbianism in Greco-Roman Culture*

Traditionally, lesbian behavior is traced to Sappho, poetess of Mitylene, from the island of Lesbos. The island was inhabited by a colony of women who wrote love poetry and "feminist" perspectives on romance, love, and even politics. However, no expressly lesbian conduct is mentioned in the literature of the poetess of Mitylene, nor can lesbianism be directly traced to it. While the word *lesbian* is derived from the island of Lesbos, that is the extent of the verifiable connection between them.

Greco-Roman literature gave relatively little attention to female homosexual conduct. K. J. Dover, who has done the most extensive study of homosexual conduct in ancient Greece, suggests that little attention was given it because male authors could not understand the attraction of woman-to-woman, or that it was "a reflex of male anxiety."[39]

---

[38] John Boswell, *Christianity, Social Tolerance, and Homosexuality* (Chicago: University Press, 1980), p. 87.

[39] Cf. K. J. Dover, *Greek Homosexuality* (Cambridge: Harvard University Press, 1978), pp. 171-172.

The first reference to lesbian conduct is found in Plato's *Symposium*, where he refers to women who "have no fancy for men: They are inclined rather to women."[40] However, Robin Scroggs maintains that Plato may have alluded to the practice of lesbianism in *Laws* 636c.[41]

Plutarch comments that in Sparta, girls became the lovers of older and more admirable women, mimicking the male pederastic practice.[42] The apostle Paul, likewise, commented that in Rome "their women exchanged natural relations for unnatural ones" (Romans 1:26). Perhaps the most complete depiction of lesbian sexual relations is offered by Lucian when describing the affair between Leana, a courtesan, and her live-in lover Megilla.[43]

Lesbian practices are also noted as having made use of an artificial penis called an *olisboi*, which one ancient author described as "cunningly contrived instruments of lechery, those mysterious monstrosities devoid of seed."[44] In photographic plates R414 and R1071, Dover includes pictures of vases depicting women with a basket full of *olisboi*. However, lesbian behavior did not always depend on a "substitute male" for sexual arousal or pleasures, as demonstrated by Dover's plates R207, B271, and B502, which depicts sexual relations between women without the use of *olisboi*.

• *Pederasty in Greco-Roman Culture*

Ronald Springett calls it the "most common form of homosexuality among Greek males," and later among the Romans.[45] Pederastic practices involved adult males having sexual relations with both boys (Gk. *pais*) and adolescents having entered puberty (Gk. *meirakion*). Craddock writes:

---

[40] Plato, *Symposium*, 191e.

[41] Robin Scroggs, *The New Testament and Homosexuality* (Philadelphia: Westminster Press, 1983), p. 141.

[42] Plutarch, *Lycurgus*, 18.4.

[43] Lucian, *Dialogues of the Courtesans*, 5.

[44] Pseudo-Lucian, *Erotes*, 28.

[45] Springett, p. 87.

> Pederasty was not uncommon, given the prevalence of slavery, the nature of tutor-pupil relationships, and the general opinion that women were inadequate as social and intellectual companions.[46]

Pederasty was *not* intended to be the beginnings of a lifelong relationship, nor was it even considered necessarily beneficial for the youth. For example, an ancient teacher, Timarchus, by age forty-five had already had several boy-lovers, "which suggests a rather rapid rate of turnover" between men and their young partners.[47] Likewise, pederasty was not to be pleasurable to the adolescent, but only for the adult male. If the youth *did* in fact consider it pleasurable, he was generally regarded as a prostitute or pervert.[48]

Pederasty was practiced in numerous contexts and for various reasons. Each form of pederastic conduct creates a new dimension from which to understand the abusive nature of the pederastic relationship.

Pederastic Prostitution: The Roman moralist and biographer Plutarch refers to "call-boys," adolescent males who prostituted themselves to adult males.[49] Similarly, Strabo comments regarding "a peculiar custom" on Crete, wherein boys are abducted for sexual relations with a nobleman.[50] Cato the Elder, a member of the Roman Senate, once commented with outrage that a "pretty boy costs more than a farm."[51]

Pederastic brothels were common both in Greece and especially in Rome.[52] Brothels were so common that Augustinian

[46] Fred Craddock, "How does the New Testament Deal with the Issue of Homosexuality," *Encounter* (Summer 1979), p. 204.

[47] Scroggs, p. 33. cf. Aeschines, *Timarchus*, 136.

[48] Dover, *Greek Homosexuality*, p. 52.

[49] Plutarch, *Lycurgus*, 18.4.

[50] Strabo, *Geography*, 10.4.21.

[51] Polybius, 31.25.

[52] Aeschines, *Timarchus*, 53, 74, 123-124, 188; Diogeneres Laterus, 2.105; Lucian, *Timon*, 22.

Rome "accorded boy prostitutes a legal holiday" and even taxed homosexual prostitution.[53] Homosexual brothels need not be considered purely as secular institutions, since some religious rituals required sexual acts "done under the guise of religious ritual . . . it was customary to use temples in search of love-adventures with men or women."[54]

Many emperors had boy concubines, including Nero,[55] Domitian,[56] and Commodus who had a harem of 300 women and 300 boys.[57] Hence, every level of Greco-Roman society had access to pederastic sexual relations.

Military Pederasty: As mentioned in our discussion of homosexual conduct in the ancient Near East, homosexual acts were frequently performed on vanquished foes. However, in Greece it became part of "basic training." Sparta, the most militaristic of the Greek city-states, propagated the idea that homosexual conduct would yield military prowess, and hence was expected during training.[58]

Slavery: The acquisition of new slaves, whether by birth, purchase, or conquest, frequently resulted in pederasty, in that masters would often require adolescent slaves to dress as women, and as they became adults required them to pluck out their beard so as to remain youthful in appearance. Seneca commented that the adolescent slave "must remain awake throughout the night, dividing his time between his master's drunkenness and his lust; in the chamber he must

---

[53] Boswell, p. 70. cf. Everett Ferguson, *Backgrounds of Early Christianity* (Grand Rapids: Eerdmans Publishing Company, 1987), p. 57.

[54] Springett, p. 105. cf. Josephus, *Antiquities*, 18.65-80; Juvenal, *Satire*, 9.22-24; O. Kiefer, *Sexual Life in Ancient Rome* (London: G. Routledge and Sons, 1934), p. 129.

[55] Tacitus, *Annals*, 15.48.

[56] Seutonius, *Lives: Domitian*, 22; Dio, *Lives*, 67.6.

[57] William Durant, *Caesar and Christ* (New York: Simon and Schuster, 1944), p. 447.

[58] Cf. Durant, *Life of Greece*, p. 83; Greg L. Bahnsen, *Homosexuality: A Biblical View* (Grand Rapids: Baker Book House, 1978), p. 50.

be a man, at the feast a boy."[59] The desire to keep adolescents youthful in appearance, and hence available for their male lovers, frequently resulted in castration, which was employed to prolong youthfulness.[60]

Educational Pederasty: Just as pederasty was the most common form of homosexual conduct in the Greco-Roman world, pederastic actions in an educational context was the most common form of pederasty until the second century A.D.[61]

The gymnasium was not only the location for formal education, but a location for teachers to watch naked boys and adolescents play and make their selection with whom they would commit homosexual acts. In fact, Lucian acknowledged that while this practice is abused, the purpose of pederasty in education was to establish a mutual *respect* between student and pupil.[62] Such acts were committed upon boys due to their "robuster nature and a large share of mind," as compared with women.[63]

In short, it was expected that teachers would have sexual relations with their youthful students.

Fear of Pederastic Practice: While pederasty was indeed prevalent, it was by no means universally accepted or condoned. According to Josephus,

> Herod the Great decided that it would not be safe for him to send Aristobulus [his son], who was then most handsome – being just sixteen – and of a distinguished family, to Antony, who . . . was ready to use him for erotic purposes and was able to indulge in undisguised pleasure because of his power.[64]

---

59 Seneca, *Epistles*, 47.7-8.

60 Seutonius, *Lives: Nero*, 28; Dio Chrysostom, *Discourse*, 21.4, 68; Juvenal, *Satire*, 10.295-309.

61 Cf. Philosophomena, 19.89b; Diepnosophists, 13.563e; Scroggs, p. 31.

62 Lucian, *Erotes*, 33-36. cf. Plato, *Symposium*, 181d.

63 Plato, *Symposium*, 181c.

64 Josephus, *Antiquities*, 15.29.

Both Lucian and Plutarch demonstrate that while pederasty in the Roman era was prevalent, differences of opinion regarding its legitimacy and morality still remained. Hence, while it was practiced and regarded by many as acceptable, this was by no means a unanimous opinion. Also, while both Lucian and Plutarch may represent opposite perspectives on pederasty, they both close with an affirmation of heterosexuality.[65] In fact, while accepted by some, it was indeed a political liability to have committed *kinaidia*, "homosexual submission" as a youth.[66] Hence, the practice of pederasty was not without its social liabilities.

The foremost educational authority in ancient Rome, Quintilian, likewise voiced his opposition to homosexual practices involving youth and adults in educational and home contexts. M. L. Clarke notes that "Roman parents and teachers were certainly concerned about" homosexual conduct between older and younger students.[67] Likewise, Quintilian did not believe that "all teachers could be trusted in this respect . . . [and] throws a lurid light on the home life of some of the wealthier Romans" who expose children and adolescents to homosexual conduct.[68]

• *Adult Homosexual Conduct in Greco-Roman Culture*

Male homosexual practices were not limited to adult-adolescent sexual relations, but in many cases developed into adult-adult homosexual conduct. In fact, male homosexual relations were oftentimes regarded as being superior to heterosexual love, since it involved *men* as opposed to involving a woman.

Not only was homosexual coitus regarded in some instances as being superior to heterosexual relations, but in some cases it was given legal favor. A married man could

---

[65] Cf. Springett, pp. 108-109.

[66] Ibid., p. 89; Dover, pp. 20-21, 75.

[67] M. L. Clarke, "Quintilian on Education," *Empire and Aftermath: Silver Latin II*, T. A. Dorey eds. (London: Routledge and Kegan Paul, 1975), p. 105.

[68] Ibid., pp. 105-106.

have extramarital sexual relations without being charged with committing adultery *if* the sex act was performed with either a licensed female prostitute or a homosexual lover.[69] Hence, violating one's marital relation with a homosexual lover was not considered adultery, and thus partially legitimized (if not sanctioned) by the Roman legal system.

Adult homosexual practices were prevalent throughout every level of Roman society, including the political and social elite. The Emperor Galba committed homosexual acts with other adults as well as with adolescents.[70] However, he was not the only emperor to engage in homosexual relations.

The sexual exploits of Nero, likewise, included homosexual relations with both adults and adolescents. He is reported to have had homosexual lovers, some to whom he was even married.[71]

2. Moral Opinion of Greco-Roman Culture on Homosexuality

As in modern America, the moralists, historians, and philosophers of the Greco-Roman world represented differing opinions regarding the ethical legitimacy of homosexuality in their civilization. For example, Aristotle maintained that homosexual behavior was natural, and hence should be condoned. While Plutarch condoned bisexuality, he could not do so for exclusively homosexual behavior. Plato argued that in a democratic republic, which was his ideal society, homosexual conduct must be tolerated on the basis of freedom of choice. As previously mentioned, Herodotus argued that Greece learned homosexual practices from the Persians, whereas Plutarch argued the exact opposite.[72]

---

[69] Lawrence E. Stager, "Eroticism and Infanticide at Ashkelon," *Biblical Archaeology Review* (July-August 1991), pp. 41, 43.

[70] Seutonius, *Lives: Galba*, 21.

[71] Miriam T. Griffin, *Nero: The End of a Dynasty* (London: Yale University Press, 1984), pp. 164-165, 168, 180.

[72] Cf. Boswell, pp. 49-59.

While homosexual conduct reached its height of toleration and acceptance in the Greco-Roman world, this was not by far the unanimous opinion of many ancient authorities. As will be demonstrated in this section, many ancient authorities restricted, limited, and even condemned homosexual practices in their culture.

Medical Condescension: The Roman physician Rufus maintained that homosexual activity was more violent than that of heterosexual contact.[73] This is primarily due to the nature of homosexual coitus, i.e., anal intercourse.[74] In fact, a "familiar medical debate on the causes of this perverse preference" existed in the medical community of the early centuries A.D.[75]

Legal Condescension: Despite earlier acceptance of homosexual marriage, even by the Emperors, the Theodosian Code (A.D. 342) outlawed homosexual marriages and instituted corporal punishment against anyone who would force a male into homosexual prostitution.[76]

In fact, prior to the Theodosian Code, a legal decision from 92 B.C. maintained that: "It shall not be lawful for Philiscus to bring in another wife besides Apollonia, *nor to keep a concubine or boy*, nor to have children by another woman while Apollonia lives . . ."[77] Hence, the adultery laws began acknowledging male homosexual lovers as a violation of marriage troth.

Boswell notes that in the third century A.D., Rome changed its open acceptance of homosexual conduct. While earlier laws did indeed contain a condescending tone toward

---

[73] Cf. Robin Lane Fox, *Pagans and Christians* (New York: Alfred A. Knopf, 1986), p. 346.

[74] Cf. Dover, p. 145.

[75] Ibid.

[76] *Theodosian Code* 9.7.3. cf. Boswell, pp. 123-124; Derrick Sherwin Bailey, *Homosexuality and the Western Christian Tradition* (London: Longmans, Green, and Company, 1955), p. 70.

[77] Sydney Page, "Marital Expectations of Church Leaders in the Pastoral Epistles," *Journal for the Study of the New Testament* (Fall 1993), 118 [Emphasis added].

passive homosexual behavior, Paulus, a Roman lawyer, argued that a passive homosexual should lose half his estate.[78] The trend to reject the legitimacy of homosexual conduct would coincide with the rise of Christianity's influence in the Roman Empire.

C. FROM THEN TO NOW: HOMOSEXUALITY AND MODERN AMERICA

For most Americans, the gay rights movement is a very recent event on the socio-political horizon, and well it should be. When Christianity gained in social, cultural, economic and political fortitude, the tolerance of homosexuality in Roman culture declined.[79] In fact, it is difficult to trace the history of homosexual conduct through the Middle Ages and modern church era for this very reason. Hence, when the modern homosexual revolution emerged on the American horizon, most Christians, churches, and denominations were caught unprepared to effectively respond to the crisis.

1. Homosexuality in America

Just how large is the homosexual community in the United States? Four researchers with the Alan Guttmacher Institute conducted a scientific survey involving 3,321 American men in their twenties and thirties. Only 1% of the men surveyed claimed to be *exclusively homosexual*. 2.3% of the men claimed to have ever had same-sex experience within the past ten years. Similar studies conducted by France in 1992 concur with these most recent findings.[80]

---

[78] *Sententiae* 2.27.12. cf. Boswell, p. 122.

[79] Cf. John Boswell, *Same-Sex Unions in Pre-Modern Europe* (New York: Villard Books, 1994); *Christianity Social Tolerance, and Homosexuality* (Chicago: University of Chicago Press, 1980).

[80] Cf. Jerry Adler, "Sex in the Snoring '90s," *Newsweek* (April 26, 1993), 55; Kim Painter, "Only 1% of Men say They are Gay," *USA Today* (April 15, 1993), 1D.

The homosexual population is indeed a minority in America, but is among the most vocal and politically aggressive. Carefully staged events receive both national and international coverage by the American media. In fact 80% of the American media community maintain that homosexuality is a valid and moral alternative lifestyle and we can only begin to appreciate and comprehend the impact of the liberal media on the American conscience in recent decades.[81] In recent history, the largest homosexual demonstration was the march on Washington D.C. While media would like for us to believe the April 1993 march on Washington D.C. was made of typical Americans who just happen to be homosexual, they must also admit that along with the marchers were "cross-dressers, leather-clad radicals, and topless lesbians."[82]

2. History of the Homosexual Crisis

In the pre-Clinton era, the homosexual constituency was on the cultural fringe of America. However, with unprecedented swiftness and publicity, the homosexual community during the Clinton administration has raced into the mainstream of American life and to the forefront of American politics. However, the foundations of the current homosexual rights movement began far earlier than the turn of this decade or the last. The following is a brief history of the milestones in the homosexual rights movement in America.[83]

1948 Alfred Kinsey's *Sexual Behavior in the Human Male* argues that 25% of U.S. male population has a degree of homosexual orientation, with 4% being exclusively homosexual.

---

[81] Joe Dallas, "Born Gay?" *Christianity Today* (June 22, 1992), 22.

[82] Mimi Hall, "Cover Story: 'You Can't Ignore Us," says Marchers," *USA Today* (April 26, 1993), 10A.

[83] Based on information gained from Randy Frame, "The Homosexual Lifestyle: Is There a Way Out?" *Christianity Today* (August 9, 1985), 34; Salholz, "The Future of Gay America," 22-23.

1950 Mattachine Society and Daughters of Bilitis formed.

1955 D. Sherwin Bailey publishes *Homosexuality and the Western Christian Tradition*, creating the foundational work of the new homosexual theological revision.

1968 Troy Perry, a homosexual Pentecostal minister, establishes the first homosexual denomination: *Universal Fellowship of Metropolitan Community Churches*.

1969 Police raid Stonewall Inn, a New York City gay bar. The incident marks the beginning of the modern gay-liberation movement.

Patrick Nidorf, a homosexual Catholic priest, forms *Dignity*, an organization for homosexual Catholics.

1970 First gay parades in New York and San Francisco, marking the anniversary of the Stonewall riots.

1972 The first mainline American denomination (United Churches of Christ) ordains the first homosexual minister, Bill Johnson.

The United Methodist Church describes homosexuality as "incompatible with Christian doctrine."

1973 Amid political pressures and threats of violence, the American Psychological Association (APA) votes to remove homosexuality from its list of mental disorders in *Diagnostic and Statistical Manual of Mental Illness*.

1975 USAF Sgt. Leonard Matlovich discharged for being homosexual, but wins a 1981 case against the Air Force.

1976 *Exodus International*, the first cooperative effort at ministering to the homosexual community, is formed.

1977 Harvey Milk elected first gay supervisor of San Francisco. He was murdered in 1978.

1981 AIDS, still unnamed, is first reported in the Center for Disease Control's *Morbidity and Mortality Weekly Report*.

1983 Massachusetts Rep. Gerry Studds announces his homosexuality, becomes the first admitted gay congressman.

The National Council of Churches tables the UFMCC's application for membership.

1984 San Francisco bathhouses closed during the Democratic National Convention. 100,000 gays march in protest.

Gay activists in the United Methodist and Presbyterian (U.S.A.) churches fail to gain support for the ordination of homosexuals.

Twenty-two states dropped their anti-sodomy statutes.[84]

1986 U.S. Supreme Court upholds states' rights to outlaw sodomy.

1987 250,000 homosexuals march on Washington for Civil Rights. AIDS Quilt is unfurled.

1989 ACT UP leads controversial protest against Roman Catholic Church at New York City's St. Patrick's Cathedral.

1992 President-elect Bill Clinton (D) announces his intention to remove the homosexual ban on the military.

1993 Largest homosexual "civil rights" march culminates in Washington, D.C.; estimates range from 300,000 by the American Park Service to 1.1 million by march organizers.

President Clinton appoints a lesbian as the chairperson of Housing and Urban Development (HUD)

1994 Twenty-fifth Anniversary march of Stonewall Riot, which began the modern Gay Rights Movement.[85]

3. The Current Crisis

In a survey of homosexuals in America, they identified the following items as being "very important" political goals:

• 77% Health-care and Social Security benefits for gay partners

---

[84] William Dannemeyer, *Shadow in the Land* (San Francisco: Ignatius Press, 1989), p. 57.

[85] Cf. Kushner, "Fireworks and Freedom," p. 46-48.

- 62% serving openly in the military
- 42% legally sanctioned gay marriage[86]

Already landmark cases involving homosexual rights have begun to set a precedent in the American legal and political scene. In July 1989 the New York State Court of Appeals became the first high court to rule that gay couples living together for more than ten years are covered under the family rent control regulations of that state. William B. Rubenstein, a lawyer for the American Civil Liberties Union (ACLU), regarded this ruling to be "the most important single step forward in American law toward legal recognition of lesbian and gay relationships."[87]

Public opinion on the subject is mixed according to a 1989 *Time*/CNN poll. For example, 65% of those polled maintained that homosexual couples should be legally allowed to inherit one another's property and 54% argued that homosexual couples should be permitted to receive medical or life insurance benefits from the partner's policy; *however*, 69% maintained that homosexual marriages should *not* be recognized by the law and 75% argued that homosexual couples should not be allowed to legally adopt children.[88] This shift in public opinion is not isolated to the United States. Canada's response to homosexuals in the role of schoolteacher, doctor, or senior politician is one of overwhelming acceptance.[89]

However, the homosexual agenda for America goes even further toward the fringe of American morality. The North American Man/Boy Love Association (NAMBLA) was founded in Boston in 1978, promoting the abolishment of age of consent laws and encouraging sexual relations between adult

---

[86] Ibid., p. 48.

[87] "Homosexual Families and the Law," *Newsweek* (July 17, 1989), p. 48.

[88] Walter Isaason, "Should Gays Have Marriage Rights?" *Time* (November 20, 1989), pp. 101-102.

[89] Nora Underwood, "Homosexual Rights," *Macleans* (January 2, 1989), p. 22.

males, adolescent, and pre-adolescent males.[90] An even more radical group in this regard, the Rene Guyon Society created in 1962, was founded for the express purpose "to actually make it possible for adults to provide sexual stimulation for virtually all *children*. . . . to convince the public that all laws controlling *nonconsensual sex* must be abolished."[91] In short, it would legalize homosexual child molestation.

---

[90] Rueda, *The Homosexual Network*, pp. 177-178.

[91] Ibid., p. 178 [emphasis added].

Chapter Two

THE POLITICS OF PLEASURE*

Dr. F. LaGard Smith

In his book, Sodom's Second Coming, *law professor Dr. F. LaGard Smith reviews the Gay agenda in America. Dr. Smith is Professor of Law and author of more than a dozen Christian books.*

Is it possible that, even as you read these words, there are gay-rights activists sitting around in boardrooms or bathhouses furtively conspiring against the American culture? As a criminal law professor who knows what it takes to prove a criminal conspiracy, I'm not one who generally favors conspiracy theories. But it is clear that somebody out there is orchestrating the gay-rights crusade. Somebody, or a group of somebodies, is zealously pursuing a course of action aimed at the homosexualization of America.

It's not happening by accident. Somebody is organizing the Gay Pride marches and convincing the mayors of big cities to participate. Somebody else is sitting behind a com-

*Taken from *Sodom's Second Coming, What you Need to Know About the Deadly Homosexual Assault* by F. LaGard Smith, Harvest House Publishers, 1993. Used by permission.

puter drafting the latest gay-rights initiative for the upcoming city or statewide election. There are teachers all across America who are discussing over coffee what would be the best way to expose your sons and daughters to the moral acceptability of a gay lifestyle.

Whether any of these people are working directly in concert, or only indirectly in sympathy with each other, we may never know. But there is one thing you can count on: *There is a gay-rights network in which many minds are working overtime to advance the goals of the gay-rights movement.*

For over two decades, much behind-the-scenes maneuvering has been going on. Consider, for example, the 1972 Gay Rights Platform drawn up by the National Coalition of Gay Organizations.[1] Among the Coalition's goals were the following:

- Repeal of all laws prohibiting private sexual acts involving consenting persons.
- Repeal of all laws prohibiting prostitution, both male and female.
- Repeal of all laws governing the age of sexual consent.
- Repeal of all legislative provisions that restrict the sex or number of persons entering into a marriage unit; and the extension of legal benefits to all persons who cohabit, regardless of sex or numbers.
- Enactment of legislation so that child custody, adoption, visitation rights, foster parenting, and the like shall not be denied because of sexual orientation or marital status.
- Encouragement and support for sex-education courses, prepared and taught by gay women and men, presenting homosexuality as a valid, healthy preference and lifestyle as a viable alternative to heterosexuality.

If you are finding some comfort in knowing that, two decades later, a substantial portion of their platform has yet to be realized, consider the success of another of their planks which 20 years ago would have been considered unthinkable,

---

[1] E. Rueda, *Homosexual Network* (Greenwich, CT: Devin-Adair Publishers, 1982), pp. 202-03.

but now reads like the leading story in a current issue of *Time* magazine:

- Issuance by the President of an executive order prohibiting the military from excluding for reasons of their sexual orientation, persons who desire entrance into the Armed Services; and from issuing less-than-honorable discharges for homosexuality; and the upgrading to fully honorable all such discharges previously issued, with retroactive benefits.

As we will see in a later chapter, the sex-education plank has also had growing success in some parts of the country, as has the plank relating to homosexual parenting and adoption. Had the Labour Party won the last election in Britain, they were pledged to reduce the age of consent for homosexuals from 21 to 16. Might this be a portent of what could happen soon on this side of the Atlantic? (You can bet that NAMBLA, the North American Man/Boy Love Association, is hoping so.)

Never underestimate the resolve or initiative of gay-rights activists. They have not hidden their sordid light under a bushel. The evidence of a premeditated, long-range gay-rights agenda is compelling – topped off by the election of a President from whom they now expect – and are getting – repayment in kind.

That is why it is so important that we examine the strategy and tactics of the movement. If gay-rights advocates are successful, then two decades from now we could be facing legalized prostitution, both male and female; the complete legalization of homosexual relations even with children; legal marriages for gays; parents losing custody of their children for disapproving of homosexual behavior; and even churches convicted of "hate crimes" for preaching that homosexual behavior is a sin.

The 12-Step Gay Agenda

With that grim prospect in mind, we turn now to a closer

examination of the gay movement's 12-step agenda:

1. Boldly claim freedom from social restraint and demand independence from the moral order.
2. Associate homosexuals with others in order to achieve legitimacy.
3. Depict decent folks with traditional family values to be the bad guys.
4. Promote the proven lie that gays constitute 10 percent of the population, so that there is legitimacy through sheer numbers.
5. Confuse the terminology so that no one realizes the difference between sexual orientation and sexual behavior.
6. Enlist science and medicine in a bogus search for some genetic cause for homosexual behavior.
7. Don't let anyone know what it is that gays actually do sexually.
8. Find creative ways to sidestep what the Bible teaches about homosexual conduct.
9. Open the door to the church and get its blessing for homosexual expression.
10. Break down legal restrictions against sodomy and instead establish legal restrictions against discrimination.
11. Dismantle the American family and make it possible for gays to marry and adopt children.
12. Perpetuate myths about heterosexual AIDS so that the disease becomes a political asset for the gay movement.

Step One: Boldly claim freedom from social restraint and demand independence from the moral order.

For homosexuals, this first crucial step is what "coming out" has been about. Before "coming out," homosexuals were collectively and individually suffocating in the seclusion of closeted guilt. As long as their homosexuality was still in the closet, there could be no relief from the guilt, no sense of moral freedom, no claim of legitimacy.

But that's mostly in the past. For today's homosexuals, the gay closet has become a relic of an unenlightened era. First one, then another, then homosexuals by the thousands have now stepped forward with ever-increasing boldness, throwing off the shackles of societal disapproval and asserting their sexuality with the fervor of political revolutionaries. Firing their first volley in the infamous 1969 Stonewall riot in New York's Greenwich Village, militant homosexuals signaled their Declaration of Sexual Independence and established themselves as a nation within a nation. "Gay and proud" became their anthem, and "gay rights" the banner to which they pledged their allegiance.

Like the self-righteous Pharisees of Jesus' day who boldly asserted their religious freedom in the face of his condemnation, today's homosexual crusaders proclaim their freedom as if it were an Emancipation Proclamation from slavery. Yet the promise of moral freedom for gays is merely illusive. What gays fail to appreciate is that in their self-proclaimed freedom they have become even more enslaved to their own passions.

That's what Jesus was telling the Pharisees in John chapter 8: "I tell you the truth, everyone who sins is a slave to sin" (John 8:34). And that is his message even today for those who would press for unrestricted sexual expression of any kind: No matter how loudly we declare our freedom, we are still shackled to whatever passions maintain their power over us.

All the more is that true when we dare to claim liberation from the moral order itself. It's one thing to *violate* the moral order through human weakness – something which all of us do. It's another thing altogether to *deny its authority over us.* It is here, in the attempt at moral emancipation, that gay activists tragically fool themselves into thinking they are free.

However much we might wish to deny it, the moral order has a way of keeping us in its grip even at the very moment we refuse to acknowledge its existence. We may *feel* free, as if we were astronauts floating in outer space. But, like them, we are tethered, whether we like it or not. And of course we ought to *like* it, for our tether is also our lifeline. Isn't that what Jesus was saying? Feeling sexually free without a moral tether is an invitation to sure destruction. Being free at the end of a morally-legitimate lifeline is being *free indeed!*

The gay-rights claim of moral freedom is a myth. That one small step out of the closet for homosexuals is one giant step toward certain disaster for both homosexuals and society at large.

Step Two: Associate homosexuals with others in order to achieve legitimacy.

In John chapter 8, Jesus was confronted by snobbish religious leaders who rested their personal righteousness on their heritage as descendants of Abraham. "How could we be religiously wrong as long as we are Abraham's descendants?" they were asking.

The gay-rights movement has ingeniously adopted a number of different ways to follow the same ploy. The idea is to somehow associate themselves with groups of heterosexuals who are unquestionably accepted throughout society, in the hope that they themselves will thereby be accepted. So far the tactic is working better than they ever could have imagined.

Just Another "Community"?

Perhaps more subtle than some of the more articulated arguments is the frequent reference to "the gay community."

The *"gay community"*? You mean, like the *black* community? The *Hispanic* community? The *Christian* community?

While no one would deny that there is a segment of society made up of homosexuals sharing common interests — and therefore a "community" in that sense — if gays can somehow be linked with the many *legitimate* communities which make up our society, their hope is that homosexuality itself might appear to take on the same legitimacy as, for instance, race or national heritage. Of course, that link is as patently contrived as if an attempt were made to confer legitimate status to the "adulterous community," or to the "tax-fraud community," or to the "white-collar-crime community."

Equally subtle is the hiding place that one might hope to find in the midst of a "community." Whereas we rightly assess personal moral character only in the case of individuals, we normally think of communities in a morally neutral sense. In "the black community," for example, one can find both moral and immoral members of the community. The same goes for "the white community," the Hispanic community," and so on.

However, when an entire community's identity is based solely upon its unique moral character, the implication is all too clear: If there can somehow be a sanitized, legitimized "gay community," then the individuals who make up that community can automatically be considered morally legitimate as well. Instead of *guilt* by association, there is a hoped-for *legitimacy* by association.

Just Another Civil-Rights Group?

Never is legitimacy by association more coveted than when the gay-rights movement attempts to link itself with truly legitimate civil-rights movements. Every effort is made by homosexuals to ride piggyback on the fortunes of blacks, women, and other legitimate minority groups. But minority groups must never be confused with special-interest groups.

As for minority groups, we champion laws prohibiting discrimination against race, gender, and national origin because they represent a status over which their members have no choice. Naturally, that raises one of the most crucial questions in the entire debate: whether homosexuals have any choice in the matter. (The issue will be more fully developed in later chapters.)

Suffice it to say for now that the burden is on the gay-rights movement to establish that homosexual conduct is *not* volitionally chosen. In that regard, their persistent reference to "sexual *preference*" and "gay *lifestyle*" betrays their attempt to deny personal volition in their sexual practices. Legitimate minority status is a bogus claim by what amounts to nothing more than a special-interest group.

Of course, gay activists point out that we also have laws prohibiting discrimination on the basis of *religion*, wherein one's faith is personally chosen. But the attempted analogy still misses the mark, because religion is a matter of constitutionally protected belief. Religious *belief* stands in sharp contrast to homosexual *behavior*, which the Supreme Court has specifically declared not to be constitutionally protected.

The Pro-Choice, Pro-Gay Connection

Far less lofty than the efforts which are made to mimic legitimate minorities is the well-documented liaison between gay-rights groups and pro-choice, pro-abortion organizations. If ever there were an unholy alliance, this is it! Considering the fact that homosexuals will never have to worry about the unwanted pregnancy that leads to abortion, it gives new meaning to the saying that politics makes strange bedfellows. How strange indeed! More importantly, instead of providing gay activists with added moral legitimacy by association with a high-profile social cause, it simply confirms how morally perverse their movement is. Pro-choice for the "men of conscience," as they are called by their pro-abortion allies, only serves to put gays in league with yet another special-interest group desperately seeking moral freedom where none exists. How much more morally bankrupt can gays be than when they are willing to trade on the lives of 1.5 million aborted babies a year in order to gain public approval of their own homosexual lifestyle!

Ironically, there is already expressed consternation over the potential convergence of two separately developing streams: 1) Gay-initiated efforts to find a "biological determinant" for homosexuality, wherein homosexual orientation is the product of perinatal chemical configurations in utero; and 2) the growing practice of eugenic abortions that would permit concerned parents to abort any fetus indicating homosexual tendencies.

Even though discovery of a "biological determinant" is about as likely as meeting Shirley MacLaine in a future lifetime, gays find themselves in the same embarrassing dilemma as feminists, who demand unrestricted choice, yet are offended when that choice results in the methodical slaughter of female fetuses in sex-selection abortions.

Once one jumps the moral cue, he has to be careful in his choice of allies. The "*immoral* order" – and there is one – tends to be as integrative and interdependent as is the *moral* order.

Parading Celebrity Comrades

Among the more visible tactics of gay-rights advocates is their concerted effort to surround themselves in a show of strength with every important personage they can muster, whether it be politicians, entertainment celebrities, athletes, or even religious leaders.

The strategy is no secret. We have it from their own pens:

> Our campaign should not overlook the Celebrity Endorsement. The celebrities in question can, of course, be either straight or gay...but must always be well liked and respected by the public.
>
> If homosexual, the celebrity jams homo-hatred by presenting a favorable gay image at odds with the stereotype. If straight, the spokesperson (who deserves the Medal of Valor) provides the public with an impressive role model of social tolerance to emulate. In either case, the psychological response among straights is the same, and lays the groundwork for conversion:
>
> I like and admire Mr. Celeb;
> Mr. Celeb is queer and/or respects queers; so
> either I must stop liking and admiring Mr. Celeb,
> or else it must be all right for me to respect queers.[2]

Naturally, many of the big names that are paraded before

[2] Marshall Kirk and Hunter Madsen, *After the Ball* (New York: Plume, 1990), p. 188.

us are homosexuals recognized and admired for their outstanding talent. Consider conductor/composer Leonard Bernstein[3] and tennis stars Billie Jean King and Martina Navratilova, to name but three.

But it is the *heterosexual* celebrities who better serve the movement's goal of achieving public acceptability. Simply consider the recent uproar over Colorado's initiative to prevent special gay-rights ordinances, and what you see is a virtual Who's Who of America's top entertainers coming to the defense of the gays. The list is long, including Barbra Streisand, Lily Tomlin, Whoopi Goldberg, Joan Rivers, Cher, Liza Minnelli, and Sidney Poitier. John Denver got in on the act by sponsoring a concert to raise $50,000 in an effort to repeal the initiative.

Even former President (and Sunday school teacher) Jimmy Carter defended his boycott-breaking appearance in Colorado by saying that his visit would help the people who were fighting that law.[4]

Sadly, there has never been a greater friend and benefactor of the gay movement than President Bill Clinton. His association with homosexual activist David Mixner is well-known. It was Mixner who marshaled the army of gays that helped elect Clinton, and the same Mr. Mixner who persuaded his friend in the nation's highest office to declare the "army of gays" in the Army official. (It was also Mixner who said he became "literally sick to my stomach" when Clinton suggested that the military might have some legitimate concerns after all.)[5]

Mixner's important political connection did not go unrewarded. During the frenzy of Clinton's many inaugural celebrations, The Gay and Lesbian Victory Fund saluted Mixner with an inaugural ball. It was attended by a host of luminar-

---

[3] Ibid., p. 52.

[4] *Boston Globe*, January 6, 1993, LIVING, p. 28.

[5] Waldman, "Battle," p. 42.

ies, among whom were actress Sigourney Weaver; White House spokesman George Stephanopoulos; three California senators, including Diane Feinstein, Barbara Boxer, and Alan Cranston (now retired); and singers Gladys Knight, Patti Austin, and Peter, Paul, and Mary.

It was a sign of the times, and of the growing public acceptability of the gay movement, when the Lesbian and Gay Bands of America played in the inaugural parade while Girl Scouts handed out American flags and AIDS ribbons.

If the gays ever wanted a calling card, they received it in President Clinton. "Bill Clinton is the Abraham Lincoln of the lesbian and gay community," said Gregory King, a spokesman for the Human Rights Campaign Fund, a pro-gay political group whose 75,000 members raised 2.5 million dollars for the Clinton campaign.[6]

"Being gay is a plus, because the president's looking for diversity," said Andrew Barrer, director of Coalition '93, an organization set up to push gay and lesbian candidates for federal appointments.[7]

On every side, gays have gained support from people of influence. The associations which they have carefully cultivated for over two decades have brought them a level of public acceptability that one could never have dreamed of happening in so short a time.

Of course, legitimacy by association misses the issue altogether. If you live by association you can also die by association. Would the gay-rights movement wish us to associate them with homosexual serial killers Elmer Wayne Henley, John Wayne Gacy, Juan Corona, and Wayne Williams?[8]

---

[6] Bob Dart, "Activists see this decade as the 'gay '90s,'" Cox News Service, Feb. 1993.

[7] Martin Kasindorf, "Clinton isn't marching but is in step with gays," *The Nashville Banner*, Apr. 23, 1993, p. A1.

[8] Kirk and Madsen, *After the Ball*, p. 47.

A Genealogy for Gays?

Yet not even the impressive list of sympathetic luminaries seems sufficient for gays. Have you heard all the historical revision going on lately? One after another historical figures are being "outed" as homosexuals. The latest coup, if it is to be believed, is "gay-hater" and former FBI chief J. Edgar Hoover, who according to biographer Anthony Summers (*Official and Confidential: The Secret Life of J. Edgar Hoover*) was homosexually involved with his assistant director, and even dallied with being a transvestite on occasion.

But just look at the revisionist strategy and why gays correctly perceive the reasons for its success:

> The honor roll of prominent gay or bisexual men and women is truly eye-popping. From Socrates to Eleanor Roosevelt, Tchaikovsky to Bessie Smith, Alexander the Great to Alexander Hamilton, and Leonardo da Vinci to Walt Whitman, the list of suspected "inverts" is old hat to us but surprising news to heterosexual America.
>
> Famous historical figures are especially useful to us for two reasons: first, they are invariably dead as a doornail, hence in no position to deny the truth and sue for libel. Second, and more serious, the virtues and accomplishments that make these historic gay figures admirable cannot be gainsaid or dismissed by the public, since high school history textbooks have already set them in incontrovertible cement.[9]

Apparently, it has become particularly important in the debate over gays in the military to dredge up great military figures of the past: Julius Caesar; the entire army of Sparta; Lord Kitchener, Frederick the Great, Alexander the Great (as mentioned), and so on.

London columnist Frank Johnson suggests, tongue in cheek, that, given the preference for anyone with "the Great" after his or her name, it's surely only a matter of time before

---

[9] Ibid.

Catherine the Great is "outed" as a lesbian![10]

And who's to know the difference? With none of them around to defend themselves, even George Washington, Napoleon, and General Patton aren't safe.

As a matter of historical fact, Frederick the Great and Kitchener probably *were* homosexuals. But apparently Alexander the Great was guilty of no greater crime than the male, Platonic friendship in which the ancient world was more interested than in the sexual craving of our own time.

Caesar, of course, was married, and spent a good deal of time with Cleopatra. Whether this precluded other, homosexual liaisons is by no means clear. But until there is more evidence, the gay-rights movement is no more entitled to him than is the other side.[11]

In all of the frenzy for establishment of a gay pedigree, it seems to be lost on gay activists that they are committing the same sin which they condemn in heterosexuals: defining a homosexual by his homosexuality. Are historical figures to be admired *because of* their homosexuality, or are they to be admired for having accomplished what they did *despite* their homosexuality?

Acceptability Through Sympathy

A final way in which the gay movement succeeds in gaining public support is not a tactic which I would guess anyone is cynical enough to purposely exploit. It just works out that way. I refer here, of course, to the many AIDS-related deaths which have seen one celebrity after another go to his grave prematurely.

It is considered indelicate to mention it, but certain sports, like men's ice-skating, have felt the brunt of AIDS more than others. The obituary in Canada alone includes

---

[10] Frank Johnson, "Of Militants and the Military," in the *Daily Telegraph*, Feb. 3, 1993, p. 17.

[11] Ibid.

such top skaters as Rob McCall, Brian Pockar, Dennis Coi, and Shaun McGill. There is also Britain's John Curry. Add to that list Ondrej Nepla, the 1972 Olympic gold medalist from Czechoslovakia, who has already died, and now Barry Hagen, the World Champion ice dancer in 1982 and 1983, who has tested positive to the HIV virus, and you begin to realize how devastating the gay lifestyle can be, even in a single sport.

On another front, who hasn't been appalled by the loss of so many people with creative talent in the field of arts and entertainment? In the past decade there have been so many funerals in Hollywood that, as one gay put it, "I'm simply weary from attending them." Many of those who died were relatively unknown behind-the-scenes writers, choreographers, and dancers. Others have been superstars whose deaths have touched us all.

For example, who among us didn't admire the strength and gracefulness that permitted Rudolf Nureyev to leap in exquisite slow motion? Or enjoy the cinematic roles played by Rock Hudson? I still remember the days of early television and the popular show-biz flair of Liberace. These people are gone now, robbed of life by the homosexual lifestyle which they shared in common. Yet they have become the heroes of the hour.

One might have thought that these tragic deaths would have been an embarrassment to the gay-rights movement. But every cause needs its martyrs, and none could be more suited for the gay movement than deaths which, in one stroke, combine unprecedented public sympathy and celebrity-status homosexuality. What could be better than legitimacy by association unless perhaps it is legitimacy by sympathy?

The connection is not difficult to draw. Were you shocked to learn how Rock Hudson died? If so, how could you possibly oppose gay rights? Hudson was a homosexual, you know.

Were you grieved at the loss which Nureyev's death

brought to the world of ballet? If so, what could possibly be wrong with gay rights? Nureyev was a homosexual, you know.

No one should underestimate the strength of the sympathy vote. In the midst of all the cynical attempts to gain public acceptability through contrived associations with legitimate minorities, civil-rights movements, and supportive celebrities, nothing grabs the American people quite like the association between AIDS and gay rights.

When faced with death, we often find a common bond that we never knew in life. In death we are neither homosexual nor heterosexual. And that is a comforting thought to the gay movement, because it means that society will then begin to look more kindly upon the special risk that homosexual men face – and thus more kindly upon their movement for social recognition.

The fact that homosexuals have virtually absolute control over that risk hardly seems to matter. For every person who blames homosexuals for the AIDS epidemic and its threat even to young innocents, there are another two or more people who let their sympathy for AIDS victims cloud the quite separate issue of gay rights.

I say "quite separate," but perhaps in another vein we would do well to make the very connection that gays would love us to make. After all, were it not for the movement for gay rights, in several decades the tragedy of the AIDS epidemic for homosexuals and many more innocents in America could literally be ancient history.

Part Two

CAUSES AND CHANGE

CHAPTER THREE

THE CAUSES OF HOMOSEXUAL BEHAVIOR

Dr. J.D. Robertson

The issue that divides the various groups is the one of cause. What specifically causes homosexual behavior? Dr. J.D. Robertson, a licensed psychologist, examines both the "nature" and "nurture" points of view and provides a well balanced conclusion based on the latest scientific research.

When discussing the causes for homosexuality, Christians and churches run the gamut. Morally, the extremes are represented by the view that homosexuality is not condemned in Scripture as opposed to the view that homosexuality is condemned in Scripture. Concerning causes, researchers run an even more complicated course: homosexuality is caused completely by genetic factors; homosexuality is caused by a complex combination of genetic factors with certain "high risk" scenarios from the environment which set a predisposition for developing a homosexual orientation; homosexuality is caused completely by environmental conditions during childhood and adolescent development; homosexuality is completely a choice.

Much of the discussion involves two "oldie goldies" from

developmental research – nature versus nurture. This issue involves how much of who we are resides in our nature – biology or genetic endowment – and is predetermined, as opposed to how much of who we are depends on how we were nurtured – childrearing practices from significant others and shaping from our unique environments – which mold us in ways that we learn and, therefore, may be unlearned. Although the verdict is certainly not in, we will attempt to explore the rationale for maintaining homosexuality has genetic origins, as well as the argument that homosexuality is environmental.

Nature

It seems we are bombarded with study after study in the mainstream media reporting that homosexuality is inherited genetically – it is someone's nature. People have no more control over their sexual preference than they do their eye color. Dr. John Money put it this way, "Despite popular assumptions, homosexuality, heterosexuality, and bisexuality are not preferences. Each is a sexuoerotic orientation or status. They are no more chosen than a native language is."[1]

David Myers maintains, "There is a growing agreement that sexual orientation is neither willfully chosen nor willfully changed. Sexual orientation in some ways is like handedness: most people are one way, some the other. Few are equally ambidextrous. Regardless, the way one is endures."[2]

He reports that Kinsey Institute interviews failed to discover any psychological cause of homosexuality. After outlining several theories involving environmental causes of homosexuality, Myers concluded "The bottom line of these conflicting theories is that after 100 years of research, the determinants of sexual orientation remain, for now, a mystery.

---

[1] "The Development of Sexual Orientation," *The Harvard Medical School Mental Health Letter*, February 1988, p. 4.

[2] *Psychology*, New York: Worth Publishers, 1992, 367.

New research hints that the mystery's eventual solution may be at least partly biological."[3]

Researchers report that homosexuality runs in families. Richard Pillard and James Weinrich recruited single men between 25 and 35 who had at least one living sibling. They found that among the brothers of heterosexual men, only about 4% were homosexuals, as opposed to about 18% of the homosexual's brothers, who were also homosexual. Reviewers said, "The authors point out that their study could not show whether heredity or upbringing were more important."[4]

Richard Pillard has continued his studies of homosexuality and families. He has found homosexuals to have homosexual siblings at 4-5 times the rate of the heterosexual population. Also homosexuals appear randomly in the birth order, which indicates a possible genetic link rather than environmental influences embedded within family dynamics. In addition, his studies have found "gender nonconformity" in childhood play among homosexuals, which poses problems for some environmental theories which maintain homosexuality emerges from adolescence.

His most compelling work was research conducted with Michael Bailey that had to do with comparing monozygotic (identical) twins with dizygotic (fraternal) twins, and adopted brothers with biological brothers. The identical twins, those having identical genetic blueprints, had the highest concordance rate which turned out to be 52%. Fraternal twins, those who are dizygotic and no more alike genetically than other biological siblings, had the same concordance rate as other biological siblings (22%). Adopted brothers, who shared the same family environment but with different genetic backgrounds, had the lowest concordance rate in the study (11%).

---

[3] Ibid., 368.

[4] "Homosexuality," *The Harvard Medical School Mental Health Letter*, February 1987, p. 6.

The greatest case for genetic influence in twin research comes when a researcher can observe identical twins, separated soon after birth, and reared apart in different environments. Pillard points out how rare such cases are, and how much rarer are those involving homosexuality. "Nevertheless, Thomas Bouchard has identified two such cases in the Minnesota Twin Study: a pair of male twins in which both were gay, and another in which one was gay and the other heterosexual with some incidental homosexual contacts."[5] Bailey and Pillard have a new study of lesbian twins that will be published soon where they have obtained similar results.[6]

Dovetailing with Pillard's findings concerning "gender nonconformity" in homosexual childhood play, Bernard Zuger has followed 48 boys who demonstrated effeminate behavior from as early as 3-6 years old from the 1960's through 1984. He found that at least 35% of the participants were clearly homosexual in adulthood. "The author considers it unlikely that the direction of sexual development could be changed in such boys even if it were desirable. He suggests explaining this to parents so they will not be made to feel guilty about something for which they are not responsible."[7]

Similarly, Dr. Richard Green of UCLA has studied gender-atypical play and concludes that such behavior in preadolescent boys reflects a homosexual orientation 75% of the time. If these studies are correct, they demonstrate powerful roots to homosexual orientation long before homosexual behavior. University of Wisconsin researcher Robert Goy has demonstrated that gender-atypical play can be created through hormonal manipulation in monkeys, which indicates the possibility that gender-atypical play in children may also

---

[5] "Does Homosexuality Have a Biological Basis?" *The Harvard Mental Health Letter*, June 1992, p.6.

[6] Chandler Burr, "Homosexuality and Biology," *The Atlantic Monthly*, March 1993, p. 65.

[7] "Homosexuals in Boyhood," *The Harvard Medical School Mental Health Letter*, July 1989, p. 7.

have hormonal roots.[8]

The Knoxville News-Sentinel picked up an Associated Press story and on August 1, 1992, ran the headline "Study Links Brain Size to Sexual Orientation." The story summarized a piece of research from the UCLA School of Medicine where researchers discovered "a brain structure called the anterior commissure to be 34% larger in homosexual males than in heterosexual males."[9] As a result, this study "adds weight to the theory that sexual orientation is not a matter of choice, but a function of biological design or development."[10] These stories seem to be a daily occurrence on radio and television news reports, as well as in newspapers and magazines.

Chief among researchers studying brain differences is Simon LeVay, a biologist at the Salk Institute in San Diego. In a small sample involving the brain tissue from 19 homosexual men, 16 presumed heterosexual men, and 6 women, he discovered a difference in size of a brain area called the third interstitial nucleus of the anterior hypothalamus (INAH 3) between homosexual and heterosexual men. He observed that the area was the same in women and homosexual men, but more than twice the size in heterosexual men. LeVay recognizes some problems with the study and allows that the brain differences may be the result of homosexuality rather than the cause. Still brain differences have been observed and demonstrated among rats and monkeys which lends credibility to the findings.[11]

Dr. Earl Wilson considers the evidence and asserts, "...homosexual behavior can be created in the laboratory by the alteration of biochemical conditions. This cannot be denied."[12]

---

[8] Chandler Burr, p. 62.

[9] *The Knoxville News-Sentinel,* August 1, 1992, p. A9.

[10] Ibid.

[11] "Is Homosexuality All in the Brain?" *The Harvard Mental Health Letter,* March 1992, p. 7.

[12] *Counseling and Homosexuality,* (Waco, TX: Word, 1988), p. 69.

He cites two examples: stress during pregnancy has demonstrated demasculinizing effects on male rat pups, and the ingestion of barbiturates by a pregnant female will demasculinize male rat pups. Likewise, high levels of androgens before birth will tend to masculinize female rat pups. Hence the inference is, "too high a testosterone level in utero may contribute to lesbianism in females and too low a testosterone level may contribute to homosexuality in males."[13] This all derives from the Adam/Eve Principle of prenatal hormonalization. Fundamentally the principle refers to the fact that sexual differentiation requires hormonalization. If the proper hormones are not secreted at the proper time the child will be female. The male gender requires hormonalization, which is what prompts Gary Smalley to say, hopefully with tongue-in-cheek, that men are brain damaged.[14] Understanding the Adam/Eve Principle makes it easier to accept that something can go wrong chemically due to maternal stress and set up predispositions as a result of faulty hormonalization (not enough for males, or accidentally hormonalizing females).

Further evidence for prenatal hormonalization comes from Dr. John Money's 1984 study of CAH women. CAH involves an enzyme defect which results in the adrenal gland producing androgens rather than the needed substance (cortisol), hence the fetus is flooded with male hormones. In Money's study, 37% of the CAH women identified themselves as lesbian or bisexual as contrasted to current estimates of 2-4% in the general population.[15]

Pillard and Weinrich hypothesize that homosexual men undergo complete masculinization because they are genetically male; however, they may not complete the defeminization process. Males require androgens to prompt masculin-

---

[13] Ibid., p. 70.

[14] *Love is a Decision*, Word Video Curriculum Resource, 1991.

[15] Chandler Burr, p. 59.

ization and an inhibiting hormone to defeminize them. The researchers maintain that homosexual men were masculinized by the androgens, yet not fully defeminized, creating a male with female aspects and homosexual orientations.[16] The gender atypical play studies are usually cited as support of this theoretical viewpoint.

Although there is clear evidence of some biological link to homosexuality, it is wise to proceed with caution. Meier, Minirth, Wichern, and Ratcliff maintain that even if a biological root was proven, it would be a mistake to blame behavior on genetics. "While our genetic makeup does have a powerful effect upon us, we are not determined solely by our genes."[17]

Chandler Burr offers a statement by William Byne, "If the prenatal-hormone hypothesis were correct, then one might expect to see in a large proportion of homosexuals evidence of prenatal endocrine disturbance, such as genital or gonadal abnormalities. But we simply don't find this."[18]

Dr. Earl Wilson quotes Dr. John Money as saying, "... sexual orientation is not under the direct governance of chromosomes and genes, and that, whereas it is not foreordained by prenatal brain hormonalization it is influenced thereby, and is also strongly dependent on postnatal socialization."[19] He also quotes Money as stating, "With respect to orientation as homosexual or bisexual, there is no human evidence that prenatal hormonalization, alone, independently or postnatal history, inexorably preordains either orientation."[20] Hence research suggests there is a predisposition for sexual orientation before birth; however, it also suggests there is a complicated group of variables and their interaction involved

---

[16] Ibid., p. 60.

[17] *Introduction to Psychology & Counseling*, (Grand Rapids: Baker, 1991), p. 272.

[18] Chandler Burr, p. 62.

[19] *Counseling and Homosexuality*,(Waco, TX: Word, 1988), p. 69.

[20] Ibid., p. 72.

and predisposition does not entail determination.

At least for the moment, genetic causes are compelling but inconclusive. Bearing this in mind concerning the "nature" studies, the consideration of arguments advanced by the "nurture" proponents can be just as compelling, and alas, just as uncertain.

Nurture

As much as it seems we are bombarded with study after study that reports homosexuality as nature, we are equally flooded with experts who claim it is properly investigated in family dynamics or other environmental situations – the domain of nurture. These experts maintain that homosexuality is learned, and can be unlearned.

Modern environmental arguments for the origins of homosexuality usually cite the works of Sigmund Freud. He believed homosexuality originated in early childhood fixations and regression.[21] Based on Freud's views on arrested sexual development, psychoanalytic theorists came to the conclusion that families with weak, passive, or distant fathers, and strong, controlling, or domineering mothers might produce homosexuality in male and female children. The thinking is that the mother dominates the son who has no strong male role model to learn from. As the boy develops, he becomes insecure in his gender identity and ability to relate to the opposite sex and therefore identifies with his mother rather than his father. In contrast, girls fail to learn to relate to the opposite sex because of the father's rejection and turn to homosexuality because they are more comfortable with women.[22] The problem with Freud's views is that there seems to be little empirical research to substantiate his opinion. As a result, "Most psychotherapists today reject this account;

---

[21] Psychodynamic Therapy: Part III, *The Harvard Mental Health Letter*, December 1991, p. 4.

[22] Gary Collins, *Christian Counseling: A Comprehensive Guide*, (Dallas: Word, 1988), p. 283.

they consider homosexuality a variation rather than a perversion of or a deviation from a normal course of development."[23] Dr. Earl Wilson points out that Freud's viewpoint seems to have face validity, yet it cannot account for the current percentages of homosexuals. "The majority of the persons I have seen who struggle with same-sex preference have not had rejecting parents of the opposite sex."[24]

A different twist on Freud's point of view comes from Elizabeth Moberly, who is persuaded that homosexuality actually originates in relational problems with the same-sex parent rather than problems with the opposite-sex parent. She maintains that homosexuality is an unconscious attempt to restore the bond or attachment with the same-sex parent. In other words, the homosexual experienced a disruption or severe stressors in the relationship with the same-sex parent and is attempting to meet early bonding needs through sexual relationships with same-sex individuals. In fact, Moberly suggests the development of non-sexual relationships with same-sex individuals as therapy for homosexuals who wish to become heterosexual.[25] "Moberly writes, '...From amidst a welter of details, one constant underlying principle suggests itself: that the homosexual – whether man or woman – has suffered from some deficit in the relationship with the parent of the same sex; and that there is a corresponding drive to make good this deficit – through the medium of same-sex, or 'homosexual' relationships.'"[26] Wilson describes this process as a "reparative urge, a desperate effort to have needs met."[27] Same-sex love is a normal human need typically supplied through the same-sex parent in a non-sexual way, however, Moberly maintains this need

---

[23] Psychodynamic Therapy: Part III, p. 4.

[24] Wilson, p. 57.

[25] Collins, p. 283.

[26] Wilson, p. 57.

[27] Ibid., p. 58.

was distorted and the pursuit of the same-sex love in a sexual relationship introduces an inappropriate method for meeting this essential need. In response to Moberly's views, Wilson offers "I have discovered that the homosexual condition in a very high percentage of the counselees with whom I work can be explained by Moberly's theory. I do not believe it explains all homosexual causality or behavior."[28]

Dr. David Seamands says, "What actually causes homosexuality is a matter of considerable debate."[29] He identifies the two dominant theories of causality as genetic and environmental, and then asserts, "There is now a general agreement that it is not something genetic or hormonal." Dr. Seamands covers several environmental scenarios which are embedded in problems in the parent-child relationship, as well as early sexual experiences. He cites these examples as not exhaustive of causes, but illustrative of how the roots for homosexuality are usually found in family or social situations during development.

Dr. Gary Collins writes, "While many homosexuals do experience disruptions in parent-child relationships, others do not. Children in the same family do not all become homosexual even though there may be similar parent-child relationships."[30]

However, certain family relationships have been shown to relate to homosexuality and Dr. Collins lists several scenarios cited by Lawrence J. Hatterer:[31]

- Mothers distrust or fear women and teach this to their sons.
- Mothers distrust or fear men and teach this to their daughters.

---

[28] Ibid., p. 60.

[29] Homosexuality, audiocassette #19, *Christian Counselor's Library*, (Waco, TX: Word Educational Products Division, 1980).

[30] Collins, p. 283.

[31] *Changing Homosexuality in the Male*, (New York: McGraw Hill, 1970).

- A son is surrounded by too many females (mothers, sisters, aunts), but he has limited contact with adult males, thus he learns to think and act like a girl.
- Parents who wanted a daughter but instead have a son subtly raise the boy to think and act like a girl (a similar situation arises when parents wanted a son but instead have a daughter); in both cases the child has great confusion about sexual identity and orientation.
- A son is rejected or ignored by his father and hence feels inadequate as a male and unsure how males relate to females.
- A daughter is rejected by her mother and hence feels inadequate as a female, thus she can't relate well to males.
- Both parents are afraid of sex, unwilling to discuss it in the home, or strong in their condemnation of sex; in all of this the child gets a distorted view of sex and as a result struggles with heterosexual adjustment.
- A mother (or father) is so overindulgent that the child is overly attached to the parent, unable to break away, and convinced that no mate could ever compare with the opposite-sex parent.[32]

Other situations discussed by Collins include early molestations or homosexual experimentation that is eventually internalized, fear (for whatever reason) of the opposite sex, or conscious, willful choice of homosexuality. It would be difficult to make the case that early sexual abuse, molestation, or same-sex experimentation leads to homosexuality because there are too many heterosexuals who have had those experiences. However, for some people these experiences may be critical in ultimately deciding they are homosexuals and many people who work with homosexuals note the presence of early sexual experiences. Fear of the opposite sex may arise from rejection or embarrassing situations among other possibilities. The rationale for this viewpoint involves awkwardness, uncertainty, insecurity, or discomfort with the opposite sex, hence retreating to relationships with same-sex individuals. The idea of deliberate choice is advanced by

[32] Collins, pp. 283-284.

authors and speakers, yet professionals and homosexuals tend to disagree. Collins maintains, "Sexual attraction to the members of one's own sex rarely if ever comes as a willful and conscious decision."[33] The realization of one's attraction to same-sex individuals usually produces anxiety or disbelief because it is so disturbing. Typically there is a long period of denial and attempts to feel comfortable heterosexually and hiding one's true feelings until eventually accepting the homosexual orientation. Therefore most professionals and homosexuals find it difficult to believe that a majority of homosexuals choose the lifestyle deliberately.

Wilson outlines the social learning theory's explanation for homosexuality. Social learning theory focuses on learning through observation and imitation. It essentially accepts operant conditioning principles, especially reinforcement, but adds cognitive components to the classic behavioral perspective and emphasizes observational learning. Wilson cites Hamachek's discussion of sexual behavior: "There seems little question that the basic components of sex-typing are undoubtedly acquired at home, largely through imitation of, and identification with, the parent of the same sex."[34] Fundamentally, children observe parents and other adults, as well as observing and participating with peers in sex-typing behavior. This begins very early and these experiences may influence sexual orientations long before adolescence. As children develop sexual behavior, some is reinforced and thereby encouraged, while some meets with negative consequences and discouraged. Reinforced behavior increases in frequency while behavior resulting in unpleasant consequences tends to decrease. The social learning perspective maintains that unwittingly homosexuals may have been reinforced for same-sex preferences and punished for opposite-sex preferences. As a result, the individual eventually begins to interpret expe-

---

[33] Ibid., p. 285.

[34] Wilson, p. 61.

riences in that way. Positive encounters with opposite-sex individuals are forgotten, while negative experiences are focused upon in a way that gives undue influence and reinforces the perception of homosexuality. Likewise, negative experiences with same-sex individuals are discarded, while positive experiences receive out-of-proportion influence. Hence once someone has accepted the homosexual orientation, a self-fulfilling prophecy is incorporated and he or she perceives and interprets incoming information in the context of the same-sex orientation. Wilson refers to this as a filtering process and observes, "...stimuli which would suggest heterosexual tendencies are denied or filtered out" and secondly, "...most of the same-sex contact seems to get filtered in."[35] In addition, Wilson maintains, "They are often shocked when they are helped through counseling to remember more clearly these experiences which have been filtered out."[36]

Conclusion

Homosexuality involves uncertainty when it comes to identifying the cause and it may be appropriate to talk in terms of "best guesses" for the causes, plural. There are several problems with accepting a totally "nature" argument. How do we know for sure biological or chemical differences determine sexual orientations as opposed to these differences coming as a result of and reflecting differences originating in the behavior? In other words, how do we know behavior is the result of biology rather than biology the result of behavior? Secondly, given a predisposition for the homosexual orientation coming from biology, should homosexual behavior be encouraged? For example, genetic links have been discovered for a predisposition to develop alcoholism in some people, yet we do not encourage these people to drink alcohol. Given biological roots, does that mean prede-

[35] Ibid., p. 68.

[36] Ibid.

termination and under no control, or predisposition with possibilities to be comfortable with heterosexuality? Finally, if biological differences in homosexuals were shown, how can we be sure those same differences are not embedded within large proportions of heterosexuals? If we were able to analyze all heterosexuals would we actually find far more of those with the biological characteristics thought to be responsible for homosexuality actually among heterosexuals? Although there are legitimate questions, enough research evidence for innate differences between homosexuals and heterosexuals exists that it becomes difficult to say each and every homosexual learned the orientation completely as a result of nurturing and environment.

Dr. Gary Collins addresses the situation in this way: "Despite probably thousands of scientific studies, one conclusion seems clear: There is no clearly identified single cause of homosexuality."[37] In order to clarify the most accepted position, Collins discusses causality in terms of nature, critical period, and nurture. There may be prenatal influences which set up a homosexual predisposition, then in a critical or sensitive period during early development there are experiences which encourage the expression of the predisposition, and finally the family and social environment serve to reinforce the expression of predisposition. Collins continues, "We are left then with the conclusion that homosexuality can arise from a variety of causes. Some inconclusive data suggest that biological influences, operating before birth, may play some role in the development of later sexual orientation, but there is even greater evidence that homosexual preferences and behaviors are determined by psychological development and social learning."[38]

Meier, Minirth, Wichern, and Ratcliff end with this thought: "The best research to date, summarized by Jones

---

[37] Collins, p. 282.

[38] Ibid., p. 283.

and Workman (1989), indicates that often (but not always) prenatal hormones influence gender orientation. When combined with certain socialization experiences, homosexuality becomes more likely; however, such influences do not force an individual to engage in homosexual behavior."[39] They allow that predispositions set potential strengths and weaknesses, however socialization and choices combine with predispositions to influence a specific person. These authors delineate several likely causes which include: insecurity in sex-role identification, sexual experiences, behavioral conditioning from environmental conditions, and biological factors.[40]

Dr. Earl Wilson concludes:

> First, there is a growing body of research which supports the idea that sex differentiation is predisposed before the child is born.... Second, the degree to which prenatal dispositions can be altered is hotly debated.... Third, there is evidence to support other causes of homosexuality.... Finally, if, as the author contends, a high percentage of cases of homosexuality are best explained by social learning or parent-child explanations, then it would follow that there is much work for the counselor to do.[41]

Although we may never be certain of the origins of homosexual attraction and orientation, we must address homosexual behavior. Christians must be concerned on two levels: we must be willing to declare God's truth concerning homosexual behavior, yet we must have a servant's heart for ministering God's grace to homosexuals.

---

[39] Ibid., p. 272.

[40] Ibid., pp. 175-176.

[41] Ibid., pp. 72-73.

Chapter Four

CAN HOMOSEXUALS CHANGE?

Dr. J.D. Robertson

Dr. Robertson compares the approaches and expectations regarding the possibility of change in homosexual behavior from both the secular and Christian perspective.

Introduction

Perhaps the best way to approach the question posed by this chapter would be to revisit an old joke concerning psychologists. Get ready, here it comes:

Comic: "How many psychologists does it take to change a lightbulb?"

Response: "I don't know, how many psychologists does it take to change a lightbulb?"

Comic: "Only one – provided the lightbulb wants to be changed!"

Although the joke may leave a bit to be desired as far as humor, it does illustrate the situation helping professionals face with any person and problem. Homosexuality is no different. The ability to change involves the individual's desire to change, willingness to take responsibility for change, and commitment to making the change no matter how long it takes. Many look for magic – "Poof! Your problem is solved!" However, such ingrained thoughts, behaviors, and feelings took years to develop and will not magically disappear through psychological "hocus-pocus."

The problem with discussing the potential for changing homosexuality involves expectations. Does the homosexual believe change is possible? Does the professional believe change is possible or even desirable? How is change defined?

Current Views

Chandler Burr provides historical study of homosexuality research and treatments for change. According to Burr, the term "homosexuality" was first used in an 1869 pamphlet published in Leipzig, Germany. Homosexuality has been observed and reported throughout history, however, this marked the first time there was a label involved. For example, "same-sex sex" was regarded as a sin and later as a crime but those who committed such acts did not wear a label that distinguished them from others. In the late 19th century this changed as psychiatry and psychology took the position that homosexuality was a form of mental illness.[1]

Burr observes that once pathology became the dominant psychiatric and psychological view, there were several treatments advanced as remedies for the condition. A 1992 documentary, entitled "Changing Our Minds" by psychologist James Harrison, reports cases of hysterectomies and estrogen injections for females, lobotomies, electric shock, castration, and aversion therapy as some of the more extreme prescriptions. However, attempts to show pathology associated with homosexuality typically failed. The Kinsey studies of the 1940's found homosexuality to be highly resistant to change. In the 1950's Evelyn Hooker conducted a study which resulted in her conclusion that homosexuality could not be de-

[1] Chandler Burr, p. 48.

fined as pathology. Finally, in 1973, The American Psychiatric Association removed homosexuality from the Diagnostic and Statistical Manual.[2] Burr summarizes the current scientific view: "Today's psychiatrists and psychologists, with very few exceptions, do not try to change sexual orientation, and those aspiring to work in the fields of psychiatry and psychology are now trained not to regard homosexuality as a disease."[3]

There are professionals who maintain the pathological view of homosexuality changed for less than empirical reasons. It must be noted that some believe homosexuality was removed from the DSM not because of scientific evidence, but because of political pressure brought by homosexual activists. In a review of the DSM, Kutchins and Kirk said, "In 1973, protests by gay activists induced APA members to vote for the elimination of homosexuality as a diagnosis. However justified, this response seemed to substantiate complaints that their decisions were influenced by political pressure."[4] Zustiak[5] relates the series of events that Kutchins and Kirk mention:

> A little known fact is that while the deletion of homosexuality from the DSM III did take place in response to a majority vote of the APA, later surveys showed that the majority of the APA membership viewed homosexuality as pathological, in spite of the vote! Four years after the vote, a survey found that 69 percent of psychiatrists believed that homosexuality "usually represents a pathological adaptation."[6]
>
> If the majority still saw homosexuality as a pathological adaptation then how did the change pass? An investigation

[2] Ibid., pp. 48-49.

[3] Ibid., p. 49.

[4] "The Future of DSM: Scientific and Professional Issues," *The Harvard Medical School Mental Health Letter*, September 1988, p. 4.

[5] "Hope and Healing for the Homosexual," *The Christian Standard*, February 14, 1993, pp. 8-9.

[6] Jones and Workman, "Homosexuality: The Behavioral Sciences and the Church," *Journal of Psychology and Theology*, Fall 1989, p. 214.

showed that the vote was taken under political pressure and under explicit threats from the gay rights establishment to continue disruptive demonstrations at APA conventions and impede research if the vote didn't pass.

Even at the very convention where the vote was taken a large voice of protest went up from specialists in the field of homosexuality. These protests resulted in a referendum vote by the entire APA body. Shortly before the ballots were due, a letter was sent out by the officers of APA urging the members to let the decision stand. It was only later that it was learned that the letter was paid for by the National Gay Task Force.[7]

It is important to know that this change in the APA Diagnostic Manual did not come about as a result of any discoveries or new theories resulting from scientific research, but was merely the result of political terrorism. This robs the decision of its credibility and force.

Regardless of whether homosexuality should or should not be listed as pathological, the fact remains that it is not so listed. Whereas professionals were once taught homosexuality was pathological, currently they receive training where homosexuality is viewed as acceptable and within the normal range of human sexuality. Usually the focus of therapy would center on how comfortable a homosexual client was with his or her orientation, rather than attempting to change the orientation. Today a person concerned about homosexual issues might seek professional assistance to overcome the sexual orientation and instead be questioned concerning why he or she was so concerned with the same-sex orientation. If the individual was not firm in the goal of the therapeutic process, it might change to helping him or her reconcile self-image and the homosexual orientation. In fact, when homosexuality and pathology are discussed, it is just as likely that heterosexual people in the client's social network will be considered pathological (homophobic) by helping professionals.

---

[7] Houck, "Neglected by Mission: The Homosexual Person," *Urban Mission*, May 1989, p. 14.

Whether we want to admit it or not, there are core beliefs that color perceptions of homosexuality and scientists and therapists are not immune. If from the late 1800's through the 1970's there was an inappropriate scientific predisposition to find homosexuality to be pathological, then the reverse may be true today. The assumption that homosexuality is not pathological and that there are biological roots may just as easily influence what questions are formed, which influences the hypotheses researched, and the discoveries that are made, and in turn which findings are written about, and finally the research findings editors choose to publish. Researchers, educators, and practitioners strive for objectivity, yet must be aware of their biases.

Carolyn Dillon, co-chair of clinical practice at Boston University School of Social Work, demonstrates the agenda professionals can bring to an issue. She asserts that in the 1970's and 1980's researchers sought to determine which strategies would be helpful to homosexuals in oppressive conditions and today professionals can assist in the "psychological liberation and empowerment" of homosexuals. Her view is, "The professional response to gay clients should involve education as well as therapy; it should be political as well as psychological."[8]

Chandler Burr provides keen insight into the potential problem of bias by allowing that many researchers had a personal stake in their research findings. "Some of those involved in the research are motivated not only by scientific but also by personal concerns. Many of the scientists who have been studying homosexuality are gay, as am I."[9] Burr's recognition of values and potential biases is a step toward objectivity.

Everyone benefits from an honest evaluation of core beliefs. This book has outlined the biases and assumptions we

[8] "Working with Lesbian and Gay Clients," *The Harvard Mental Health Letter*, February 1993, p. 4.

[9] Burr, p. 48.

as authors bring to this material. Understanding one's bias and admitting it brings about the possibility for a sincere search for truth. Currently, most psychological professionals would assume that homosexual tendencies are essentially innate and the focus of therapy with homosexuals would be to assist in the healthy acceptance, internalization, and incorporation of the homosexual identity. The problem would not be considered to be homosexuality, but how one feels about one's homosexuality. This view expresses a certain set of assumptions and reflects a particular worldview. However, there are some who hold a different set of assumptions concerning homosexuality and approach the issue from a different perspective. One of these different perspectives involves Christian practitioners and the Christian worldview.

Christian View

Again, we as authors have already taken a clear position on the morality of homosexual behavior based on the core assumptions outlined earlier. Our core assumptions do not diminish the desire to understand the dynamics of homosexuality or our commitment to minister to homosexuals in the name of Jesus. Yet in many cases Christian values put professionals at odds with certain psychological schools of thought, and not just concerning homosexuality.

For example, consider a man who seeks out a professional because of anxiety and guilt. The professional explores this problem with the client in order to find the origins of his negative emotions. At first, the man is hesitant and hedges, but finally he relates his involvement in an extramarital sexual relationship with a woman. The client finds the affair to be irresistible and laced with excitement. Yet at the same time, he can hardly look his wife and children in the eyes. He is petrified they will discover his secret activities, yet he does not want to end the extramarital relationship. The professional is then confronted with what must be done to address the man's anxiety and guilt.

Although no one can predict the exact course each and every professional would take, there are essentially two alternatives representing the extremes and each can remedy the man's negative feelings. Although both tacks are successful they end in vastly differing situations and represent opposing worldviews and core assumptions.

One view involves changing the man's values. The anxiety and guilt originates in the man's belief that he is engaging in wrong behavior. His conscience is possibly viewed as too strict and punitive, hence the prescription is to relax the man's rigid and stifling moral code. He might be questioned why he believed the extramarital relationship was wrong. Discussion could cover whether the relationship was consenting and mutually beneficial. Also questions of whether the relationship was hurting his marriage or children might be reviewed. If the determination was made that no one was hurt by the relationship, the man might actually begin to feel differently and the anxiety and guilt would possibly disappear. At termination of the helping relationship, the man feels better; however, he still is involved in an extramarital relationship and his family does not know his secret.

A second view involves changing the man's behavior. Because the anxiety and guilt originates in the man's belief that the relationship was wrong, then the negative emotions will likely disappear by quitting the wrong behavior. Here the assumption is that the client experiences negative emotions because he is behaving inconsistently with his values and the prescription is to behave consistently with his values. At termination of the counseling relationship, the man feels better because he has ended the affair, hopefully confessed the secret to his family, and is focused on restoring trust in his family life.

Although this hypothetical situation is obviously broad and simplistic, it does demonstrate the two very different approaches to a problem based on core assumptions. Both therapists can be concerned, empathic, skilled, and successful in assisting the client to overcome the present problem. Yet they succeed through very different approaches with very different resulting situations.

Christian professionals must be concerned, empathic, and skilled, yet recognize their core beliefs put them in a specific context. Hence the Christian view works to balance the "grace" of interpersonal compassion and ministry, and the "truth" of the scriptural stand on homosexuality.

Zustiak illustrates the dilemma well:

> As strongly as we want to take a stand against the practice of homosexuality, we must also strongly take a stand against our unwillingness to reach out and evangelize, counsel, love and convert those struggling with homosexuality.
>
> Two new Christians approached a pastor for help with homosexual issues. They were told by this pastor, "Commit suicide! God understands suicide better than homosexuality." One jumped off Seattle's George Washington Bridge, the other is drinking himself to death.[10]
>
> It is not possible for the church to pray, "Oh, God, heal that person, but please don't involve me." The homosexual can change. It takes place through the love and power of Jesus Christ. It will not happen overnight. It takes patience and great commitment on the part of the church. But it does happen.[11]

Fundamentally most evangelical Christian professionals would maintain that even if we cannot be certain of its causes, homosexual behavior is wrong, and it can be changed. Dr. David Seamands suggests that change involves commitment and struggle. The place to start is identifying what constitutes change in the mind of the person who wants change. Seamands believes it may be impossible for some people to totally change the homosexual attraction or tendency, but is absolutely convinced homosexual behavior can be changed. Factors that influence the potential for change

---

[10] Houck, p. 15.

[11] Ibid., p. 9.

include the age of the individual, the extent of the person's involvement in homosexual behavior or lifestyle, and his or her motivation for change. Change may not mean heterosexuality for every person who seeks assistance with same-sex struggles, it may mean celibacy. Dr. Seamands' audiotape provides some general guidelines for consideration. There is a need to analyze the possible underlying reasons for developing the homosexual orientation, as well as honestly coming to grips with God's view of homosexual behavior and lusts. Also attempt to consider what "payoffs" come with the homosexual orientation. Usually when we have developed deeply ingrained patterns of behavior or attitudes and wish to change, we have to address the needs which are being met by those activities or beliefs. The brakes must be applied to behavior with a determination to stop all homosexual activities and rid oneself of all reminders of it. Finally, the need for developing a "plan of renewal" is discussed. The components of the plan involve: 1. activities centering on Christian growth, such as praying, Bible reading, reading Christian literature, attending church, becoming involved in Christian fellowship, ministering to others, and honestly evaluating oneself; 2. activities of self-discipline, such as exercising, sleeping and eating properly, coping appropriately with life stressors, and choosing to actively change lifestyles; 3. developing a relationship with a mentor or role model who has spiritual maturity, is trustworthy and deserving respect; 4. establishing friendships and developing deeper relationships with people of the opposite sex; 5. setting appropriate goals in counsel with one's mentor, developing plans for attaining goals, realistically adjusting goals, and working to realize goals.

Dr. Jay Adams proposes his response when helping homosexuals who wish to change. The place to begin according to Adams involves the acceptance of two truths: First, acknowledge homosexuality as sin; and second, realize that Jesus Christ holds the keys to lasting change. Once those two truths are understood, Adams offers practical guidelines for change. The person must break off homosexual relationships and associations. Also places which are associated with the homosexual lifestyle or contacts should be avoided. Another component involves the recognition of the dominating place homosexuality holds in one's life. He says that homosexuals often learn to lie as a result of the "double" life they sometimes lead. Hence one concern is to be vigilant for truth and sensitive to the temptation of taking liberties with the truth. This process involves what Adams terms "total structuring" which means "looking at the problem in relationship to all areas of life."[12] Just as Christians view their faith as the cardinal trait of their identity and as such, permeating all areas of their lives, so too, homosexuals tend to view their same-sex orientation as the cardinal trait of their lives, hence all areas of life should be examined for its effects. Dr. Adams summarizes by saying:

> There is hope for the homosexual. That hope, then, lies in the following.
> 1. Christian conversion;
> 2. An acknowledgement and confession of the sin of homosexuality leading to forgiveness;
> 3. Fruits appropriate to repentance, such as
>   a. Abandonment of homosexual practices and associates (I Corinthians 15:33);
>   b. Rescheduling of activities, etc.;
>   c. Restructuring of the whole life according to biblical principles by the power of Christ's Spirit;
>   d. Less emphasis upon sexual experience;
> 4. Unless God gives the gift of continence, seeking to learn and manifest a life of love by giving oneself to his spouse within the bounds of heterosexual marriage.[13]

Dr. Gary Collins advises, "The place to begin counseling is with your own attitudes . . . Jesus loved sinners and those

---

[12] Jay Adams, p. 410.

[13] Ibid., pp. 411-412.

who were tempted to sin."[14] Collins pleads for an empathic understanding of the struggle many homosexuals endure. He agrees with Richard Foster who addresses the difficulties involved in balancing grace and truth, "Because this issue has wounded so many people, the first word that needs to be spoken is one of compassion and healing . . . . All who are caught in the cultural and ecclesiastical chaos over homosexuality need our compassion and understanding."[15] Collins then squarely confronts the issue of change:

> One idea that must change is the myth that homosexuality is a disease that cannot be cured. Homosexuality is not a disease; it is a tendency that often but not always leads to habitual fantasies or acts of homoerotic behavior. If homosexuality is primarily a learned condition, as the evidence suggests, then it can be unlearned. If homosexual behavior is sinful, as the Bible teaches, then forgiveness is available and so is divine help that can keep a homosexually oriented person from sexual sin.
>
> Change is never easy for homosexuals and their counselors. The counselee dropout rate is high, and enthusiastic reports from ex-gay ministries often appear to be overly optimistic. Nevertheless, change (even to heterosexual tendencies and behavior) is possible, especially when some of the following are present (the more that are present, the better the chance for change):
>
> - The counselee honestly faces his or her homosexuality.
> - The counselee has a strong desire to change.
> - The counselee is willing to break contact with homosexual companions who tempt the counselee into homosexual behavior.
> - There is a willingness to avoid drugs and alcohol since these leave one more vulnerable to temptation.
> - The counselee is able to build a close nonsexual intimate relationship with the counselor or other same-sex person.
> - The counselee experiences acceptance and love apart from homosexual friends and contacts.

[14] Collins, p. 287.

[15] Ibid., p. 280.

- The counselee is under thirty-five and/or is not deeply involved in homosexual attachments to others.
- The counselee has a desire to avoid sin and to commit his or her life and problems to the Lordship of Jesus Christ.[16]

Conclusion

The primary concern from a Christian perspective is balancing grace and truth. This cardinal concern is not just for serving the brother or sister grappling with problems related to homosexuality, it is the core tension in the Christian's approach to the world. Sinful behaviors and attitudes must be separated from people who are sinners. People who are sinners need love while sins must be confronted. Christians are committed to God's unyielding truth, expressed in God's unconditional love. Christians are absolutely called to minister with grace, yet they are also called to be completely faithful to God's absolute truth. For dealing with homosexuality, this means Christians must oppose the proliferation of the gay rights movement's social and political agendas because of the call of God's truth, yet remember each individual who faces same-sex orientations and practices remains a child of God who deserves the ministry of God's grace.

The popular television and radio host, Rush Limbaugh, asserts that people must have the courage to face the truth. When there is an open, genuine, and courageous examination of the truths involved in homosexuality, the effects are sobering:

(1) Homosexual behavior is wrong according to God's Word.

(2) We are uncertain of its causes; it is probably a combination of factors for each homosexual.

(3) Homosexual behavior puts people at risk for sexually transmitted diseases, especially AIDS.

(4) According to a June 1993 television news report,

[16] Ibid., p. 288.

AIDS is becoming the leading cause of death in major cities among young adult males.

(5) AIDS is a horribly devastating disease. One testimony is Silver Lake Life, a documentary airing on PBS in June of 1993, chronicling the relationship of a same-sex couple and the progression of AIDS from onset to death, as well as its aftermath for those who survived the victim's death.

(6) According to one television news report in June 1993, the average life expectancy for homosexual males is now 42, while life expectancy for homosexual females is presently 45, a little over half the life expectancy of heterosexual males and females.

(7) According to June 1993 newspaper reports of the European meeting of leading AIDS researchers, there are no likely cures for AIDS on the immediate horizon, despite the large sums of funding for research.

(8) AIDS is spread primarily through behavior and the only sure prevention has to do with avoiding behavior that puts one at risk.

(9) Although many researchers and mental health professionals believe the origins of homosexuality are innate and there is no need for change, many Christian professionals maintain homosexuality is wrong and change is possible regardless of its origins. These Christian practitioners are called to ministries of God's grace to the person, yet dedication to the truths of God concerning homosexuality.

(10) God offers immediate mercy, real restoration, and ultimate hope for those who seek Him.

PART THREE

AIDS

Chapter Five

THE AIDS AGENDA*

Dr. F. LaGard Smith

In this chapter, Dr. Smith explodes the myths surrounding heterosexual AIDS and traces the history and politicization of this issue.

The year was 1987. Oprah Winfrey dramatically opened her show, "Women Living with AIDS," with the ominous words:

> Hello, everybody. AIDS has both sexes running scared. Research studies now project that one in five – listen to me, hard to believe – one in five heterosexuals could be dead from AIDS at the end of the next three years. That's by 1990. One in five. It is no longer just a gay disease. Believe me.[1]

---

*Taken from *Sodom's Second Coming: What You Need to Know About the Deadly Homosexual Assault* by F. LaGard Smith, Harvest House Publishers, 1993. Used by permission.

---

[1] "Women Living With AIDS," *Oprah*, transcript of Feb. 18, 1987, p.2, as quoted in Michael Fumento, *The Myth of Heterosexual AIDS*, p. 3.

We are now several years beyond 1990. Not one in five, nor one in ten, nor even one in a hundred heterosexuals have died from AIDS as Oprah predicted. In fact, *not one in 3500 heterosexuals have died from AIDS!*

In just over a decade since AIDS was first diagnosed (in 1981), a total of 70,000 nongays have died from the disease, the vast majority of whom were intravenous drug abusers, followed far behind by a combination of hemophiliacs and those receiving blood transfusions infected with HIV, and a somewhat larger percentage of heterosexuals of Haitian or East African descent. What this means for heterosexuals of all categories is that, out of 250 million Americans, only .0003 percent have died in a decade from AIDS-related deaths!

It's not just Oprah, of course, who predicted the gloom. She was in good company. Teamed together with the media, the former Surgeon General C. Everett Koop had launched a campaign to "inform" America that not only was AIDS easily transmitted among heterosexuals, but that soon the "epidemic" would reach astronomical proportions.

In the same year that Oprah made her dramatic prediction, across the ocean in Great Britain the Communicable Diseases Surveillance Centre advised the Government to expect 3000 new cases (both heterosexual and homosexual) to be diagnosed in the following year. As it turned out, there were only 755 cases (predominantly homosexual). A forecast made only one year ahead was wrong by a factor of 400 percent![2]

Global predictions have been equally excessive. The U.N.'s World Health Organization (WHO) has predicted catastrophe for years among heterosexuals worldwide – a catastrophe which has yet to take place. As we will see momentarily, its predictions – focusing mainly on the continent of

---

[2] Jenny Rees, "Cut AIDS research urges economist," in *The Daily Telegraph*, June 14, 1991.

Africa — may have been based upon a number of false premises.

Both at home and around the globe, the coming heterosexual AIDS apocalypse has been — and for the most part continues to be — conventional wisdom. But where is the evidence? Why hasn't it happened? Did that many promiscuous heterosexuals immediately stop sleeping around? Did the panicky use of condoms bring the predicted epidemic to a screeching halt? If so, how do we account for an almost minuscule number of AIDS-related deaths resulting from the wide-open sexual activity going on in the incubation years before AIDS was discovered and the brakes put on?

It just doesn't add up. Rampant heterosexual AIDS is a myth!

You've Got a Transmission Problem

To say that heterosexual AIDS is a myth is not to say that heterosexuals can't have AIDS. Thousands of heterosexuals have AIDS or have been diagnosed as HIV-positive. As we have already seen, however, the vast majority of such heterosexuals are in the high-risk intravenous drug-abuser group. On the other hand, sadly, there are also completely innocent victims of the disease who did nothing at all to bring it on themselves. Most of these contracted AIDS through tainted blood transfusions (like tennis great Arthur Ashe) or through infections which were passed on to children by their infected mothers.

A case in point demonstrates both the good news and the bad news of heterosexual AIDS. People all across the nation were saddened to learn that Elizabeth Glaser, wife of actor/director Paul Michael Glaser (who played Starsky on the '70's detective show "Starsky and Hutch") had contracted the virus in 1981 through a blood transfusion received after giving birth to her daughter.

The bad news was compounded when she unknowingly passed the disease on to her baby, Ariel, through breast milk.

Seven-year-old Ariel eventually died of AIDS complications in 1988. Their son, Jake, was also infected in utero before the Glasers knew Elizabeth was HIV-positive.

The good news is that Paul Michael never contracted the disease. And as he put it, "Until we found out that our family was infected, Elizabeth and I had a natural sexual relationship. I wasn't infected by either child, and they did everything a child can do to a parent. They bled on me, they crapped on me, they hugged me, and they kissed me. And I still don't have it."[3]

Elizabeth Glaser's Pediatric AIDS Foundation is a poignant reminder of the passivity with which HIV and AIDS can be received. In far too many cases, AIDS has walked in uninvited. To that extent, AIDS is *not* exclusively a gay disease, and deserves every effort we can make to control it.

On the other hand, we have to be careful in assessing the extent of its impact through heterosexual intercourse. Paul Michael Glaser's case tells us what any number of other studies are also showing: that AIDS is extremely difficult to get.

University of California's Nancy Padian, often referred to as the queen of partner studies because of her vast work in the field, reports that only about 20 percent of women who sleep with HIV-positive men *over a period of years* become infected. And for infection going in the other direction – from infected women to uninfected men – the figures are even less. Far less! "Of 61 HIV-positive women studied, only one transmitted the virus to her partner – and that was as a result of a highly unusual sex life."[4]

What these and other studies show is that, statistically, it is unlikely (though possible) for HIV to be transferred from a man to a woman through acts of vaginal intercourse. And the odds of it being passed from a woman to a man through vagi-

---

[3] *The Jerusalem Post*, Aug. 31, 1989, Features.

[4] Mona Charen, "The Curious Ways of AIDS Activists," in *Newsday*, Jan. 22, 1992, Wednesday, City Ed., Viewpoints, p.76.

nal intercourse are simply negligible.[5]

Further proof of the difficulty of female-to-male transmission is found in the mandatory health checks required of prostitutes in Nevada, where brothels are legal. The 32 legal brothels take in some 600,000 "dates" each year. Despite the busy traffic in heterosexual sex, *not one case* of HIV infection has been reported among the brothel's many "working girls."[6]

The reason for the relatively rare instances of people being infected through heterosexual contact is that, without some other factor being involved, there is simply a *serious transmission problem.*

How HIV Travels

The often-repeated phrase "exchange of body fluids" is itself misleading. You don't catch AIDS from toilet seats, airborne bacteria, insect bites, or even saliva or urine. That is why we have no reason to shun AIDS victims as if merely touching them will infect us. They are not lepers!

And as indicated above, normal heterosexual intercourse (and probably in most cases even oral sex) is not a good vehicle for HIV transmission. HIV, which usually (though not always) leads to AIDS, is a "blood-borne" virus. For the HIV infection to be transmitted, it must have some passage whereby it may enter the bloodstream. Without such an entry, there can be no infection.[7] Again, remember what Glaser said about his children bleeding *on* him. That kind of blood contact wasn't a threat.

What this means is that normal heterosexual intercourse

---

[5] Merle A. Sande, M.D. and Paul A. Volberding, M.D., *The Medical Management of AIDS* (Philadelphia: W.B. Saunders Company, 1988), p. 20.

[6] "Study of Brothel Prostitutes Finds Little Venereal Disease," in the *Los Angeles Times*, Aug. 26, 1991, Part A, p. 3; Legalized Prostitution," in *The Economist*, Sep. 7, 1991, American Survey, p. 28.

[7] Denise Grady et al., "Just how *Does* AIDS Spread?" in *Time*, Mar. 21, 1988, p. 61.

(vaginal) is typically not suited to HIV transmission, whereas homosexual intercourse (anal) definitely is. With the latter, there is frequently a skin breakage that occurs during the act, usually to both parties. The same is not true of vaginal intercourse. (Sex during a woman's menstruation could possibly alter this scenario, but even then it would probably require the man to have an open lesion.)

Even where there is no skin breakage, the risks of anal intercourse are greatly enhanced because of the functional nature of the rectum. In rather simple terms, the walls of the rectum are porous, or absorbent, so that the last bit of nutrients entering the body can get into the bloodstream before being totally eliminated. That absorbency can be the HIV's best friend.

Vaginal-penile sex may be more apt to transmit HIV if the partners already have any other sexually-transmitted diseases (STD's), but this is still associated with the blood system. Sores, ulcers, and lesions caused by the STD's can open up pathways for the virus-infected semen to travel into the bloodstream.

The fact that typical HIV transmission occurs through anal intercourse explains why lesbians – although homosexuals – are almost completely unaffected by AIDS. (Female-to-female transmission has been reported in one case where "a woman infected through intravenous drug abuse appeared to have transmitted HIV to a female partner through traumatic sex practices that resulted in exposure to the blood of the drug abuser."[8]) Relative to lesbians, it can properly be said that AIDS is not a "gay disease."

Unfortunately for gay men, because of the unnatural way they have sex, AIDS is very definitely a "gay disease." Likewise, for intravenous drug-abusers AIDS is very definitely an "addict's disease." They too provide the conduit for HIV by sharing needles which inject not only drugs but also the

---

[8] Sande and Volberding, *Medical Management of AIDS*, p. 20.

"blood-borne" disease into their veins.

As a "gay disease," AIDS is not even the most frequent blood-borne disease affecting homosexuals. That dubious honor goes to Hepatitis B, which, being one hundred times more infectious than AIDS, kills more people in a day than AIDS does in a year.[9] According to one authority, Hepatitis B "infects the majority of homosexual men within three years of their becoming sexually active."[10]

Other False-Positive Theories

The doomsayers can be excused for having made wildly wrong predictions, because knowing what AIDS is all about has been a difficult learning process in what necessarily has been a crash course. We simply haven't understood the disease well enough, and have therefore erred on the side of caution.

One of the early misconceptions about the disease was the supposed ability of the infection to travel rapidly via sexual intercourse from one person to another and to another and to another, after first being obtained from an initial member in one of the high-risk groups. That is how other sexually-transmitted diseases (STD's), like gonorrhea and syphilis, spread.

That is what is so mystifying about HIV relative to heterosexuals. With heterosexuals, it works the exact opposite way from all other STD's. STD's thrive on multiple partners, or promiscuity. But HIV will be transmitted, if at all, only after significant sexual contact with *the same partner*.

The belief that the virus would be transmitted rapidly to distant third parties probably accounts for all the doomsday figures. But the fact is that, if such transmission happens at all, it happens only in the rare case. Virtually all cases have

---

[9] Green, *Dead-End*, p. 99.

[10] John Seale, M.D., MRCP, "The Aids Epidemic and its Control," in the *British Medico-Chirurgical Journal*, Vol. 102(iii), Aug. 1987, p. 66.

been members of high-risk groups and their immediate sexual partners.[11]

Enter Earvin "Magic" Johnson. I can still remember where I was and what I was doing when I first heard the broadcast. In my memory, the shocking news will always stand right up there along with President Kennedy's assassination and the explosion of the space shuttle Challenger. I was a diehard Lakers – and Magic Johnson – fan. My mind raced: "Magic has tested positive for HIV? Like everyone else in America, I simply couldn't believe it!"

Looking back, I suspect that gay activists, while struck by the tragedy like all the rest of us, had other thoughts as well, since this universally admired superstar was proof positive that even heterosexuals could get HIV. After all, hadn't Magic confessed to "accommodating as many women as possible"? What more proof could you ask for? "If it can happen to Magic, it can happen to anybody."

We may never know for sure how Magic contracted the disease. What we do know is that it's unlikely he got it through "third party" transmission. This fact suggests contact with someone in a high-risk group – in other words, blood-related contact. It galls me to even think it, but if Magic hasn't told us the whole truth about how he contracted the virus, then he has some serious apologies to make to the media, to his fans, and particularly to the young people who look up to him on the subject of AIDS.

However he got it, one simply *has* to ask why Magic's wife, Cookie, did not test HIV-positive, despite a longstanding sexual relationship with Magic. Or why we haven't had a rash of major news conferences announcing the infection of Wilt Chamberlain (who claims 20,000 sexual partners) or other NBA superstuds with similar sexual habits as Wilt and Magic.

---

[11] "Why the Course of AIDS is Defying Africa's Precedent," in the *New York Times*, Feb. 21, 1988, Late City Final Ed., Sec. 4, p. 6.

No matter how well-intended, Magic's crusade for kids to use condoms misses the whole point. Unless they are part of some other high-risk group, their risk is not from unprotected heterosexual intercourse. Their greatest risk – ever present – is a moral risk, and not all the magic condoms in the world can spare them from its spiritual consequences.

Finally, what could prove to be a third major problem with the predictions of heterosexual AIDS is surfacing more each day in the escalating debate over whether HIV is the cause of AIDS. Several experts are beginning to question even that sacred cow. Among them, Professor Peter Duesberg, virologist at the University of California, argues that HIV itself is harmless and must be related to other factors in order for it to end up as AIDS.[12]

The coming months and years are likely to see the rise and fall of one theory after another regarding HIV and AIDS. The bottom line, however, is that at this point there is simply no evidence of widespread heterosexually transmitted infection in the United States and western Europe.

Out of Africa: More Fiction

However, if you listen to the World Health Organization and to virtually all major AIDS research bodies, you will hear a chorus of voices telling you that Africa is in the grip of a heterosexual AIDS epidemic, and that the continent is being devastated by HIV. According to WHO, we can expect half a million sub-Saharan Africans to die from AIDS each year by the turn of the century – all because of unprotected heterosexual sex.[13]

But is it true? Is the African "heterosexual AIDS" experience a dire warning to the West of what could happen to us?

Right off the bat, one would do well to consider carefully

---

[12] Neville Hodgkinson, "Epidemic of Aids in Africa 'a tragic myth,'" in *The Sunday Times* (London), Mar. 21, 1993, News 2.

[13] Ibid.

what is meant by the term *heterosexual AIDS*. As typically used, the term refers to AIDS which is acquired through heterosexual sex. That's what all the television warnings are about. That's what the new-moralists are talking about when they encourage "safe sex" through the use of condoms.

But it is easy – especially in Africa – to get caught in the trap of saying that there is evidence of "heterosexual AIDS" (AIDS transmitted through heterosexual intercourse) simply because people who have AIDS (from whatever cause) *happen to be heterosexual*. To personalize the point, Elizabeth Glaser and her daughter Ariel are properly classified under the heading "heterosexual AIDS" (because they were both heterosexuals when they were infected); but this doesn't mean that either of them acquired the disease as a result of heterosexual sex.

Just because thousands of heterosexuals in Africa have been diagnosed as having AIDS doesn't mean that they *acquired it* through heterosexual relations.

That said, it is even more important to appreciate that just because thousands of heterosexuals in Africa *have been diagnosed as having AIDS* doesn't necessarily mean that they either actually *have* AIDS or that it was caused by HIV. Study after study is beginning to show that AIDS diagnosis in Africa is faulty on a grand scale.

Dr. Harvey Bialy, Scientific Editor of *Biotechnology*, a sister publication to the science journal *Nature*, has been visiting Africa since 1975 and has spent eight years there.[14] Dr. Bialy says that HIV tests in Africa react to non-HIV antibodies as well as to HIV itself, producing up to 80 to 90 percent false-positives. "There is vast literature showing this," he emphasizes.[15]

Even in America, it is well-known that the HIV tests can

---

[14] Ibid.

[15] Joan Shenton, "AIDS and Africa," in *Dispatches*, Channel 4 (London) programme aired Mar. 24, 1993.

often produce false-positives, and multiple tests are recommended to confirm HIV findings. In Africa, where there is even less funding to support HIV testing, there is simply no opportunity in most cases to verify initial screening, if there is any test at all. What relatively few tests are given which indicate that the patient is HIV-positive are accepted at face value and added to the burgeoning statistics.

As suggested in the careful wording of the previous paragraph, *most AIDS diagnosis in Africa involves no HIV testing whatsoever.* Diagnosis is made on the basis of a standard Clinical Case Definition which looks at a combination of symptoms (fever, pronounced weight loss, diarrhea, and prolonged, dry cough) – all of which are virtually indistinguishable from other diseases such as malaria and tuberculosis. As a result, almost all malaria and TB cases are diagnosed today as AIDS – and so they too end up in the grim statistics.[16]

The plain fact is that "AIDS" in Africa is as likely to be related to poverty, malnutrition, inadequate medical supplies, and bad water as to HIV.

In the Ivory Coast, the relationship between AIDS and HIV is particularly suspect. In one maternity clinic in Koumassi, for example, there is a higher incidence of HIV than in the West, but there is not a frequent progression to AIDS. At the same time, many women are classed as HIV-negative, yet they meet the definitions for AIDS![17] It suggests once again that there must be cofactors which make possible the progression from HIV to AIDS.

Among the interesting data from Uganda is another study among a hundred discordant heterosexual couples (one partner originally testing positive, the other negative). Over a two-year period, both partners became HIV-positive in only five of the couples. The significance? In 95 percent of

---

[16] Ibid.

[17] Ibid.

the couples, HIV had *not* been passed on through heterosexual intercourse.[18] (That mirrors the studies already noted in the United States.)

The raw statistics alone are enough to make one sit up and take notice that something is odd indeed about the research figures coming out of Africa. Since 1984, in the West one million people have been diagnosed as having HIV, yet there are only 129,000 reported cases of AIDS.[19] How does that stack up with 1) all the horror stories about Africa, or 2) the validity of AIDS diagnosis in the dark continent?

In Tanzania, volunteers working for Partage, a French charity in aid of adoptions, asked its staff of 160 people and a whole village of 842 people to undergo HIV testing. The results were only 5 percent (among the staff) and 13.8 percent (among the villagers) who were HIV-positive. The results were *five times lower* than WHO's statistics for the region.[20]

In fact, AIDS research in Africa is severely criticized by local health officials for focusing in on some particularly chosen "epicenter" and then extrapolating the results as if they accurately represented a much larger region or even an entire nation.[21]

In the same light, Africa's prostitutes are getting a lot of attention from AIDS researchers, with their obvious potential for verifying heterosexual AIDS. And sure enough, the studies come back one after another confirming what the researchers hoped to find: a high incidence of AIDS among the prostitutes. Local health officials complain that foreign researchers pack up and leave after gathering figures for research purposes rather than assessing the figures for patient care. Hardly anyone stays around long enough to consider that the use of hard drugs among prostitutes has greatly esca-

[18] Ibid.

[19] Ibid.

[20] Ibid.

[21] Ibid.

lated over the same period as the rise in AIDS.

According to Dr. Bialy, "The only utterly new phenomenon I have seen is in the drug-using prostitutes in Abidjan in the Ivory Coast," he said. "These girls come from Ghana, from families of prostitutes who are brought in by the busload. They have been doing this for generations, and never became sick until now."

So why now? And why do they *look like* they have AIDS? "What is new is that these girls are addicted to viciously adulterated, smokable heroin and cocaine. It completely destroys them. They look exactly like the inner-city crack-addicted prostitutes of the United States."[22] Bialy's overall conclusion about Africa and AIDS? "There is absolutely no believable, persuasive evidence that Africa is in the midst of a new epidemic of infectious immuno-deficiency."[23]

Assuming some avenue of blood transmission through one's skin, Dr. John Seale puts the prostitution issue in stark perspective: "You are more likely to get AIDS by helping an African prostitute clean up after a nose-bleed than by having sex with her."[24]

Perhaps the most compelling bit of evidence coming out of Africa is the study reported in *The Lancet* by a group of Japanese doctors. Out of a group of 22 diagnosed "AIDS" patients who had all the classic clinical signs qualifying for AIDS under the WHO definition, 59 percent showed no trace of HIV in their blood.[25]

And out of all the "AIDS cases" reported in Abidjan's three main hospitals, there were 2400 "documented" cases of AIDS that turned out not to have HIV present![26]

What's the point of this statistical parade? Simply to

---

[22] Hodgkinson, "Epidemic."

[23] Ibid.

[24] John Seale, M.D., in *The Daily Telegraph*, Nov. 1986.

[25] Hodgkinson, "Epidemic."

[26] Shenton, "AIDS and Africa."

demonstrate that there are serious questions about the African AIDS figures which have been bandied about so glibly in America as proof of so-called "heterosexual AIDS."

Reducing Human Tragedy to Politics

And what is the point of that point in a book dealing with gay rights? Hopefully, to expose the politics of AIDS, particularly as it relates to the gay movement's cry that "AIDS is an equal-opportunity destroyer." Gay activists are concerned about the stigma that would result (at least in America) from AIDS being correctly associated primarily with homosexual behavior. The implication that they wish us to draw from the myth of heterosexual AIDS is that "we're all in it together."

If we're all equally at risk (they would have us ask ourselves), then how different can we be? If AIDS affects heterosexuals as well as homosexuals, then AIDS is not a "gay disease" and should not give anyone reason to lash out at gays for the many innocent deaths which have been caused by the disease. If AIDS is more than just a "gay disease," then it can't possibly be a sign from God that homosexual behavior is sinful. Need I go on?

Most of all, promoting AIDS as equally heterosexual helped persuade the public that any classification of homosexuals was pointless and could have no other motive than invidious discrimination.[27]

On a practical level, gay activists knew that badly needed research funds for AIDS research probably never would be received unless society felt that, as a whole, they were at risk.

And don't for a minute think that gay activists aren't aware of the enormous implications of the "heterosexual AIDS" argument. Nor that they aren't actively doing whatever it takes to keep the myth alive.

---

[27] Rhonda M. Robinson, "AIDS: The Mismanagement of a Tragedy," paper presented in Law and Morality seminar, Pepperdine University, Fall 1990.

If you have any doubts, just ask Michael Fumento, former AIDS analyst for the Commission on Civil Rights. His book *The Myth of Heterosexual Aids*[28] has been the victim of censorship by the gay lobby both in America and Britain. Bookstores in New York received letters threatening boycott if they carried the book. (I can personally testify to the book's unavailability. I nearly wore out a good pair of shoes searching New York City in vain for a copy.)

The campaign to censor Fumento's book proved so successful that now even its publisher (Basic Books) has embargoed all remaining copies. You simply cannot obtain one.

In Britain, only 20 copies of Fumento's book were imported into the United Kingdom. Following gay reaction to the serialization of his book in London's *Sunday Times*, no publisher would touch it.[29] Of course, innuendos of a conspiracy were vehemently denied by Britain's publishers.

Back in the States, when *Forbes* magazine published an article favorably profiling Fumento and his views, gay activists from ACT-UP picketed the publisher's Fifth Avenue offices. The gays won a personal capitulation from Malcolm Forbes, who said that the article was "asinine," and that he would have "killed" it had he not been traveling at the time.[30]

Freedom of the press? What freedom of the press? When gay rights come to town, everybody else's constitutional rights are forced to leave. No Serbian ethnic cleansing was ever more complete. Dare question the myth of "heterosexual AIDS" and you'll have gay activists on your back before you can say "Sodom's second coming."

---

[28] Michael Fumento, *The Myth of Heterosexual Aids* (New York: Basic Books, Inc., 1990).

[29] Deirdre Fernand and Jasper Gerard, "Don't Believe the Hype," in the *Sunday Times* (London), Mar. 1, 1992, Features; *Sunday Telegraph* (London), Mar. 11, 1990, p. 21.

[30] Patricia Cohen, "The Myth of Heterosexual AIDS" (book review in the *Washington Monthly*, Nov. 1989).

Putting a Price on Tragedy

Of course, it's not only the gay lobby that wants in on the action. In London, Auberon Waugh zeroes in on what he calls "the dollar dimension:"

> I wonder what persuaded the Observer this week to lead its front page with the dismal headline: "New Aids virus threatens heterosexuals." Ever since people started talking about Aids 10 years ago, medical researchers have been desperately trying to convince the world that it is a heterosexual affliction, reckoning on all the billions of dollars in research budgets which might become available.
>
> This week's scare comes from a symposium in Boston, which heard Dr. John Sullivan, of the University of Massachusetts medical centre, proclaim a global epidemic yet again. The only solution, he said, was to double biomedical research efforts and budgets. Ah yes, budgets.[31]

For researchers, grants are dependent upon the myth of heterosexual AIDS. And since the figures in the United States wouldn't even begin to be sufficiently persuasive, the scientists have turned to Africa for the supposed evidence.

Dr. Bialy says that "it has become a joke in Uganda that you are not allowed to die of anything but AIDS. A favorite story is that a friend had just been run over by a car; doctors put it down as AIDS-related suicide!"[32]

But the AIDS scare in Africa is no joke. The hysteria itself may have as serious side effects as the disease. Local health officials tell horror stories of people all over Africa who are so afraid that they will be diagnosed as having AIDS that they won't go to the hospital. And so they die at home of malaria or tuberculosis or simply malnutrition.

If fear doesn't kill them, they slowly waste away from despair. Why keep trying to live if they are going to die anyway?

---

[31] Auberon Waugh, "The dollar dimension," in *The Daily Telegraph*, Feb. 17, 1993, p. 21.

[32] Hodgkinson, "Epidemic."

And everyone is telling them they are going to die.

The AIDS scare has turned families and villages against their own. Those who are diagnosed with AIDS are shunned and kicked out of the village. AIDS-infected homosexuals in America aren't the only ones who suffer from AIDS stigmatization.

It just doesn't get any more callous than when the gay lobby and the scientific community are willing to trade on the lives of others to put across their own agenda. In Uganda alone, the government has less than one dollar per person to spend on health care each year. Last year it received six million dollars in foreign funding for AIDS. What could be a greater incentive to classify people as AIDS sufferers?

But it gets worse. Of that six million, $750,000 came from the World Health Organization, which at the same time gave only $57,000 for the prevention and treatment of malaria, which kills an estimated one million people in sub-Saharan Africa every year.[33] Unlike AIDS, malaria is curable. But are the drugs available to do the job? No. And why? Because malaria is not a politically correct disease!

But that's still not the worst of it. The double-whammy comes when you realize that a significant number of all the reported "AIDS cases" are nothing more than curable malaria cases to begin with!

And who knows just how deceptive it gets? The World Health Organization and its colleagues in the US-AID organization are notorious for their family-planning, birth-control bias. AIDS funds go to counseling, education, and condoms – not medicine. Could there be a connection between the big budgets for condom distribution and their push for eliminating the teeming underclass in Africa?

A spokeswoman for US-AID did not deny the bias, but demurred, saying that condoms had never been the method of choice for birth control.[34] Perhaps that is true historically,

---

[33] Shenton, "AIDS and Africa."

[34] Ibid.

but are we to believe they wouldn't take advantage of the current AIDS hysteria and kill two birds with one stone? AIDS as a political football has never been kicked in so many different directions!

Back home, those of you who are parents should also be aware that the political football is being kicked directly at your children. It's happening in the campaign to pass out condoms on school campuses all over the country. In the past, we've been able to keep the Great Condom Giveaway – with its implied moral acceptance of promiscuity – out of the classroom. Both Christian and non-Christian parents steadfastly opposed the distribution of condoms as long as the primary risk was nothing more than teenage pregnancy. (That risk has been around for a long time.) But the supposed threat of *death through AIDS* if condoms weren't used by sexually active teens was a risk that few parents were willing to take.

So now, thanks to a threat that in most communities is nothing more than a gay-promoted hoax, condoms have become as much a part of the students' wardrobe as gym shorts and Reeboks. Thanks to the immorality of *homosexual* behavior, parents and school officials have caved in to the immorality of *heterosexual* behavior.

More Callous by Comparison

If someone asked you to name a disease that is reaching crisis proportions among Americans, that often ravages people in the prime of life, that does not discriminate on grounds of race or gender, and that suffers from a lack of government funding, you would probably think of AIDS. But the correct answer, of course, is cancer.[35]

As Mona Charen reports, "In the 10 years since the AIDS epidemic began, about 120,000 Americans have died from the disease. During the same period, 40 times that many have

---

[35] Charen, "Curious Ways."

succumbed to cancer."[36] And heart disease kills five times as many as AIDS in a single year!

To put it into perspective, AIDS-related deaths are not even in the top ten killers, but we pour more government money into AIDS than any other illness, despite its comparatively narrow impact.[37] AIDS research funding is already 10 times that of cancer on a per-death basis, and 20 times on a per-patient basis.[38] (Certainly there is no disputing that the "start-up money" has to be spent in huge sums in order to catch up with funding for other diseases where there have been years of costly research.)

Britain's figures are similarly skewed. In 1989/90, when there were 553 AIDS-related deaths, the government spent 240 million dollars on AIDS research and education. In the same year, in which 200,000 people died from heart disease, the government spent 15 million dollars for heart research. That works out to about 75 dollars for each person who died of heart disease, and 433,000 dollars for each person who died of AIDS!

In human terms, Britain's director of the Committee on Population and the Economy, Robert Whelan, reminds us that "people will die from cancer and heart disease who would not have died if additional funds had been available. Their names will never be embroidered in a quilt, and they will never be celebrated at gala entertainments. But they will die just the same."

There is no effort here to pit AIDS sufferers against those who suffer from cancer and heart disease. No one I know would begrudge the announcement that a cure for AIDS had been discovered. No one I know wouldn't wish that we could have prevented little Ariel Glaser's death. The plea here is

---

[36] Ibid.

[37] Ibid.

[38] Michael Fumento, "What You Can Do to Avoid AIDS," in the *Washington Monthly*, Dec. 1992, Vol. 24, No. 12, p. 46.

not to cut off funding for AIDS research. The plea is that we put everything in its proper perspective.

A large part of that process is ridding ourselves of the myth of heterosexual AIDS. As Robert Whelan puts it, "After at least 30 years in the community, AIDS remains tightly confined to members of high-risk groups, such as male homosexuals and drug addicts. The much-heralded 'homosexual explosion' has failed to materialize despite the earnestly-expressed hopes of some workers in the AIDS field."[39]

Rather than reducing the current level of AIDS funding, society would do better to redirect where that money goes. Programs that aid intravenous drug-abusers in cities like New York desperately lack the funding necessary to deal with even a fraction of the demand for help. There is where the focus must shift. If there is any truth at all to the fears surrounding heterosexual AIDS, you can find it in the inner city.

In some areas of the south Bronx, 1 in 22 young mothers have tested positive for HIV. And what breaks your heart is that the same is true of 1 in 40 infants.[40] Naturally, the children aren't getting HIV from heterosexual intercourse, and their mothers aren't necessarily sleeping around. The mothers are either intravenous drug-abusers themselves, or have partnered on a long-term basis with a man who is. In high-risk-group communities like the south Bronx, the escalation of AIDS among heterosexuals promises to be a continuing serious threat. For those who are caught up in a culture of cocaine and crack addiction, every penny spent on prevention of drug abuse and on AIDS research is well worth the investment.

When it comes to the highest-risk group of all, however, in the long range *absolutely no public funding is needed or warranted.* Finding a cure for those already infected is one thing.

---

[39] Rees, "Cut AIDS."

[40] Cohen, "Myth."

Let's do it if we can, as soon as we can. But *preventing* AIDS-related deaths among homosexual males is not a matter of medical research. Common sense tells you that, if AIDS results primarily from anal intercourse, then the solution ought to be obvious! No, not condoms, but homosexual abstinence.

In 1986/87, the taxpayer-funded National Centers for Disease Control made two grants totaling almost $675,000 to the Gay Men's Health Crisis, Inc. of New York, following its proposal to spend the money in part upon a manual for conducting "Eroticizing Safer Sex Workshops." According to the grant application, the workshops were intended to "discover and share information on how to be sexually active in low-risk ways."[41]

Taxpayer-funded programs to educate gays about AIDS is a sick joke. No group of individuals knows better how AIDS is transmitted than male homosexuals. Why else do they "negotiate" safe sex? (They don't even have the excuse of addicts that their perception is so altered by drugs that they can't put two and two together.) And this gets us to the heart of the matter: What gays really want is *risk-free sodomy*!

Gays don't want to stop their homosexual behavior – only to pressure the government into discovering the equivalent of "the pill" for males wishing to have intercourse with each other. And then when "the pill" – whatever in the future it might turn out to be – happens to fail, they want the rest of us to foot the bill for hospitalization. At the present time, the cost of treating the average AIDS patient from diagnosis to death is $100,000.

And, of course, the quicker the government can discover a medical means of prevention, the better. But the money/time factor itself is nonsense. You get the idea among many gay activists that if twice as much money is spent on the AIDS budget, then the disease will be cured

---

[41] James Kilpatrick, "Encouraging safe sodomy," in Universal Press Syndicate, Nov. 14, 1987.

twice as fast. That if three times as much is spent, then the cure will come three times as fast. But medical research doesn't work that way. If it did, we probably would have beaten cancer and heart disease by now.[42]

For homosexual males, AIDS is a self-inflicted fatality. If they want a speedy end to the crisis, it is within their own power to make it happen. (Proof of that is the statistical plateau that apparently has already been reached in the incidence of AIDS among homosexuals.) Playing on the fears of heterosexuals (and jumping the cue to get ahead of those who suffer from other diseases) in order to continue their self-destructive behavior is a callous game indeed.

Our Own Mismanagement of AIDS

One of the grand ironies of the myth of heterosexual AIDS is that it has been widely perpetuated by the Christian community. It is just one more way in which we have mismanaged the entire AIDS affair. We hurt our credibility from the very start by saying that AIDS was a plague from God specifically to single out and punish homosexuals. We didn't stop to think that lesbians were left untouched by the plague; or that many innocents were also plagued, or that the figures for white homosexuals and homosexuals from other ethnic groups were often greatly disparate. It should have been enough to say that sin always has built-in consequences, often *physical* consequences.

But turning around and virtually arguing against ourselves, we took up the gay movement's banner of heterosexual AIDS in order to denounce heterosexual promiscuity as well. Proclaiming the widespread heterosexual nature of the epidemic as fervently as any gay activists, we (rightly) called for sexual abstinence and monogamous, married sex. And with that proclamation in aid of a biblical cause, we played directly into the hands of the gay lobby. How they must have

[42] Fumento, "Avoid."

snickered behind our backs!

Ironically, the same Michael Fumento who angered the gays by daring to suggest that the AIDS focus ought to be on high-risk homosexuals was demoted from his position as AIDS analyst for the Reaganesque Commission on Civil Rights because he suggested that the religious and conservative right were also manipulating the AIDS crisis to their own ends. Can the Christian community not face up to self-criticism?

It must be asked, What did we gain by jumping on the gays' "heterosexual AIDS" bandwagon? Morality by fear? The previously promiscuous heterosexual who gives up sex in order to avoid AIDS is not suddenly more moral – just more practical! Although the words look very much alike, there is a vast spiritual gulf between being *sacred* and being *scared*.

Can we not see that, in using heterosexual AIDS as an argument against extramarital sex, we run the risk of having no moral persuasion left should the time come (and it likely will) when some medical prevention or cure for AIDS is discovered? Why make morality so vulnerable to science? The moral issue can, and should, stand on its own.

Whatever the issue, pragmatism is never good theology. With the myth of "heterosexual AIDS," good theology has not even been truly pragmatic. It is not the *myth* that we should perpetuate, but the *message*.

Chapter Six

AIDS: THERE WILL NEVER BE A CURE!

James Taylor

James Taylor is a consultant and speaker whose AIDS material is listed with the Centers for Disease Control and Prevention. This challenging chapter assesses the true success of AIDS research past and present.

> The word 'cure' is not even in the vocabulary.[1]
> –Dr. Michael Gottlieb, UCLA immunologist

In order for us to understand why there will never be a cure we must first understand how the HIV operates. Our bodies were created with very distinct, complicated, and methodical operations. These operations function so routinely we never give them much thought. As an example, when was the last time you thought about breathing? You don't, you just breathe. If you have had the "wind" knocked out of you, you know how precious the moment is when you can breathe normally. Without breathing you would die. Breathing is one of the many functions of our bodies that we take for granted.

---

[1] G. Antonio, The AIDS Cover-up? *The Real and Alarming Facts About AIDS*, (San Francisco: Ignatius Press, 1986) p. 125.

The human immunodeficiency virus (HIV) is a retrovirus which means that it is RNA (genetic material) surrounded by protein. This is the virus that leads to acquired immunodeficiency syndrome (AIDS). It is acquired because we cannot inherit AIDS and it is not the result of an illness. We do not become sick and then come down with AIDS. We will see that it has a great deal to do with our behavior. It is immunodeficiency because the immune system is not protecting the body against unusual diseases or infections. It is also a syndrome because a variety of specific diseases can occur.

How our Bodies and the Virus Operate

Our white blood cells (T-Lymphocytes) house our immune system. It is important to know who the major players are in this fight and their functions. I will use the analogy of a military battle to help understand how our bodies work.

T-4 Helper, Inducer cell: He is the General, he is the one that tells the rest of the cells what they are to accomplish. He is the boss.

The Macrophage: He is like a scout that roams around looking for the enemy. When he spots the enemy he reports to the T-4 (The General).

B Plasma cell: This guy is in the infantry. He is the one that does the actual fighting. He attaches himself to the antigen (foreign object in the body) and begins to create antibodies (protein) to dissolve the antigen.

B Memory cell: This cell is like a super-duper-computer-secretary rolled into one. What this cell does is records what the antigen looks and acts like. Also, it records what the body did to expel the antigen from the body. This helps expedite the process if the body is exposed to the same antigen in the future.

T-8 Cytotoxic/Suppressor cell: He is kind of like a janitor and a coward. What he does is sneaks up to an infected cell, pierces its membrane, and then runs and hides behind the General. This allows the antibodies to go directly to the infected cell. Another function is that of the janitor. After the body has dissolved the antigen the T-8 helps expel the residue from the body.

An Illustration

Let us say that I am the "JT bacteria" and I have entered the body. As the scout (Macrophage) is making his rounds, he spots me and reports to the General (T-4) that something strange is in the body. The General then sounds the alarm and sends out the infantry (B Plasma cells). The infantry attaches to the JT bacteria and is now making the JT antibodies (protein) to dissolve the JT bacteria. But before the job is complete, the B memory cell (the secretary) records everything about the JT bacteria and everything the infantry did to dissolve the antigen, so that the next time the JT bacteria enters the body the memory cell can pull up the files and expedite the procedure. After the job is done the janitor (T-8) does his job and expels the residue. This procedure is repeated all the time in your body and you give it no thought.

Here is what happens when your body is infected with the HIV. The process is the same, except when the infantry is sent out. Keep in mind, the HIV is a retrovirus, RNA, surrounded by "protein." When the infantry attaches themselves to the HIV, they are making the HIV antibody dissolve the virus. But there is a problem, the HIV antibodies (protein) do not kill the virus, they actually protect it. They act like a "big brother," so that the body's natural functions are interrupted. The virus uses the protein as a type of fuel for survival.

Remember, we are fighting in a war. If you were a general in a war, as is the AIDS virus, who out of the five major players would you probably attack first? The General (T-4) because he is the boss and tells the rest of the cells what they are to do. That is exactly what the HIV does. It attaches itself to the General and the two become one. It is as if you took two different colors of paint and mixed them together. Once they are mixed you have a new color. It is now impossible to separate the new color into two distinct colors. That is what happens with the HIV and the T-4 cell. Now, if you want to destroy the virus you have to destroy the cell as well. If the cell dies, our immune system is gone and soon we are dead.

The HIV and the T-4 (the General) have literally set up a little HIV baby factory where they are spitting out HIV at an astronomical rate. The infantry is still making HIV antibodies, and the virus is saying, "Good, because my babies have to eat and be protected." Keep in mind, each one of their babies is going to a new cell and doing the exact same thing. The General is a little preoccupied with his new "marriage" and he is on a little "honeymoon." The General no longer stimulates the cellular defense response and the immune system begins to weaken. Eventually the General collapses on himself and the boss is dead. Some experts believe he commits a type of suicide (apoptosis).[2] Now there is no one to stimulate the cell's defenses and this gives way to opportunistic infections. These are infections that take advantage of the fact that there are no defenses and they enter the body and wreak havoc. Most people who die from AIDS die from these opportunistic infections. But make no mistake about it, people do die directly from AIDS. In 1992, 26% of all the people who died from AIDS related causes died directly from AIDS.[3]

Out of all the major players in this war who else would you probably attack? The scout (Macrophage) because he has mobility. The HIV attacks the scout by catching a ride. The scout penetrates the blood brain barrier and the HIV looks around and sees fertile ground and says, "It's party time."

---

[2] CDC, "Human Immunodeficiency Virus Infection in the United States: A Review of Current Knowledge," *Morbidity and Mortality Weekly Report*, Supplement, December 18, 1987, Vol. 36, No. S-6. cf. *The Arizona Republic*, March 28, 1993, p. A2.

[3] CDC, *HIV/AIDS Surveillance Report* Year End Edition, February 1993, p. 16.

The HIV hops off the scout and sets up another HIV baby factory in the brain. This is when HIV encephalopathy (dementia) sets in and the person begins to lose his/her mind.

The Progression of HIV Disease

A person gets exposed to the HIV and the process of infection has begun. The virus enters the Lymphocytes; at this point a blood test cannot detect the HIV antibodies. Usually a person has an acute illness; for a brief time, the person experiences a mild illness similar to the flu. The virus has been detected, the body is now making antibodies. You recover from your illness and have no clue you have been infected with the HIV. Usually six to twelve weeks is how long it takes for your body to produce enough antibodies to be detected by a blood test.[4] This process of being detected by a test is called Seroconversion. 95% of all people seroconvert in 12 weeks (3 months).[5] However, it is recommended that you wait six months to be on the safe side. At any stage of the disease infected people can pass the virus on to others. Even if you have not seroconverted.

After seroconversion you now test positive for the HIV antibodies. The virus enters a latent or incubation period that can last as long as ten years. This does not mean that if you get tested it will be negative. If you get tested it will still be positive. This simply means you show no physical signs that you are sick (asymptomatic), but you can pass the virus on to others. You look healthy, feel healthy, and no one would be able to tell if you are ill by visual means. Using the term latent does not truly capture what is taking place with the HIV. The AIDS virus can hide for years in the lymph nodes before launching a final, lethal attack on its victim.

---

[4] Department of Labor/Department of Health and Human Services, *Joint Advisory Notice: Protection Against Occupational Exposure to Hepatitis B Virus (HBV) and Human Immunodeficiency Virus (HIV)*, October 19, 1987, p. 4.

[5] Ibid.

The virus is never idle.

Two studies published in the March 25, 1993 journal *Nature*, reported that once a person is infected with the virus the HIV can congregate in lymphoid organs, such as the tonsils, spleen, adenoids and lymph nodes, where it steadily infects key blood cells and breaks down cells that filter out viruses. Eventually the filter cells in the lymph organs are destroyed; infected blood cells spill out into the body's circulation system, leading to a collapse of the immune system.[6]

Dr. Anthony Fauci, director of the National Institute of Allergy and Infectious Diseases and a co-author of one of the studies published in *Nature*, said:

> This discovery answers one of the key mysteries about the course of the disease. Many patients infected with HIV experience an initial bloom of virus particles in their blood, a condition called viremia, within weeks of exposure. But then traces of virus disappear from blood tests and patients often live without HIV symptoms for up to ten years. Eventually there is another explosion of viremia, usually followed by death from opportunistic infection. Since there was little virus in the blood, it was a puzzle why this process inevitably progressed and occurred. The bottom line of the study is that this virus is present in the lymph nodes ... and it is actively replicating ... even when there is little or no virus activity detected in the blood.[7]

In effect, Fauci said, the period that doctors call the latent or symptomless stage of HIV is not latent at all. The virus is thriving in the lymph nodes and insidiously eroding the body's immune system.

The second study, co-written by Dr. Ashley T. Haase of the University of Minnesota, confirmed that the HIV thrives in the lymphoid tissue during the so-called latent period of the disease. He said the virus in the lymph nodes actively in-

---

[6] *Nature*, March 25, 1993.

[7] *The Arizona Republic*, "AIDS Virus Can Hide For Years In Lymph Glands," Thursday, March 25, 1993, p. A2.

fects lymphocytes, called CD4 T-cells (the General), that reside in the lymph nodes or which are passing through.[8]

Towards the later part of HIV infection, some symptoms appear, lasting a few months to several years. The antibody level will decline because the T-4 cell (General) is getting weaker, and the B plasma (infantry) is overwhelmed at the rate of reproduction of the HIV. They are simply, grossly, outnumbered. The virus gradually kills off the Lymphocytes (part of your immune system) and you develop symptoms of immune deficiency. You are now symptomatic and you are showing visible signs that you are sick. Some people call this stage: ARC – AIDS Related Complex.

The only exception to all of this is if you become infected by someone who has full blown AIDS. Case in point – Kimberly Bergalis, Richard Driskill, and John Yecs, Jr., the victims of Florida dentist David Acer. It was 3 years from the time Kimberly was intentionally infected by Acer until the time she died. For Richard, and for John it was 5 years. The so-called "incubation" period was decreased substantially.

Many experts believe that the incubation period is going to increase to longer than ten years as an average. I do not agree with that assessment. If person "A" is HIV infected and is taking the drug azidothymidine (AZT), the drug most commonly given, the virus will eventually develop an immunity to AZT. The virus will incorporate the AZT into its own genetic code and continue to mutate. If person "A" passes HIV on to person "B," person "B" also receives person "A's" mutated form of the virus. Now person "B" has an immunity to AZT, but doesn't know it. More AIDS patients are showing early resistance to AZT.

Dr. Wendell Ching of the School of Medicine of the University of California at Los Angeles, said:

> Blood tests are turning up increasing numbers of AIDS-infected patients who have never taken AZT and are sick with

[8] *Nature*, March 25, 1993.

> a virus that is naturally resistant to the drug. Some of the patients may have gotten the virus from other patients who had been taking AZT and who are now transmitting the resistant virus.[9]

In the January 1, 1993, report published in the *Proceedings of the National Academy of Science,* Ching said:

> People usually are infected with various strains of HIV. Once they start taking AZT, the resistant strains are the ones that survive. Eventually the resistant strains become the dominant HIV population in the patient's body. If the virus is spread to another person at that point, then the new patient develops an HIV infection that is dominated by a resistance to AZT. If this occurs widely among new cases of HIV, then there is a risk that AZT would become of little value.[10]

AZT might be of little value anyway. A recent study published by *Lancet* on April 3, 1993, of 1,749 volunteers indicates that patients who got the drug were just as likely to succumb to the disease or die as those who got a placebo. Conducted over three years, it is the longest trial comparing AZT with a placebo among infected but symptom free volunteers.

Dr. Ian Weller, an AIDS expert at University College London Medical School who participated in the study, said:

> . . . results are not encouraging for early intervention. Those physicians and patients who felt certain giving AZT early would be beneficial will be more uncertain. Those who waited, like myself, will be more sure we've been doing the right thing.[11]

---

[9] *The Arizona Republic,* "New Drugs Vital in Fight on AIDS, Because AZT is Losing Punch, Study Says," Friday, January 1, 1993, p. B16.

[10] *The Proceedings of the National Academy of Science,* January 1, 1993.

[11] *Lancet,* April 3, 1993.

Nick Partridge, director of the Terrence Higgins Trust, a British patient advocacy charity based in London, described the results as:

> . . . very depressing for infected people who are well. It rocks the foundation of the small house of believers for using early intervention and shows how far away we are from adequate treatment of HIV.[12]

Signs of HIV Infection

- Unexplained, extreme tiredness.
- Unexplained fever, shaking chills or night sweats lasting longer than a few weeks. The night sweats are not as if you woke up and had a little drool on your pillow; it is as if someone took a bucket of water and poured it on you. That is how much moisture is left in your sheets.
- Swollen glands (enlarged lymph nodes) at multiple sites, such as in the neck, armpits or groin which are otherwise unexplained and persistent.
- Pink or purple flat or raised blotches, usually about the size of a quarter, occurring on or under the skin, inside the mouth, nose, eyelids, or rectum. At first they may look like bruises, but they are firmer than the surrounding skin, are painless, and do not disappear.
- An unexplained and unintended weight loss of more than 10% of your total body weight over a period of one or more months.
- A persistent thick, whitish coating on the tongue or in the throat.
- A dry cough which has lasted too long to be caused by a common respiratory infection, especially if accompanied by a shortness of breath.
- Pain in the esophagus (food pipe) when swallowing.
- Confusion, personality changes, loss of memory and equilibrium.

---

[12] *The Arizona Republic*, "Study Disputes Early Use of AZT Against AIDS," Friday, April 2, 1993, p. A2.

- Chronic diarrhea that usually lasts a couple of weeks to a month. It is not uncommon for a patient to expel ten liters of diarrhea in a single day. This leads to the wasting syndrome.[13]

Each of the symptoms listed above can appear in illnesses that are not associated with AIDS. For example, everyone occasionally experiences tiredness, headaches, fevers, or diarrhea. Anyone, particularly those who have participated in high risk behaviors who had one or more of the listed symptoms for a prolonged period of time, and cannot identify another cause for the problem, should see their physician.

After symptoms of immune deficiency appear this leads to full blown AIDS. Your immune system is doing everything it can to fight off any infection. Any infection you get is devastating to you. Because you can not fight off infections, opportunistic infections take advantage of your weakened condition.

Opportunistic Infections

- *Pneumocystic carinii Pneumonia (PCP)*: The number one killer of people with AIDS. This parasite infects the lungs. Patients experience shortness of breath, sharp chest pains when inhaling deeply and a persistent, wheezing cough. There is a feeling of suffocation.
- *Kaposi's sarcome (KS)*: This invasive form of skin cancer involves the internal organs. This is the number three killer of people with AIDS. Unlike cancers which originate from a single malignant cell and then spread to other parts of the body, independent cancerous growths of KS occur in different areas even without metastasis. KS can develop in the lungs, lymph nodes, liver, stomach, spleen

[13] The Arizona Department of Health Services, *HIV Guidelines and Information*, "Questions and Answers About AIDS," Module 1-Revised June 30, 1989, p. 2.

and intestines. These are the quarter sized spots that appear all over your body. Both PCP and KS can appear together in the same patient.

- *Candidiasis*: A fungal infection which produces a condition in the mouth known as thrush (white patches like milk curds lining the mouth and tongue). Along with swollen lymph glands, candidiasis is one of the most common early warning signs of AIDS. This infection can spread to the esophagus and into the bloodstream and central nervous system. Patients develop chest pain and difficulty in swallowing.
- *Cytomegalovirus (CMV)*: A devastating viral infection which commonly attacks the lungs and can spread throughout the body. CMV can cause blindness. Half of the young adult population in America have been infected with CMV at one time or another. There is no cure for CMV. As with other opportunistic infections, the consequences in AIDS patients are much more serious than usual. Among homosexuals, persistent repeated reinfection with CMV, often including different strains, has been implicated in the high rate of KS occurring mainly in their group.
- *Herpes simplex (HSV)*: This causes painful, severe ulcers around the mouth and perianal (around the rectum) areas. Colitis (inflammation of the colon) may also occur with bleeding, cramps and weight loss. In AIDS patients this is serious and often has fatal consequences.
- *Herpes zoster*: Causes skin eruptions commonly known as "shingles." In AIDS patients it may lead to oozing blisters and large black scabs over the infected areas, such as the mouth, nose, and rectum.
- *Toxoplasmosis*: Caused by a small intracellular parasite which is often found in cat feces. For healthy people this is not a serious problem; however, for AIDS patients this can create havoc. It is found in AIDS patients in association with CNS symptoms such as headaches, severe

lethargy (abnormal drowsiness), seizures, vomiting, fever, and psychological disturbances.

- *Cryptosporidiosis*: An intestinal disease caused by a parasite often found in farm lifestock, dogs, cats, and other animals. It is spread by direct contact with infected feces. In AIDS patients it may cause a devastating cholera-like syndrome, producing as much as ten liters per day of diarrhea. This leads to severe dehydration and malnutrition, causing drastic weight loss. Unlike some of the other opportunistic infections whose symptoms may be alleviated, at least temporarily, by treatment, cryptosporidiosis in AIDS patients is resistant to all therapy.
- *Cryptococcosis*: A fungal infection which, in AIDS patients, may cause diffuse meningitis (affecting your brain and spinal cord). Symptoms include stupor, mental disturbances, and personality changes, accompanied by severe headaches, double vision and facial weakness.
- *Oral "Hairy" Leukoplakia*: Hairy leukoplakia appears to be associated with the papilloma virus and a virus of the herpes family. It appears on the tongue as white raised areas of thickness on the tongue. It first appeared in 1981 in San Francisco exclusively in the mouth of male homosexuals.
- *Malignant lymphoma*: This viral form of lymphoma associated with AIDS virus infections has been found to attack extranodal sites in the central nervous system, rectum and/or anus in persons at risk for AIDS.
- *Tuberculosis*: In the US TB was on the decline since the 1950s, however, the disease is making a dramatic comeback due to AIDS. Now there is a form of TB that is resistant to all medication.
- *HIV Wasting syndrome*: This where your body is literally wasting away. Other opportunistic infections can contribute to this but you die from dehydration. HIV wasting syndrome was the second leading cause of deaths (20%) in 1992 for all patients who died from AIDS-related

causes – dying directly from AIDS.

- *HIV encephalopathy (dementia)*: You are losing your mind and literally going crazy. This differs from toxoplasmosis and cryptococcosis, both of which have similar symptoms. The difference is that you can die directly from HIV dementia. In 1992 6% of all the people who died from AIDS-related causes died of HIV dementia – dying directly from AIDS.[14]

After a patient has gone through the three stages of AIDS (asymptomatic HIV infection, symptomatic HIV infection, and full blown AIDS) the only other step is death. With this destruction that is taking place in the body one wonders about the prospects for a cure or a vaccine in the near future. Hopefully there will be a vaccine, but there will never be a cure.

Why There Will Never be a Cure for AIDS

1. In the history of mankind we have **never** cured a retrovirus. Every retrovirus that has ever been with us is still with us today. Yes, we have made some vaccination, but even that is not 100 percent. It is highly unlikely that this will be the first virus cured. Patrick Dixon in his book, *The Whole Truth About AIDS*, says,

> All our technology has failed to produce a single drug that attacks and destroys a virus directly.[15]

Even as late as March 28, 1993 in *Science*, the journal of the American Association for the Advancement of Science, the top researchers were saying,

> Despite the high-powered arsenal of contemporary biology, there is nothing on the horizon remotely resembling a cure for AIDS. Nor is there anything like a workable vaccine.[16]

---

[14] G. Antonio, op. cit., pp. 15-20.

[15] Patrick Dixon, *The Whole Truth About AIDS* (Nashville: Nelson, 1989), p. 40.

[16] *Science*, March 28, 1993.

2. In May of 1990, the *Cold Institute* closed their doors.[17] They were in existence for 40 years to find one thing – a cure for the common cold. They said there will never be a cure for the cold because it mutates too fast. The cold is caused by a virus, also. If we could not cure the common cold that moved at a snail's pace, we will not touch the HIV. The AIDS virus reproduces much more rapidly.

> The common cold virus is also unstable. That is why we are always getting colds. I probably have antibodies in my blood now to 50 or 100 different shaped cold viruses. By the time one of those viruses has infected people between here, North America, Japan, Korea, India, Greece, and back again, its shape has changed so much that I can catch the same cold all over again. That is why we are light years away from a vaccine against the common cold.[18]

> "The kind of readout of genetic information we see in this system is absolutely astounding," asserts Dr. William Haseltine, a prominent investigator at Harvard's Dana-Farber Cancer Institute. "Nobody would have thought this level of transcription [gene activity] was possible before we did these studies. We were shocked. It's about 1000 times faster than the... genes we know about.
> This system is very potent in permitting viruses to replicate at a ferocious rate. It's one reason this is such a devastating disease. It's one of the reasons this virus can be transmitted so easily from person to person."[19]

Not only does the virus mutate rapidly but once inside the body disappears quickly, making early detection almost impossible.

> The trouble with antibodies is that the body takes three days to produce the right antibody for the right virus. During this

---

[17] The Centers for Disease Control and Prevention, Confirmed.

[18] Patrick Dixon, *The Whole Truth About AIDS*, p. 45.

[19] *Forth Worth Star-Telegram*, 30 July 1985.

> critical three-day period the body is totally unprotected. Yet only an hour or two after viruses have entered the bloodstream, they have completely disappeared. You can hunt throughout the entire body, cell by cell, with the best electron firing microscope and find nothing. Why? Because every particle has disintegrated. Each one has burst like a child's soap bubble when it touches the ground. The virus bag has disintegrated and vanished. What about the contents? They too have disappeared without trace, but the cell it touched has received the kiss of death.[20]

3. Once the virus has attached to the T-4 cell (The General), you cannot kill the virus without killing the cell. Even Surgeon General C. Everett Koop doubts that a cure for AIDS will ever be found:

> I don't see how it is going to be possible to attack a virus that works its way into the nucleus of a cell, combines with DNA of that cell, and kill that virus without doing damage to the cell.[21]

4. There are at least five genetically distinguishable groups of the AIDS virus. This creates difficulty in coming up with a cure or a vaccine. The AIDS virus is continually mutating. Whatever we give it, it incorporates that into its genetic structure and keeps on going, somewhat like the Energizer Bunny. The same person can harbor multiple forms of the virus.[22] These multiple forms could interact with one another and cause the virus to compromise the immune system at a faster pace.

Dr. John Seale, an eminent British venereologist, comments:

---

[20] Patrick Dixon, *The Whole Truth About AIDS*, p. 40. cf. *Science American* 255 (1989), pp. 78-88 and 256 (1987), pp. 38-48.

[21] *The Arizona Republic*, October 13, 1992, p. B6.

[22] "AIDS-Associated Virus Yields Data to Intensifying Scientific Study," *Journal of the American Medical Association*, 22/29 November 1985, pp. 2865-2866.

> The almost unlimited varieties of antigenic strains of lentiviruses produced by antigenic drifts, combined with the inability of antibody produced by the host to eliminate the virus from circulation, have rendered ineffective all attempts to produce vaccines to prevent lentivirus diseases in animals. Effective protection against infection with the AIDS virus using existing vaccination techniques would seem to be theoretically impossible.[23]

By 1991, more than one hundred HIV-1 isolates had been identified from ten countries on four continents, and in 1989 French researchers discovered what may be a much more virulent form of HIV-1, far more powerful and contagious than either HIV-I or HIV-II. In fact, all HIV infected people are apparently infected with several mutant forms of the virus.

> HIV can change shape in subtle ways in the same person over the course of a few months, and a person can be infected with several differently shaped viruses at once, possibly with varying abilities to cause disease. Even worse, HIV occasionally changes its shape radically. We are currently seeing new HIV-like viruses emerging every year or two somewhere in the world. There are probably at least four [1988 figures; now some estimate fifteen] HIV-like viruses already. An increasing number of people are infected with more than one type of HIV. Every time someone is infected, there is a minute chance that radical new changes will occur. As the number of infected people worldwide continues to double each year, so does the risk of new strains emerging. Incidentally, most of our tests for infection are for the earliest virus type found. The others can be missed.[24]

5. Any vaccine developed would be ineffective for those already infected. Any person who is currently infected is capable of spreading the infection to others. By the time any

---

[23] Seale, "AIDS Virus Infection: Prognosis and Transmission," *Journal of the Royal Society of Medicine*, 1985; 78: 614.

[24] Patrick Dixon, *The Whole Truth About AIDS*, p. 45.

agent is developed that is capable of preventing the AIDS virus from invading the immune system and the brain after it has entered the body (assuming that it is even possible), it will be too late for the millions who will have become infected. The earliest date for a projected vaccine is the turn of the century. In the year 2000 it is estimated there will be 120 million to 150 million people who will be HIV positive in the world.[25] And that is the earliest date for a vaccine; that is why we need to get a handle on this now before it is too late.

6. Even if there were a vaccine, it still would not guarantee noninfection of the virus. Many people get a flu shot each year to avoid the flu. The flu is also caused by a virus. The reason you need a new flu shot each year is because the flu virus mutates. It takes the vaccination we create and incorporates that into its own genetic makeup. So, if you received last year's flu shot it would do you no good. Also, there is a certain number of people who after receiving a flu vaccination still come down with the flu. This is one of the potential problems with a vaccination for AIDS. No one wants to receive a vaccination for AIDS and come down with the HIV. Plus, there are at least five major strands of AIDS; there would have to be at least that many vaccines. But we are not even close to a vaccine.

Dr. John Seale has noted, "If...we wait perhaps 20 years before we take drastic preventive action, half the population of the Western World will be wiped out.[26] In his forward to the text, *AIDS: The Unnecessary Epidemic*, AIDS authority Stanley Monteith, M.D., warns:

> When historians of the future record the history of this [AIDS] epidemic, they will record a story of malice and mis-

---

[25] Jonathan Mann, Daniel J.M. Tarantola, and Thomas W. Netter, Editors, *AIDS in the World 1992*, (Cambridge, MA: Harvard University Press), October 1992, pp. 5, 6.

[26] ISIS, *What Homosexuals Do*, Institute for the Scientific Investigation of Sexuality, 1988 (2940 S. 74th St., Lincoln, NE 68506), p. 6.

takes, illusions and delusions, deceit and deception, of dying and death. They will record how the liberal media, highly placed government officials, and the US Public Health Service worked in collusion to deceive the American public and convince them that every effort was being made to monitor and control the spread of the disease when, in truth, exactly the opposite was done.

It is my sincere hope that I am wrong about a cure.

PART FOUR

HOMOSEXUALITY AND THE BIBLE

Chapter Seven

GAY THEOLOGY?*

F. LaGard Smith

Dr. Smith looks at some of the popular "biblical" arguments used by homosexuals to defend their lifestyle.

'Twas guilt that taught my heart to fear,
And pride my fears relieved;
How precious did that pride appear,
The hour I first believed!
–Revised lyrics to "Amazing Grace" as sung at San Francisco's (gay) Glide Memorial United Methodist Church.

In the gay-rights assault against the American culture, no citadel is more coveted than the church. Getting the church's imprimatur on the homosexual lifestyle would be the ultimate stamp of legitimacy. But no matter how seductive that idea is for many mainstream churches – in keeping with the spirit of Christian tolerance and love – there is always that

*Taken from *Sodom's Second Coming: What You Need to Know About the Deadly Homosexual Assault* by F. LaGard Smith, Harvest House Publishers, 1993. Used by permission.

one last hurdle to cross: the Bible.

Have you ever wondered how gays attempt to get around the many passages in the Bible that condemn homosexual conduct as sin? Those who pay homage to the Bible (most don't even bother) have become incredibly sophisticated in the unholy art of sidestepping God's revelation.

In his book *Just As I Am – A Practical Guide to Being Out, Proud, and Christian*, pro-gay theologian Robert Williams attempts a biblical justification of homosexual conduct by asking, "What's the most loving course of action? What would Christ have you do?" As implied in the perversely fashioned title to his book, the most loving thing to do is what Christ himself would do: Accept gays *just as they are*.

He then tells us what we already knew, that "without interpretation, without placing it in its cultural, historical, and literary context, the Bible can be used for evil."[1] And from that point forward, Williams proceeds to demonstrate the very evil of which he speaks by systematically reconstructing each and every passage which threatens his freedom to enjoy homosexual relations.

As for the whole of the Pauline letters, Williams highhandedly concludes:"What the Holy Spirit tells you is a greater authority for *your* life than what the Holy Spirit may or may not have told Paul."[2]

In the Footsteps of Feminists

To get around obvious biblical proscriptions against homosexual acts, pro-gay theology borrows heavily from feminist theology. It's basically a matter of *hermeneutics*. If that's a new word for you, it simply refers to the *method* whereby we read, interpret, and apply Scripture. Not everyone wears the same set of glasses when they open their Bibles. Recently, in order to get around the numerous passages that expressly

---

[1] Williams, *Just As I Am*, p. 39.

[2] Ibid., p. 54.

call for different roles for men and women in the church, feminist theologians have taken to radical, revisionist methods of interpreting Scripture.

For example, Elisabeth Schüssler Fiorenza, a New Testament scholar and author of *Bread Not Stone: The Challenge of Feminist Biblical Interpretation*, promotes what she calls a *hermeneutic of suspicion*, a hermeneutic which rejects any biblical text that appears to have a patriarchal bias.[3] With that, she blithely dismisses the gender distinctions called for in Paul's writings.

To a lesser extent (undoubtedly because there are fewer Scriptures with which to take issue), black activists have done the same thing. James Cone, the black theologian of liberation, asserts that "any interpretation of the gospel in any historical period that fails to see Jesus as the Liberator of the oppressed is heretical."[4] And with that, Paul's instructions that slaves be content with their lot in life are scissored out of Scripture.

Whether gay, feminist, or black activist, today's cultural priests and priestesses are applying radical, revisionist, and reconstructionist approaches to the biblical text, with predictable, self-serving results. Their method? Imaginative narrative interpretation, or "reading between the lines."

Feminist author Dorothee Solle (*Beyond Mere Obedience*) calls the method *Phantasie* (German for phantasy), a process of creative imagining – not passive escapism, but an active imaging of the possibilities within a given text.[5] Robert Williams explains:

---

[3] Elisabeth Schüssler Fiorenza, *Bread Not Stone: The Challenge of Feminist Biblical Interpretation* (Boston: Beacon Press, 1984), p. xiii.

[4] James H. Cone, *God of the Oppressed* (New York: Seabury Press, 1975), p. 37.

[5] Dorothee Solle, *Beyond Mere Obedience*, translation of *Phantasie und Gehorsam*, Lawrence W. Denef, trans. (Minneapolis: Augsburg, 1970), pp. 30ff.

> The technique is simply one of creative visualization. You select a biblical passage, read it carefully and thoughtfully, then close the Bible and allow yourself to *experience* the passage. It works best with narrative passages, such as those in the gospels . . . .
>
> As with any visualization, the secret is to set the scene as vividly as possible. When you close your eyes and imagine the setting you just read about, imagine it in the most intense detail you can muster. Pay attention to colors, sounds, smells. Notice what people are wearing, what color their eyes and hair are, what their facial expressions are.[6]

Using such creative visualization, Williams informs us that David and Jonathan were gay lovers;[7] that the story of Ruth and Naomi is "the account of a deeply committed, intergenerational, lesbian love affair;"[8] and that – yes – Jesus himself was a homosexual! After all, "the disciple whom Jesus loved" *was* close by in the upper room, "snuggled up against Jesus' chest."[9]

In previous generations this form of hermeneutical interpretation was called by another name – *blasphemy!*

The Old Testament Through Revisionist Glasses

Gays realize that they must deal with the whole of Scripture if they are to have any chance of convincing us – or themselves – that homosexual conduct is pleasing in the eyes of God. It's a daunting task, but they set forth in confidence, undeterred by even the most explicit biblical teaching. It begins at Creation, where they know that the most fundamental principles of gender, marriage, and sex are established.

---

[6] Williams, *Just As I Am*, p. 26.

[7] Ibid., p. 56.

[8] Ibid., p. 58.

[9] Ibid., pp. 116-17.

Genesis 1:28
God blessed them and said to them, "Be fruitful and increase in number; fill the earth and subdue it. Rule over the fish of the sea and the birds of the air and over every living creature that moves on the ground."

With this opening passage, gay theology goes for the jugular of Roman Catholic teaching on sex: that sex is for the purpose of procreation. Gays answer weakly that they sometimes *do* procreate, either before "turning gay," or as bisexuals, or through alternative technologies (e.g., lesbians being artificially inseminated).

On firmer territory, they bask in a false sense of correctness, due to the weakness of the Catholic interpretation of this passage. Neither here nor elsewhere does the Bible teach that procreation is the *only* purpose of sexual relations.

Where gays go wrong on this point is in assuming that the pleasure which God intended sex to bring in addition to the act of procreation is without moral limitations. Procreation, requiring as it does both male and female, is as defining of proper sexual relations as it is of procreative roles. It's not just male and female for reproduction; it's also male and female for legitimate sexual enjoyment.

Genesis 2:24
For this reason a man will leave his father and mother and be united to his wife, and they will become one flesh.

All it takes for gays to make this passage gender neutral is the simple replacement of the word *companion* for the word *wife*. That the woman was made to be "a helper" for man suggests the idea of companionship, say gay theologians, and not just a difference in gender. By pro-gay thinking, loving companionship of any type is what God wants, for truly "it is not good for man to be alone."

It should be enough to point out that this convenient translation is nothing more than taking the liberty of literally rewriting Scripture. God neither created another *man* for

Adam's companion, nor a third person of either sex, as if to indicate the insignificance of gender. It was to be one *man* (male) and one *woman* (female) for life. Man would have his "companions," as would woman, but not for sexual expression.

Genesis 19:1-13, 24, 25

The two angels arrived at Sodom in the evening, and Lot was sitting in the gateway of the city. When he saw them, he got up to meet them and bowed down with his face to the ground. "My lords," he said, "please turn aside to your servant's house. You can wash your feet and spend the night and then go on your way early in the morning."

"No," they answered, "we will spend the night in the square."

But he insisted so strongly that they did go with him and entered his house. He prepared a meal for them, baking bread without yeast, and they ate.

Before they had gone to bed, all the men from every part of the city of Sodom – both young and old – surrounded the house. They called to Lot, "Where are the men who came to you tonight? Bring them out to us so that we can have sex with them."

Lot went outside to meet them and shut the door behind him and said, "No, my friends. Don't do this wicked thing. Look, I have two daughters who have never slept with a man. Let me bring them out to you, and you can do what you like with them. But don't do anything to these men, for they have come under the protection of my roof."

"Get out of our way," they replied. And they said, "This fellow came here as an alien, and now he wants to play the judge! We'll treat you worse than them." They kept bringing pressure on Lot and moved forward to break down the door.

But the men inside reached out and pulled Lot back into the house and shut the door. Then they struck the men who were at the door of the house, young and old, with blindness so that they could not find the door. The two men said to Lot, "Do you have anyone else here – sons-in-law, sons or daughters, or anyone else in the city who belongs to you? Get them out of here, because we are going to destroy this

> place. The outcry to the Lord against its people is so great that he has sent us to destroy it. . . ."
>
> Then the Lord rained down burning sulfur on Sodom and Gomorrah – from the Lord out of the heavens. Thus he overthrew those cities and the entire plain, including all those living in the cities – and also the vegetation in the land.

This passage is so definitive of homosexual conduct that our modern-day reference to *sodomy* is based on it. No wonder gay theologians are anxious to minimize its impact any way they can! Whatever the men of Sodom were up to, there is no question but that it drew God's wrath!

The first line of attack for all revisionists is to cast doubt on the meaning of the translated word when compared with the original. Pro-gay theologians therefore point out that the Hebrew verb *yadah*, translated in the King James Version "to know," may either mean "get to know" or be a euphemism for sex (as in "carnal knowledge" or he "*knew* her in a biblical sense").

The latter usage, "to have sex with," is adopted in the New International Version, quoted above. However, we are told that such a meaning is unlikely, since the word is used in the Hebrew Scriptures 943 times, and in only ten of those does it have the connotation of "carnal knowledge."

I suppose one would be foolish to ask how, using the same logic, one can be sure that *yadah* meant "having sex" in the ten cases cited. Couldn't the same argument be used in each case?

And what are we to make of any consistent interpretation of *yadah* in verse 8, which the King James version renders, "I have two daughters which have not *known* man"? Are we to presume that Lot's daughters were "not acquainted with" any men? Surely the point was that they were *virgins*, never having *had sex* with a man. As used in each case, *yadah* contemplated sexual relations.

More to the point, the context simply defies any other interpretation. Are we supposed to believe that the men of

Sodom were rebuked by Lot for merely wanting to make the acquaintance of the visitors? Are we being asked to believe that God rained down fire from heaven because the men of Sodom comprised some kind of a Chamber of Commerce welcoming committee?

Pro-gay theology responds that it was *violence* for which the men of Sodom were condemned, not homosexual sex. Williams goes so far as to say that "virtually all mainstream biblical scholars, including those who are somewhat conservative, agree that the point of the story, the 'sin of Sodom,' is not about sex, but about violence."

I've had enough courtroom experience to know that one can always find an "expert" to testify in his behalf on virtually any position imaginable, but I must demand a "bill of particulars" on this one. What "conservative," even "mainstream" scholars are we talking about? I've consulted a number of respectable conservative and mainstream scholars on Genesis 19, and so far I have found none who would take issue with the assertion that the "sin of Sodom" encompassed the sin of homosexual conduct, whether or not violently intended.

Certainly, Sodom's wickedness was not exclusively related to homosexual conduct. Even before the two angels visited Lot, Abraham was negotiating with God over the wickedness that was endemic in Sodom. And, writing centuries later, Ezekiel the prophet notes that Sodom's wickedness included pride, materialism, and injustice:

> Now this was the sin of your sister Sodom: She and her daughters were arrogant, overfed and unconcerned: they did not help the poor and needy (Ezek. 16:49).

But never doubt that Ezekiel's dirty laundry list on Sodom included other "detestable" sins as well:

> They were haughty and did detestable things before me. Therefore I did away with them as you have seen (Ezek. 16:50).

In an attempt to shift the blame away from its homosexual implications, Genesis 19 is presented by pro-gay theologians as preaching the sin of *inhospitality*, and that therefore "when a family or a church group disowns one of its members after discovering his or her homosexuality, *they* are committing the sin of sodomy. When Cardinal O'Connor preaches against gay rights, he is committing the sin of sodomy."[10]

Certainly there is no justification for shunning the penitent sinner, but Lot was saved from Sodom's destruction precisely because he called sin *sin*, no matter how "inhospitable" or "intolerant" it seemed to those who were bent on flaunting sin in the sight of God.

On its face, a more difficult problem posed by pro-gay theologians concerns Lot's offer to give over to the men of Sodom his two virgin daughters. That offer (as well as a similar one made in the strikingly parallel story of the Levite in Judges 19) does indeed shock one's modern sensibilities. Williams says, "Lot's lack of concern for his daughters ought to render this story useless as a moral and ethical model!"

As uncomfortable as we might feel about Lot's offer of his daughters, the one thing we cannot say is that the story is "useless as a moral and ethical model." In his short New Testament letter, the inspired writer Jude employs the incident as exactly that – a moral model – specifically naming "sexual immorality and perversion" as the sin for which God brought down his judgment (Jude 7). Peter does likewise in his second epistle (2 Peter 2:6-8).

We may never feel good about the moral propriety of offering the daughters. Yet one cannot help but wonder if the enigmatic reference to Lot's daughters is simply to further highlight the kind of sex the men of Sodom were after. Unlike the wicked Benjamites in Judges 19, who saw the Levite's concubine as a "consolation prize" and raped her to

[10] Williams, *Just As I Am*, p. 48.

the point of death, the men of Sodom weren't after just any kind of sex. Rape alone was not good enough for the Sodomites. It was *perverse sex only* that they demanded.

Deuteronomy 23:17, 18
No Israelite man or woman is to become a shrine prostitute. You must not bring the earnings of a female prostitute or of a male prostitute into the house of the LORD your God to pay any vow, because the LORD your God detests them both.

Initially, pro-gay advocates objected to the King James translation, which used the words "sodomite" and "dog" in reference to the male cult prostitutes. But even the modern translations, as above, leave gay critics unsatisfied: "The sex, whether homosexual, heterosexual, or transvestitism, was not the issue; the issue was idolatry."[11]

As for the passage's focus on idolatry, the point is well taken. But any inverse implication – that male prostitution itself is somehow thereby legitimized – is a kind of tortured logic in which only someone desperate for self-justification can indulge.

Leviticus 18:22
Do not lie with a man as one lies with a woman; that is detestable.

What pro-gay theologians say of this explicit passage ought to win some kind of award for creativity! "The operative and telling phrase here," says Robert Williams, "is *as with a woman.*" He goes on to explain that the prohibition is not against having same-gender sex, but against having it in any manner that would perpetuate class distinction. In other words, a man should not have sex with another man in the degrading way in which men have sex with women, treating them as inferiors. As long as sex is enjoyed with mutual respect, it doesn't matter who is doing what with whom!

[11] Ibid., p. 50.

Are we to take it that the same explanation applies to the very next verse?

> Do not have sexual relations with an animal and defile yourself with it. A woman must not present herself to an animal to have sexual relations with it; that is a perversion.

I appreciate how unfair it is to bring up bestiality in the same sentence as homosexuality, but the absurdity or the "class distinction" explanation for verse 22 is exploded by even the most cursory look at verse 23.

The Levitical prohibition neither assumes that heterosexual sex deems the woman to be man's social inferior nor that any amount of mutuality between two members of the same gender would legitimize sex between them.

In this regard it is interesting to note the penalty attached to the prohibition. Leviticus 20:13 instructs that "if a man lies with a man as one lies with a woman, *both of them* have done what is detestable. *They* must be put to death; *their* blood will be on their own heads." The punishment had nothing to do with "class distinctions." It assumed that *both* men were doing *with each other* that which was detestable.

As a last-ditch effort to get around the plain teaching of this passage, gays make a feeble attempt at damage control. They point to other prohibitions which were considered "abominations" (to use the King James terminology for "detestable"), including various "unclean" dietary foods, different forms of idolatry (Deut. 7:25), blemished sacrifices (Deut. 17:1), acts of divination (Deut. 18:12), remarrying a divorced wife (Deut. 24:4), and even "haughty eyes" and "a lying tongue," in the words of Proverbs (6:17).

Of course, it's a "this sin is no worse than any other sin" argument – which is true as far as it goes. All sin is an affront to God. The problem for gays (and for any of the rest of us, for that matter) is that such an argument never goes far enough to make any sin "not a sin," as they try to imply, and that is the ultimate, futile aim of pro-gay theologians.

Culturally Updating the New Testament

What you run into in discussing New Testament passages with pro-gay theologians is a hermeneutical ploy that introduces "the cultural argument." At the center of the argument stands the apostle Paul, who – so it is said – is writing either from his own personal biases or who reflects the patriarchal standards of his day.

This cultural argument goes on to say that times have changed, and with them God's will. "*Their* story" in the first century is not "*our* story" today. Paul's perspective is no longer relevant; it is out of step with the twentieth century. Scripture must constantly be updated so that it can minister to the needs of people in whatever circumstances they may be found. And with that hermeneutical approach, we once again see both radical reinterpretation of familiar texts and something new – the sheer rejection of biblical authority!

Again, Robert Williams says it most chillingly: "The point is not really whether or not some passage in the Bible condemns homosexual acts; the point is that you cannot allow your moral and ethical decisions to be determined by the literature of a people whose culture and history are so far removed form your own. You must dare to be iconoclastic enough to say, 'So what if the Bible does say it? Who cares?'"[12]

Romans 1:18, 19; 24-27

The wrath of God is being revealed from heaven against all the godlessness and wickedness of men who suppress the truth by their wickedness, since what may be known about God is plain to them, because God has made it plain to them....

Therefore God gave them over in the sinful desires of their hearts to sexual impurity for the degrading of their bodies with one another. They exchanged the truth of God for a lie, and worshiped and served created things rather than the Creator – who is forever praised. Amen.

---

[12] Ibid., p. 42.

> Because of this, God gave them over to shameful lusts. Even their women exchanged natural relations for unnatural ones. In the same way the men also abandoned natural relations with women and were inflamed with lust for one another. Men committed indecent acts with other men, and received in themselves the due penalty for their perversion.

This is a particularly painful passage for gays. And especially so for lesbians, since it is the only passage making direct reference to female homosexuals.

Initial protest is made that the passage seems to blame homosexuality on the idolatrous practice of worshiping "created things rather than the Creator." But here Paul seems not to be thinking specifically of wooden idols or stone gods of some kind – only the fact that homosexual conduct, like all other sin, *dethrones God* (the Creator) and *enthrones man* (the creature).

The primary assault comes against the obvious implications for homosexuals: that homosexual conduct is "unnatural." That's the *last* thing gays would ever want to hear the Bible say about what they do. To be absolved of responsibility for their sexual acts, they absolutely must prove that what they do is completely natural in every sense of the term.

It's a question of whether Paul was right in saying that homosexual acts stem from "sinful desires of the heart" and "shameful lusts." If Paul was right, then homosexual acts are plainly sinful and subject to God's condemnation. So the stakes are high, and everything possible must be done to favorably explain what Paul means by "unnatural."

Their best shot is similar to their attack on Leviticus 18:22. Says Williams, "It is precisely the social equality of the sexual partners that causes Paul to label the same-sex relations 'unnatural.' Sex that was 'natural,' in Paul's view, necessarily involved males dominating females!"[13]

This hardly needs refuting. Even Williams realizes that

---

[13] Ibid., p. 53.

any attempt to get around the plain meaning of Paul's words is hopeless. So he turns to decanonizing the passage altogether: "Perhaps Paul is condemning homosexuality in this passage, or at least labeling it as 'unnatural' (which is not *exactly* the same thing as calling it sinful). But the bottom line for you is: So what? Paul was wrong about a number of other things, too. Why should you take him any more seriously than you take Jerry Falwell or Anita Bryant or Cardinal O'Connor?"[14]

Well, there we have the real truth of the matter: Who cares what the Bible says if it disagrees with what we believe or want to do! And from there it just goes downhill altogether.

> **1 Corinthians 6:9, 10**
> Do you not know that the wicked will not inherit the kingdom of God? Do not be deceived: Neither the sexually immoral nor idolaters nor adulterers nor male prostitutes nor homosexual offenders nor thieves nor the greedy nor drunkards nor slanderers nor swindlers will inherit the kingdom of God.

> **1 Timothy 1:9-11**
> We also know that law is made not for the righteous but for lawbreakers and rebels, the ungodly and sinful, the unholy and irreligious; for those who kill their fathers or mothers, for murderers, for adulterers and perverts, for slave traders and liars and perjurers – and for whatever else is contrary to the sound doctrine that conforms to the glorious gospel of the blessed God, which he entrusted to me.

After quibbling about the various words translated in these two lists of sinners – whether "sodomites," "sexual perverts," "sexually immoral," "male prostitutes," or "homosexual offenders" – gay theologians finally throw up their hands in despair.

---

[14] Ibid.

For Williams, there is nothing left but to say, "Paul, like most of us, had his good moments and his bad moments."[15] And then he takes us back to the feminist test of canonicity: "*It cannot be believed unless it rings true to our deepest capacity for truth and goodness.*"[16] With that, he concludes: "Any discussion of the household of God, then, that degenerates into a list of those who will not get into the club should strike you as misguided. It does not ring true to our deepest capacity for truth and goodness. This passage, then, simply has no authority for you."[17]

Here we go again. Take what feels good from the Bible and dump the rest of it! So why all the pretense at scholarly debate over the meaning of individual biblical passages? Why even bother opening the Bible in the first place?

Once we ourselves become the highest moral authority, the Bible is irrelevant at best and a nuisance at worst. Williams, writing to fellow homosexuals, makes no bones about it: "As a queer Christian, you can draw from other sources, particularly from the sacred writings of your own people, past and present, as well as from the 'rather grossly overrated' Bible."

Up Close and Personal

Throughout this chapter I have purposely chosen to liberally quote from Robert Williams even though there are many other sources available at my fingertips. By now the basic arguments are fairly standardized. However, for a reason which I will share with you momentarily, I want you to know this man up close and personal.

Robert Williams began his spiritual saga at the age of 11 by walking down the aisle of the Pioneer Drive Baptist

---

[15] Ibid., p. 51.

[16] Margaret A. Farley, Feminist Consciousness and the Interpretation of Scripture," in Letty M. Russell, ed., *Feminist Interpretation of the Bible* (Philadelphia: Westminster Press, 1985), p. 43.

[17] Williams, *Just As I Am*, p. 52.

Church in Abilene, Texas, to "accept Jesus as his personal Lord and Savior." From there he "followed Jesus" through dozens of different churches in at least four denominations, to New Age study groups and gay religious caucuses, and finally into "high church" Anglo-Catholic worship. You may have read about him in conjunction with his ground-breaking place in history as the first openly gay priest to be ordained in the Episcopal Church.

The ordination took place under the auspices of Williams' mentor, the controversial John Spong, bishop of the Diocese of Newark, who was once quoted as saying that if the church could bless the hounds at a fox hunt, it could bless committed same-sex couples![18] But not even Bishop Spong could keep back the hounds in the church and media when Williams suggested in a forum on celibacy that Mother Teresa's life would be greatly enhanced if she "got laid." Spong himself turned out the light in Williams' priestly office!

However, you should not dismiss Williams as a nut case. His understanding of Christian theology is as deep as it is perverse. At times his book is uncannily perceptive, and even profoundly spiritual – perhaps owing to the fact that he has been diagnosed as having AIDS, and is therefore forced to struggle with life's meaning.

His is not the only book written on pro-gay theology. Indeed, I have rummaged through a long shelf-full of such books. But none is more personal, and thus revealing, of the mind of one who is *convinced* that he is doing God's bidding as a practicing, proud, and – in his own words – "queer Christian."

A Struggle of Conscience

And that brings me to the point I want to make about not just Robert Williams but millions of gays whom I think he represents: *The gay-rights movement is aimed primarily at gain-*

[18] Ibid., p. xvi.

ing public legitimacy for the homosexual lifestyle. Not just legalization, but *legitimacy*. Yet there is another process going on behind the scenes that is far more personal: *a struggle of individual consciences.*

Let me go back to the questions I asked earlier: Why all the pretense at scholarly debate over the meaning of individual biblical passages? Why even bother opening the Bible in the first place? The answers to both of these questions, I propose, is that homosexual men and women *have* to deal with the Bible! Intuitively, they *know* that what they are doing is wrong, and they can't live with it.

Sadly for many homosexuals, they literally can't live with their consciences and tragically end up among the deplorable suicide statistics that haunt the nation's gays. Facile attempts to put the blame for their deaths on an unaccepting homophobic society only serve to perpetuate the problem.

Those who do not choose "the easy way out" are left to struggle within themselves. I suspect that the guilt is overwhelming. (It can be bad enough for heterosexual sin!) And that very guilt is the strongest experiential evidence possible that homosexuality is neither natural (in terms of what God intended) nor morally acceptable when acted upon (in terms of what God demands).

Longing for Acceptance

But it's not always just the guilt, and that brings me back to Robert Williams. He would probably deny it (he's far too feisty to beg sympathy), but laced throughout his book are what seem to be telltale cries for help, subtle pleas for love he never received, and a desperate longing for acceptance — from family, friends, the church, and most of all, his God.

Just catch the tone of these snippets strewn through his book:

> [Said by a friend,] "You are a very angry young man."[19]

[19] Ibid., p. xii.

> Chances are you grew up believing in a God who did not truly love you. A God who – like your human parents, perhaps – was disappointed in you, ashamed of you.[20]

> The person in my life who has consistently offered me the closest thing I have ever experienced to truly unconditional love is not my father or mother or lover, but my grandmother.[21]

> While my father seemed to be always working, and my mother was often too busy with her own work, I can't remember Grannie ever telling me not to bother her.[22]

> For many of us, it is difficult if not impossible to imagine our fathers ever saying to us, "You are my beloved child. I am proud of you."[23]

> Pride, far from being a sin for queers, is the remedy against sin. Our greatest sin is self-hatred, self-denigration ....[24]

> [Of his first visit to a gay bar,] Suddenly, this twenty-three-year-old man who had grown up feeling like an outcast, a sissy, felt affirmed, attractive, *wanted*.[25]

Am I reading too much into these statements, or has Robert Williams just told us how innocent babies grow up to be homosexuals? How different might Robert's life have been if his father had not always been working, and his mother not so busy with her own work? What if his father had said to him, "Son, I love you. I am proud of you"? What if from an early age Robert could have sung "Jesus Loves Me" with real confidence that it was truly so?

Somehow I have to believe that there might have been one less pro-gay theologian out there doing scholastic flip-flops in order to find a God who might accept him *just as he is*.

---

[20] Ibid., p. 87.

[21] Ibid., p. 91.

[22] Ibid.

[23] Ibid., p. 92.

[24] Ibid., p. 150.

[25] Ibid., p. 172.

People don't just intentionally set out to go Bible-bashing. Behind every feminist and gay theologian is likely to be some early relationship gone terribly wrong. How many more "rebellious gay activists" are there out there, trying desperately to overcome their upbringing and somehow connect with God? And how many precious little ones are there in homes across America today, even in *Christian* homes, who one day will grow up fearing what the Bible teaches so much that they are willing to trash it, if necessary, to get some misguided sense of God's acceptance?

> *Jesus said, "Let the little children come to me, and do not hinder them, for the kingdom of heaven belongs to such as these" (Matt. 19:14).*
>
> *"But if anyone causes one of these little ones who believe in me to sin, it would be better for him to have a large millstone hung around his neck and to be drowned in the depths of the sea."*
>
> *"Woe to the world because of the things that cause people to sin! Such things must come, but woe to the man through whom they come!" (Matt. 18:6,7).*

CHAPTER EIGHT

THE BIBLE DOES HAVE SOMETHING TO SAY ABOUT HOMOSEXUALITY

Dr. Carl Bridges, Jr.

Many gay writers have promoted the idea that the Bible is silent or even approves of homosexual behavior. In this study, Dr. Carl Bridges reviews the key passages and arguments that support biblical interdiction against homosexuality.

Much has been written on the homosexual issue, including many books and articles which have appeared over the past few decades. A bibliography published thirteen years ago, dealing only with homosexuality as it impacts the Judeo-Christian tradition, contained 459 entries![1]

As one might expect, these writings reflect all kinds of viewpoints. The viewpoint that concerns us here is the claim made by some scholars in recent years that the Bible does not condemn homosexual behavior.

"The Bible doesn't condemn homosexuality," or, "The Bible doesn't say anything about homosexuality." To some-

[1] Tom Horner, *Homosexuality and the Judeo-Christian Tradition: An Annotated Bibliography*, ATLA Bibliographical Series 5 (Metuchen, NJ: Scarecrow, 1981).

one who knows Scripture, these statements seem surprising when we hear them. Our tendency is to turn up a passage or two and say, "See, it says right here . . . ."

This response is not good enough. When people claim the Bible has nothing to say about the homosexual issue, they usually do not mean that homosexual behavior is never mentioned in Scripture. Instead, they usually mean one of two things, either (1) that homosexuality *as practiced today* never appears in Scripture, or (2) that even though the Bible does speak against homosexuality, what the Bible says does not apply to the present situation. We suspect that there may be a third group also, people who do not know much Scripture and really believe the homosexual issue is never discussed there.

Our strategy will be to look at the relevant biblical texts, then to discuss what pro-homosexual interpreters have made of them, showing the weaknesses in their arguments and explaining why the traditional understanding is largely true. Following the textual discussion we will discuss the nature of human sexuality in theological terms.

The Sodom Account

The first mention of homosexual behavior in the Bible appears in Gen. 19:1-11, the account of the angel visitors to Abraham's nephew Lot in the city of Sodom. The visitors' mission, which Lot does not know about, is to discover if the rumor of Sodom's wickedness is true, in order to find out if God should punish its people (Gen. 18:20-21). Once Lot persuades the two men to accept his hospitality for the night, the men of Sodom surround the house, demanding that Lot send the visitors out so the Sodomites may "know" them (vv. 4-5).

One Old Testament word for "know" often serves as a euphemism for sexual intercourse. Adam, for example, "knew" his wife and she conceived a child (Gen. 4:1, 25), as did his son Cain (Gen. 4:17) and many others. Lot's reply to the men of Sodom shows that he understood their demand in sexual terms: "No, my friends. Don't do this wicked thing" (v. 7). His offer of his virgin daughters to the Sodomites as substitutes for the male visitors also indicates that their demand was sexual.

An incident appears in Judges 19 which has close parallels to the Sodom account. In this case the near-victim is a Levite from the territory of the tribe of Ephraim, traveling home through Benjaminite territory with his concubine and a male servant. As in the Sodom account, a man of the town of Gibeah, like Lot a member of a different tribe, takes the travelers in to keep them from spending the night in the public square, only to see them besieged by the men of the city, who again want to "know" them (v. 22). Just as Lot did, the man of Gibeah begs his neighbors not to do such a wicked deed (v. 23), and again he offers women as a substitute, in this case his visitor's concubine and his own virgin daughter (v. 24). In the event, the traveler pushes his concubine out the door to be raped all night and eventually to die of the abuse (vv. 25-28). Once again it is clear that the Gibeahites intended homosexual rape, though the offenders in this case were willing enough to abuse a woman instead if they could get her.

Old Testament Legal Passages

In two legal passages, Lev. 18:22 and 20:13, the God of Israel forbids a man to "lie with" another man "as with a woman." From a Christian perspective we are interested in knowing if these rules might be purely ceremonial ones, like the requirement to wear tassels on one's robe (Num. 15:37-39), or obviously moral requirements, like "You shall not steal" (Exod. 20:15). We conclude that homosexual intercourse is not only a matter of ceremonial purity here, for it is discussed in the same context with such moral offenses as incest (18:6-18, 20; 20:11-14, 17, 19-21), adultery (20:10), idolatry (18:21; 20:1-6) and bestiality (18:23; 20:15-16). The only apparently ceremonial matter mentioned in this context is lying with a menstruating woman (18:19; 20:18).

Paul's Writings

In the New Testament Paul speaks to the issue of homosexual behavior in Rom. 1:24-27. Because the people of the Gentile world have largely "suppressed the truth" (v. 18) by failing to glorify God to the extent that they understand him (v. 21), God has "handed them over" to indulge their lusts (v. 24). Just as pagans have "exchanged" God's truth for falsehood, so also their women have "exchanged the natural use for the unnatural" (v. 26), a probable reference to female homosexuality, and if so the only one in the Bible. Moreover, pagan men "burn with lust for each other," "abandoning the natural use of the female" (v. 27). Here is the closest thing we find in Scripture to a natural law argument against homosexual behavior, and here also is perhaps the clearest statement that homosexual intercourse is wrong.

In two other places in the Pauline letters we find strong statements against homosexual intercourse. Homosexual behavior appears in two vice lists, one in 1 Cor. 6:9-10 and the other in 1 Tim. 1:9-10. In the Corinthians passage Paul includes "fornicators, idolaters, adulterers, . . . thieves, drunkards, slanderers [and] swindlers" among the "unrighteous" who "will not inherit God's kingdom." Along with these he places *arsenokoitai* and *malakoi*, two words unfortunately lumped together in the Revised Standard Version ("homosexuals" in the first edition; "sexual perverts" in the second). These words denote the active and passive partners in a homosexual relationship, the first word referring to a man who "beds" another, the second to a "soft" or "effeminate" man, here specifically a male who plays a female sexual role with another man.[2] The reference to homosexual behavior in the

---

[2] Robin Scroggs, in *The New Testament and Homosexuality: Contextual Background for Contemporary Debate* (Philadelphia: Fortress, 1983), pp. 62-65, 106-109, argues that these two words refer in a restricted sense to homo-

Timothy passage is similar. There *arsenokoitai* appear alongside people called "ungodly, sinners, . . . killers of fathers and mothers, . . . kidnappers, liars, perjurers" and others. There can be little doubt about the intent of these passages to describe homosexual intercourse as morally reprehensible.

Another Approach

We might think that these passages settle the issue, and perhaps they do settle it for people who believe that the Bible teaches eternally true moral principles in clear, understandable language.[3] Things are not so simple, however, for those who do not believe that Scripture and morality are related in such a direct, simple way. In 1955 Derrick Sherwin Bailey published an influential book called *Homosexuality and the Western Christian Tradition*, in which he called into question much of what appeared certain in our understanding of the Bible's teaching on homosexuality.[4] Based on Sherwin Bailey's ideas, or ideas like his, some people today make surprising claims about the biblical attitude toward homosexual behavior. Even though we do not share the presuppositions

---

sexual prostitutes (*malakoi*) and the men who use them (*arsenokoitai*). However, even if Paul does not refer to homosexual behavior generally in this passage, he certainly does so in Romans 1:26-27, which Scroggs appears to admit (116-117). P. Michael Ukleja, "Homosexuality in the New Testament," *Bibliotheca Sacra* 140/4 (October-December 1983): 350-358, argues for the more general meaning of the two words which we believe is correct. See also two articles by David E. Malick, "The Condemnation of Homosexuality in Romans 1:26-27, *Bibliotheca Sacra* 150/3 (July-September 1993): 327-340, and "The Condemnation of Homosexuality in 1 Corinthians 6:9," *Bibliotheca Sacra* 150/4 (October-December 1993), pp. 479-492.

[3] Marva J. Dawn, *Sexual Character: Beyond Technique to Intimacy* (Grand Rapids: Eerdmans, 1993), in a useful "hermeneutical excursus" (pp. 96-98), deals with the question of how the present-day church should deal with the biblical passages on homosexuality.

[4] Derrick Sherwin Bailey, *Homosexuality and the Western Christian Tradition* (London: Longmans, Green, 1955); reprint, Hamden, CT: Archon, 1975. John R. W. Stott, in "Homosexual 'Marriage,'" *Christianity Today* 29/17 (November 22, 1985), p. 22, refers to Sherwin Bailey as "the first Christian theologian to re-evaluate the traditional understanding of the biblical prohibitions regarding homosexuality."

of those who think they find scriptural material in favor of homosexuality, we need to examine what they do with Scripture, if only in order to refute it.

In his book Sherwin Bailey does not sound a bit like a gay activist of today, and as many of his points argue against homosexual behavior as those which might seem to argue for it. For this reason we find much in his work to agree with. However, in two major areas his work tends to weaken the traditional Christian understanding of homosexual behavior, and his foundational work has provided others since then an opportunity to take his ideas much further.

Sodom Reinterpreted

The first of these areas is the interpretation of the Sodom account. Sherwin Bailey argues that the traditional Christian understanding of the destruction of Sodom is wrong in that the men of Sodom did not intend homosexual rape of the angels. Because of this supposedly wrong understanding, a picture of the Sodomites has built up over the years which presents them as vicious perverts when they really were nothing of the kind. The sin of Sodom, Sherwin Bailey argues, was inhospitality. However, because of the belief that their sin was homosexual, Christians came to think that God's destruction of their cities shows that God hates homosexual behavior more than other sins. Partly on the foundation of this belief, Sherwin Bailey maintains, Christians built a longstanding attitude toward homosexuals that resulted in severe legal penalties against them, as well as a general abhorrence of them which is unjustified by the biblical text.

We need to examine Sherwin Bailey's study of the Sodom account in some detail, because his understanding of that passage provides a major building block for his thesis. To begin with Sherwin Bailey claims that when the Sodomites said they wanted to "know" the visitors, they did not intend homosexual intercourse with them (pp. 2-4). As we have seen, one of the Old Testament words for "know" sometimes refers to sexual intercourse. Sherwin Bailey points out that this use appears only ten times in the Old Testament (excluding this debated reference and the related one in Judges 19), and five of these always refer to heterosexual intercourse. Further, another word was available which would have made the sexual meaning unmistakable, but the writer did not use it.

So far Sherwin Bailey's argument sounds convincing. In the Old Testament to "know" does not always mean "to have sex with," and other meanings are certainly possible. But the sexual interpretation of the Sodom account does not rest on the meaning of a word alone; contextual considerations, in our opinion, make that interpretation certain. If the Sodomites did not want to rape the angels, what did Lot mean when he begged them "not to do this wicked thing" (Gen. 19:7)? And what was his point in offering his neighbors his virgin daughters instead of the men (v. 8)?

Sherwin Bailey attempts to answer these questions. He points out correctly that Lot, as a resident alien in Sodom, may have brought suspicion on himself by taking in foreigners. His neighbors may have wondered who these men were and whether Lot was planning something subversive. Lot himself may have had no right as an alien to take strangers in without first letting the people of Sodom make sure the visitors were harmless. Sherwin Bailey concludes, then, that when the men of Sodom said they wanted to "know" the visitors, they meant only what they said; they wanted to check up on the visitors and make sure they posed no threat to the city. In Sherwin Bailey's view the "wicked thing" Lot begged them not to do referred to the Sodomites' willingness to "flout the obligation of hospitality" (p. 5) by making Lot give up the visitors he had promised to protect. Lot offered his daughters not as a sexual substitute but as "simply the most tempting bribe that Lot could offer on the spur of the moment to appease the hostile crowd" (p. 6).

Sodom in Ancient Literature

In support of his view that the sin of Sodom was not homosexual, Sherwin Bailey next discusses the approach to the Sodom account which other ancient writers take. He correctly points out that elsewhere in the Old Testament the writers do not emphasize, or even mention, homosexual behavior in connection with the people of Sodom. Two prophetic references to Sodom's sin contain nothing about homosexual behavior. In condemning evils common in the sixth century BC, Jeremiah mentions adultery, lying and condoning evil in connection with Sodom and Gomorrah, but he does not mention homosexual acts (Jer 23:14). In the same way Ezekiel describes the "sin of . . . Sodom" in terms of its people being "arrogant, overfed and unconcerned; they did not help the poor and needy. They were haughty and did detestable things before [God]" (Ezek 16:49-50 NIV). In the Ezekiel passage only the "detestable things" might refer to homosexual behavior but, as Sherwin Bailey points out, the term is general enough that most likely it has "no warrantable homosexual implications" (p. 10). In addition he cites twelve other Old Testament passages which use Sodom "as a symbol of utter destruction, and its sin as one of such magnitude as to merit exemplary punishment," but contain no reference to homosexual behavior (p. 9).

Moving into the period between the testaments, Sherwin Bailey points out three passages from the Apocrypha which refer to the sin of Sodom in terms of pride, inhospitality and moral blindness, but which have nothing to say about homosexual behavior (Wisd. of Sol. 10:8, 19:8; Eccles. 16:8). In the same way several authors of pseudepigraphical writings – nonbiblical Jewish religious works from the period between the Testaments – accuse the Sodomites of fornication but not of homosexual behavior (Jubilees 16:5-6, 20:5-6). The first indication that a post-Old Testament writer considered the sin of Sodom to be homosexual appears in the Testament of

Naphtali, part of the larger work called The Testaments of the Twelve Patriarchs, which Sherwin Bailey dates around 109-106 BC (p. 13). There the writer condemns the men of Sodom for "changing the order of nature" (Testament of Naphtali 3:4-5). This statement, Sherwin Bailey believes, forms the background for Jude's remark that the men of Sodom "went after strange flesh" (Jude 7 in Sherwin Bailey's literal translation, p. 16). Although most English translators take this "going after strange flesh" to refer to sexual perversion (so NIV, RSV, NRSV, Phillips, TEV; AV and NASB translate the phrase literally), Sherwin Bailey argues that the sexual intent of Jude's statement is secondary and that his main focus lies on the forbidden mingling of two kinds of "flesh," the human and the angelic (p. 16).

Here then is where Sherwin Bailey's argument leads. He claims that the original Sodom account was not about homosexual behavior, and that later Old Testament writers knew nothing of the homosexual interpretation of the story. Only in the period between the Testaments, and not universally at that, did Jewish writers begin to interpret the sin of the Sodomites as homosexual, an interpretation which influenced the only New Testament reference (Jude 7) which identifies the Sodomites as homosexuals. In Sherwin Bailey's view Christians, beginning with Jude, have condemned homosexual behavior on slender grounds, based on a misunderstanding of the Old Testament text.

We have only briefly summarized Sherwin Bailey's argument, but we have tried to be fair to him. He cites more evidence from the intertestamental and early Christian periods than we can repeat here, but the result of it all is his conclusion "that the Sodom story has no direct bearing whatever upon the problem of homosexuality or the commission of homosexual acts" (p. 28). Here lies one root of the statement so often heard, that "the Bible doesn't condemn (or even, the Bible doesn't say anything about) homosexuality."

Critique

What can we make of the claim that the Sodom story is irrelevant to a Christian understanding of homosexuality? To begin with, Sherwin Bailey's argument that the Sodomites did not intend to rape the angels will not hold water. The evidence for a homosexual understanding of the Sodomites' demand is cumulative. They wanted to "know" the visitors. As John Stott points out, most of the uses of "know" referring to sexual intercourse occur in Genesis, which would lead us to expect that meaning here.[5] Lot referred to their proposed action as a "wicked thing." Such language makes more sense if Lot was trying to prevent a rape than if he were trying to assert his right to offer hospitality. And he offered them his daughters in exchange, an action for which Sherwin Bailey (p. 6) offers no convincing explanation unless the motive were sexual. As Derek Kidner neatly puts it, "it would be grotesquely inconsequent that Lot should reply to a demand for credentials by an offer of daughters."[6] In the parallel account of the outrage at Gibeah, the wicked men did eventually commit rape, though against a woman. Even if no single piece of evidence is conclusive, all the evidence taken together points clearly to the homosexual interpretation.

Sherwin Bailey may be on firmer ground, however, in maintaining that the men of Sodom did not practice homosexuality habitually. The Sodomites' attempt on the angels did not necessarily result from their sexual orientation but from a desire to bully the strangers. What we see here is a case of a gang of men trying to humiliate and control men weaker than themselves, in this instance strangers who have

---

[5] Stott, 23. See also Scroggs, p. 73, who although in general he concludes that Scripture does not forbid homosexual behavior today, still "believe[s] the traditional interpretation [of the Sodom account] to be correct."

[6] Derek Kidner, "Additional Note on the sin of Sodom," in *Genesis: An Introduction and Commentary* (Downers Grove: InterVarsity, 1967), pp. 136-137. See also Coleman, p. 34.

no strong local protector, through homosexual rape (cf. Sherwin Bailey, pp. 31-32). This kind of behavior, well known in prisons, may have nothing to do with the offender's sexual orientation. He may be a heterosexual person using homosexual rape as an offensive weapon.[7]

If this is true, however, it still makes little difference to the issue of homosexuality today. We will argue that, just as it is wrong for a heterosexual to practice homosexuality, it is also wrong for a sexual invert – a "natural" homosexual, if such exists – to engage in homosexual activity. In the biblical account, whether the Sodomites usually practiced homosexual behavior or not, whether or not they would be considered inverts today, their attempt on the angels was wrong and perverse. And in the same way today, whether one is gay or straight, Christian behavioral standards require believers to abstain from homosexual activity.

More than that, Sherwin Bailey's argument implies that a New Testament writer – Jude – may have misunderstood the Old Testament, and that if he did, we have no reason to accept his interpretation. Those of us who hold a high view of Scripture cannot accept such a conclusion. As Stott put it, ". . . for those of us who take the New Testament documents seriously, Jude's unequivocal statement cannot be dismissed as merely an error copied from Jewish pseudepigrapha" (p. 23).

In dealing with the clear prohibition of homosexual activity in Lev. 18:22 and 20:13, Sherwin Bailey admits that "the Biblical text condemns such practices in the strongest terms" (p. 37), a position which "cannot be lightly dismissed by the church" (p. 156). From this point, however, he moves to the question of inversion, concluding that Scripture has little to say about the question of people who are genuinely oriented

[7] White, p. 112, calls temporary homosexuality associated with prison life and similar circumstances "situational homosexuality." Eleanor Daniel, *What the Bible Says About Sexual Identity* (Joplin: College Press, 1981), pp. 161-162, prefers to call such people "contingent homosexuals."

toward others of their own sex (p. 157). He appears to accept the obvious reading of the Leviticus passages without accepting their moral content as permanently normative, which again involves a view of Scripture we do not accept.[8]

We agree fully with Kidner's conclusion on Sherwin Bailey's argument, that

> . . . the doubt created by Dr. Bailey has travelled more widely than the reasons he produces for it. Not one of these reasons, it may be suggested, stands any serious scrutiny.[9]

The Question of Inversion

Above we mentioned that Sherwin Bailey's conclusions, if accepted, tend to weaken the traditional Christian understanding of homosexuality in two areas. The first area had to do with our understanding of Scripture, especially the Sodom account, whether it stands as an indication of how much God hates homosexual behavior. The second area is the question of sexual inversion, an area in which Sherwin Bailey makes certain suggestions but leaves it to others to draw firm conclusions.

Sherwin Bailey carefully distinguishes between "perverts," whom he identifies as heterosexual people who choose to engage in homosexual activity, and "inverts," who are people attracted to others of the same sex due to genetic or environmental factors. In dealing with Paul's condemnation of homosexual behavior in Rom. 1:27, Sherwin Bailey says that Paul, unaware of this distinction between pervert and invert, condemns the behavior of both (p. 38), but that Paul's words, and those of the rest of the New Testament, simply do not apply to the issue facing us today (p. 157). He concludes that

---

[8] For an argument that the Leviticus passages are normative for Christians as we believe, see P. Michael Ukleja, "Homosexuality and the Old Testament," *Bibliotheca Sacra* 140/3 (July-September 1983): 259-266, especially 264ff. on "The Relevance of the Law."

[9] Kidner, p. 137.

> the Western Christian tradition [including, but not limited to, Scripture]. . . is . . . defective, in that . . . it is ignorant of inversion as a *condition* due to biological, psychological, or genetical causes; and consequently of the distinction between the invert and the pervert. Therefore, . . . it assumes that all homosexual acts are, so to speak, "acts of perversion" – a term which does not happily or accurately describe the acts to which the invert may be impelled by his condition.[10]

At this point an important question arises: Is some behavior objectively natural or unnatural, or is the question of natural behavior purely a matter of subjective taste? Does "natural" as Paul uses the term mean "natural for me" or "natural for everyone"? Some homosexual people would argue that heterosexual contact is unnatural, even disgusting, for them, and that homosexual behavior, because it is natural for them, is justified. What are we to make of this claim?

We need to move carefully here, neither abandoning the idea of natural law nor making too much of it. We hold as a hermeneutical principle that natural law is a valid theological category, if only because biblical writers make use of it from time to time. We do not want, however, to go beyond Scripture and make natural-law claims without biblical support. Simply put, if a biblical writer makes a natural-law claim, our view of Scripture leads us to consider it valid; if someone else makes a claim based on natural law, we feel free to question it.[11] It is clear that Paul did not mean "natural for me" when

---

[10] Sherwin Bailey, pp. 172-173; author's emphasis. Freud used the terms "inversions" and "perversion" somewhat differently; see Coleman, p. 13.

[11] An alert reader might notice that Paul uses a natural-law argument in favor of women keeping their hair long, and men cutting theirs, in 1 Cor. 11:14-15, and that we find an argument from creation, similar to a natural-law argument, for the silence of women in church in 1 Tim. 2:13-14. If we say that we are bound to condemn all homosexual behavior because Paul argued against it on the ground of natural law, are we also obligated to keep our hair short (or long, as the case may be) and keep women quiet in church on the same grounds? We believe these are different cases.

Paul condemns homosexual behavior *as sin* in Rom. 1:26-27, while he does not discuss variations in hairstyle or women's speaking in church on

he spoke against men who "abandoned natural relations with women" (Rom. 1:27); he was talking about an objective condition of depravity experienced by people who rejected God's will. Since this is so, it goes a long way toward settling the issue for those whose view of Scripture does not allow us to claim that we know better than the biblical authors because of their supposed ignorance of some aspects of the human condition.

We will have more to say about natural law later, but for now we may say that Paul's alleged ignorance of the matter of sexual inversion does not invalidate what he says about sexual behavior. If we believe that God gave the writers of Scripture, if not all knowledge, at least enough knowledge to avoid error, we will hesitate to second-guess them. If Paul did know about sexual inversion, he believed it to be the consequence of sin, so that God

> gave them [Gentile sinners] over to shameful lusts. Even their women exchanged natural relations for unnatural ones, [. . . and] the men also abandoned natural relations with women and were inflamed with lust for one another . . . (Rom. 1:26-27).

On the other hand, if he did not know about sexual inversion, he still condemned perverse behavior as a violation of God's will. The "lusts" Paul talks about are "shameful" and "unnatural." If we could speak to Paul today and enlighten him – as though he really needed instruction – on the matter of sexual inversion, would he really change his approach and agree that homosexual activity might be "natural" for some

---

the same terms. We might say that for Paul, homosexual behavior was a moral matter, while hairstyle was a symbolic one – standing for a wife's submission for her husband (see 1 Cor. 11:5, 7) – or a customary matter (see 1 Cor. 11:16), while the question of women speaking in church was a practical, not a moral, issue (see 1 Cor. 11:5, 14:33b-35). Paul's use of a natural-law argument in discussing a non-moral issue does not necessarily imply that he considered hairstyles or women's silence part of the moral order of creation.

people and "unnatural" for others? We believe not.[12]

We have seen that Sherwin Bailey's conclusions, though based on a carefully nuanced examination of primary sources, will not stand up in the main. The Sodom account in Scripture does refer to an attempted homosexual rape, and the biblical condemnations of homosexual activity, based as they are on a concept of objectively natural behavior, may not be criticized as defective.

Another Challenge

Robin Scroggs, a New Testament scholar, has dealt with the New Testament evidence, setting it in the broad context of first century Greek and Roman attitudes toward homosexual activity.[13] When he concludes that "Biblical judgments against homosexuality are not relevant to today's debate" (p. 127), he agrees with Sherwin Bailey, who concluded that "it can hardly be said that the New Testament speaks" to the problem of sexual inversion.[14] We need to examine this conclusion in detail, since it serves as a foundation for the claim that a Christian can be a practicing homosexual without doing wrong.

Scroggs begins with a helpful summary of various attitudes that students of this issue hold toward the biblical evidence. To begin with he describes four different views held by those who believe that "the Bible opposes homosexuality" (p. 7):

> "1. The Bible opposes homosexuality and is definitive for what the church should think and do about it" (p. 7).
>
> "2. The Bible opposes homosexuality, but it is just one sin among many. There is no justification for singling it out as

[12] Coleman, p. 91, calls that attempt to read Paul as only condemning homosexual acts by heterosexual people "an attempt to read the old texts with modern presuppositions."

[13] See note 9.

[14] Sherwin Bailey, p. 157.

more serious than other sins castigated in the Bible, but because of which ordination is not denied" (p. 8).

"3. The Bible opposes homosexuality but the specific injunctions must be placed in the larger biblical context of the theology of creation, sin, judgment, and grace" (p. 9).

"4. The Bible opposes homosexuality but is so time- and culture-bound that its injunctions may and should be discarded if other considerations suggest better alternatives" (p. 11).

It appears to us that views #1 and #2 are compatible. This is, in fact, the conclusion we have reached: that Scripture does indeed identify all forms of homosexual intercourse as sinful, but not as a special category of sin. We believe that Christians today must do all they can to avoid and discourage homosexual behavior yet deal with it in a pastoral way. In the same way, views #3 and #4 appear compatible with each other – though not with our views – #3 being a theological attempt to find room for legitimate homosexual behavior today, and #4 a sociological attempt to do the same thing.

Next Scroggs describes two views held by those who believe that "the Bible does not oppose homosexuality" (p. 11):

"1. The Bible does not oppose homosexuality because it does not speak of true or innate homosexuality but rather of homosexual acts by people who are not homosexuals" (p. 12).

"2. The Bible does not oppose homosexuality because the texts do not deal with homosexuality in general" (p. 12).

As before, it appears that one could hold both of these views at the same time. We have dealt with #1 already under "The Question of Inversion," answering Sherwin Bailey's arguments on the subject. #2 represents the viewpoint closest to Scroggs' own conclusions.

New Testament Evidence

In examining three New Testament passages on homosexuality (1 Cor. 6:9-10; Rom. 1:26-27; 1 Tim. 1:9-10), Scroggs holds the "beginning presupposition that these passages all oppose one form or another of pederasty, insofar as they speak of male homosexuality" (p. 101). This assumption, which runs throughout his work, colors his conclusions at every point. As Scroggs sees it, homosexuality in the New Testament world consisted only of relationships in which the strong exploited the weak. The strong person might be an older man who corrupted a youth, or a slave owner who used a slave against the slave's will, or the customer of an "effeminate call boy," but in every case mutual caring and unselfish concern were absent.

In writing against these evils, Scroggs maintains, Paul could only have been thinking about the kind of exploitative relationships he knew about in his world: "Paul . . . must have had, *could only have had*, pederasty in mind" (p. 122, author's emphasis). In fact Scroggs' whole argument depends on "what Paul is thinking about" (p. 116, cf. p. vi), and we learn what Paul is thinking about by doing the kind of background study already presented.

Here lies Scroggs' point. Although Paul's opposition to homosexuality "is not to be denied" (p. 116), the fact that he considered homosexual behavior unnatural and wrong springs mainly from the kind of homosexual behavior he knew about. Since Paul did not explain why he opposed homosexual activity, "Paul's theology leaves one in the same ambiguous position that the church finds itself in today. Theological or ethical assertions without adequate rationale," even those contained in Scripture, are not sufficient grounds for making moral decisions today (p. 117). To put it crudely, we do not have to listen to what Paul said on the subject because he did not sufficiently explain himself. Even though the language Paul used in Rom. 1:26-27 condemned homosexual behavior generally, Scroggs believes Paul really intended to condemn only pederasty in particular. Scroggs' final conclusion is that "biblical judgments against homosexuality are not relevant to today's debate" (p. 127), because the writers of Scripture were not arguing against the kind of homosexual relationships which (we are told) predominate today: relationships between people of a similar age, in which mutual love and faithfulness are the norm.

Critique

In dealing with the New Testament evidence, Scroggs makes use of a sound hermeneutical principle which we believe he has taken too far. The principle is this: In order to apply biblical teaching to today's situations, "the context today must bear a reasonable similarity to the context which called the biblical statements into existence" (p. 125). This is a good principle.

For example, the Old Testament prohibition of tattooing and certain kinds of haircuts (Lev. 19:27-28) likely springs from some association with ancient near eastern religious practices, pagan actions Israel was supposed to avoid out of devotion to God. Since in our present cultural context these actions no longer carry any pagan meaning, Christians today are not much concerned about these matters.

In interpreting scriptural statements about moral behavior, Scroggs maintains, the main issue is "What are the authors against?" (p. vi). If Paul opposed only one particular form of homosexual activity, we may not take his words to prohibit homosexual activity generally. Scroggs' arguments tend to support the position he describes in these words: "The Bible does not oppose homosexuality because the texts do not deal with homosexuality *in general*" (p. 12, emphasis added), only exploitative pederastic relationships in particular.

But we believe Scroggs applies this principle too narrowly. He maintains that since the only type of homosexual behavior the biblical authors knew about was pederasty – though in talking about it they appear to condemn all homosexual behavior – we have no idea what attitude they would take toward today's mutual and caring homosexual relationships (p. 122). We would say, in contrast to Scroggs' viewpoint, that the authors condemned homosexuality in general terms in order to fight both the pederasty of their day and any kind of homosexual intercourse in any day. Since they spoke against homosexual activity in general terms, we conclude that they were against all kinds of homosexual intercourse. If they had only objected to dehumanizing pederasty, which Scroggs believes was the only variety of homosexuality they knew, they would have had ample opportunity to say so. Since instead they spoke against homosexuality generally, we ought to take their words at face value.

An imaginary example may serve to make our position clearer. A few decades ago when premarital sex was less approved socially than now, a common scenario involved a young man getting a girl pregnant and then "running out" on her, refusing to take responsibility for her or their child. Suppose a Christian writer of that day wrote, "God hates premarital sex." An interpreter of those words a thousand years later might reason like this: "The primary model of premarital sex in mid-twentieth century America involved a young man impregnating a girl and then leaving her. Since this was the only kind of premarital sex the author knew about, his general statement that 'God hates premarital sex' must refer to that situation alone, so that we cannot learn from the writer's statement what he would say about premarital sex generally." A better way to understand the writer's general statement, however, would be the conclusion that what he said in general terms he meant in general terms. We believe we should extend the same courtesy to the apostle Paul as to our imaginary writer.

Biblical Homosexuals?

At this point a few words are in order about whether some biblical characters were gay, as some prohomosexual writers maintain. To begin with, not one individual named in the whole Bible is clearly identified in the text as a homosexual, even for the purpose of condemning his/her behavior. None of the alleged homosexual pairs in Scripture – Cain and Abel, David and Jonathan, Ruth and Naomi, Jesus and the "beloved disciple," the centurion and his servant, or Paul and Timothy – will stand any scrutiny; the evidence cited is flimsy at best.[15] We suspect that the suggestion that some or all of these people may have practiced homosexuality represents an attempt by some homosexuals to claim biblical support for their way of living.

God's Plan

Our argument against homosexual behavior so far has been a negative one. But as Stott points out,

> ...the negative prohibitions of homosexual practices in Scripture make sense only in the light of its positive teaching in Genesis 1 and 2 about human sexuality and heterosexual marriage. Without the wholesome and positive teaching of the Bible on sex and marriage, our perspective on the homosexual question is bound to be skewed.[16]

The more we understand of God's original creative plan, the more it becomes apparent that homosexual behavior involves a perversion of that plan.

God created the human race in two complementary sexes. Man and woman together make up "humankind" (Gen. 1:27 NRSV). God intends them to "be fruitful" (Gen. 1:28), to find companionship with each other (Gen. 2:18) and to realize that in a deep sense they are part of each other (Gen. 2:23).

Marriage is a part of God's plan for his creation: "For this reason a man will leave his father and mother and be united

---

[15] Both Daniel, pp. 171-173, and Sherwin Bailey, pp. 56-57, agree that the evidence is weak. For an argument that David and Jonathan did have a homosexual relationship, see Tom Horner, *Jonathan Loved David: Homosexuality in Biblical Times* (Philadelphia: Westminster, 1978), pp. 26-40.

[16] Stott, p. 24, (author's emphasis).

to his wife, and they will become one flesh" (Gen. 2:24 NIV). As Walter Trobisch has pointed out, the "leaving" involves a public commitment, the "cleaving" (AV for "being united to") involves lifetime faithfulness, and the "one flesh" comes as the result of the union.[17] Sexual love is a good thing, if enjoyed in a context of public, permanent commitment. No one who reads the Song of Solomon can come away with the impression that God hates sex.

Earlier we mentioned the idea of natural law and suggested that we as biblical interpreters should accept the concept but not take it too far. Specifically, we said that natural-law arguments are valid if a biblical author, such as Paul, uses them, and arguable if another writer uses them. Such caution in expanding the area covered by natural law may help us at this point.

The Genesis account suggests that heterosexual marriage is natural and says nothing about homosexual activity. If this were all the Scripture we had, we might believe that because heterosexual marriage is right, homosexual unions are wrong, but we could not be completely sure of the biblical attitude toward homosexuality. Yet when we see another biblical writer drawing a distinction between natural and unnatural relations (Paul in Rom. 1:26-27), we go back to Genesis with our earlier impression strengthened. The New Testament writer confirms the natural-law interpretation of the Old Testament passage.

We would not want to go any further, however. We could spin out questionable natural-law interpretations of Genesis for a long time, e.g., that family planning is wrong ("be fruitful" in Gen. 1:28) or even that nudity, since natural, is good (Gen. 2:25). These interpretations are arguable, since no New Testament writer confirms them. The principle of accepting

---

[17] Walter Trobisch, *I Married You*, in *The Complete Works of Walter Trobisch: Answers about Love, Sex, Self-Esteem and Personal Growth* (Downers Grove: InterVarsity, 1987), pp. 376-386.

natural-law arguments if they are confirmed by New Testament writers, and questioning them if they stand alone, will go a long way toward helping us construct a clear, supportable biblical theology that (in theory) all Christians could agree on.

In summary, then, we may say this: Homosexual behavior is wrong because God, through his inspired writers, forbids it. It is wrong also because something else is right. God created heterosexual marriage, with all its responsibilities and all its joys, for his children to enjoy.[18]

So far we have surveyed the Scriptures to find evidence for a biblical view of homosexuality, attempting to make valid theological statements about human sexual nature and behavior. We have found that since the fall of the human race some people have experienced sexual inversion. Thinking theologically, we conclude that such people should regard their orientation as a perversion of God's original creative plan and not "the way God made us." If their inversion does not spring from conscious choice but from genetic or environmental factors, they do not need to repent of their orientation, but they do need to control their behavior and seek healing for their inversion. We have seen that the writers of Scripture regard homosexual behavior as sin, whether it results from one's orientation or from conscious choice.[19] However, we have found no evidence that homosexual activity oc-

---

[18] Marva Dawn's near-poetic description of sexual Shalom" (pp. 161-168) paints a compelling picture of God's design for sexuality as revealed in Scripture.

[19] Here we must part company with Helmut Thielicke, who in his work *The Ethics of Sex*, trans. by John W. Doberstein (New York: Harper & Row, 1964) refers to homosexuality as a "borderline situation" (p. 199). Although he argues that the homosexual orientation is a perversion of the created order (pp. 282-283), he seems to leave the door open at least for the theoretical possibility that a given individual might live an ethically responsible life as a practicing homosexual (pp. 283-286). In practical terms, however, Thielicke admits that "Christian pastoral care will have to be concerned primarily with helping the person to *sublimate* his homosexual urge" (p. 287, Thielicke's emphasis).

cupies a special category of sin; instead, it is morally equivalent to heterosexual fornication. Each of us has his or her own temptations; it is not wrong to be tempted either homosexually or heterosexually, but it is wrong to sin with someone of the same or the opposite sex.

No doubt what we have written seems judgmental to some readers. If so, we need to understand clearly that God's grace covers every kind of sin for the believer in Jesus who decisively turns from sin and toward God. God can forgive homosexual sin as well as heterosexual sin, sin which is socially acceptable and sin which is not. But the first step in receiving forgiveness is to recognize our wrongdoing as sin. We have tried here to show that homosexual behavior is wrong in God's eyes, not in order to condemn but to enable people to receive God's grace and extend it to others.

CHAPTER NINE

ANSWERING PRO-GAY THEOLOGY*

Joe Dallas

No one is better equipped for the rapid-fire response to the pro-gay arguments than Joe Dallas, former president of Exodus International and director of the ex-gay ministry, Genesis Counselling. In his book, Desires in Conflict, *he lists and answers the most common arguments for the gay lifestyle.*

As of this writing (July 1991) five major denominations have considered or are considering a revision of their traditional views on homosexuality. The General Assembly of the Presbyterian Church (USA) has overwhelmingly rejected a committee report asking for, among other things, acceptance of premarital sex, homosexual relationships and teenage sexual activity. By a 534 to 31 vote the general assembly said no to all of the above.

It remains to be seen whether the United Church of

*Taken from *Desires in Conflict, Answering the Struggle for Sexual Identity* by Joe Dallas, Harvest House Publishers, 1991. Used by permission. Scripture quotations in this chapter are from *The Holy Bible, New King James Version,* © 1982, Thomas Nelson, Inc.

Christ, the Episcopal Church, the United Methodist Church, and the Evangelical Lutheran Church in America – all of whom are currently involved in similar debates – will follow suit. Much depends on the influence of the more liberal factions in each group, and how much pressure they can apply to their denominations at large.

Although church groups supporting acceptance of homosexuality seem to be in the minority (a telephone poll of 100 adults taken for *Time*/CNN showed that 81% of the respondents who frequently attend church feel that sexual contact between men is always wrong),[1] they are a powerful minority indeed to have made such inroads that the subject is even under discussion!

The debate over homosexuality and the Bible – specifically, whether or not the Bible condemns homosexual acts in all cases – will do no less than rip the body of Christ apart within the next decade. It will force believers to declare, in black and white terms, where they stand on issues of sexuality and biblical interpretation. And the emotions generated during the debate will, as always, color and cloud the issue.

You are already participating in the battle. Whether you're a Fighter, a family member impacted by a loved one's homosexuality, or an interested party, at some point you'll be approached by someone who will claim that Scripture doesn't forbid homosexual practices. That person's argument will force you to give an answer for your beliefs, part of which should include a response to what I call the "Pro-Gay Theology."

In essence, Pro-Gay Theology argues that, while the Bible is authoritative, it is either not *fully* authoritative (it is subject to error in certain social issues) or it has been traditionally misinterpreted in the area of homosexuality. It is, as I see it, a system of beliefs based on objections to the traditional

---

[1] "The Gospel on Sex," *U.S. News and World Report*, June 10, 1991, vol. 110, no. 22, p. 50.

viewpoint of Scripture and sexuality.

"Our pews are empty and our outdated attitudes about sex have a great deal to do with it," complains Marvin Ellison, professor of Christian Ethics at Bangor Theological Seminary in Maine.[2] The good professor would have us believe that our attitudes toward sex should reflect those of our culture, that filling pews is more vital than objective truth. Yet Dr. Greg Bahnsen of the Southern California Center for Christian Studies insists that "when the church begins to look and sound like the world, there is no compelling rationale for its continued existence."[3]

The dilemma of homosexuality for many Christians also fuels the objections of many pro-gay advocates. They claim that their attraction to the same sex feels perfectly normal and natural. "If it seems natural," they say, "must it not therefore be God-given?"

While a specific scriptural response to this question is detailed later, a general look at the question and a bit of history will shed some light on the beliefs of the pro-gay apologist.

The advent of the Universal Fellowship of Metropolitan Community Churches (UFMCC), founded in 1968 sparked a new approach to homosexuality and religion. The UFMCC, attended largely but not exclusively by self-identified Gay Christians, claimed there was no conflict between homosexuality and Christianity. The initial precepts that the church (and the budding Gay Christian movement) was founded on were rather general: God loves gays as much as He loves anyone else, the gospel invitation is extended to everyone regardless of orientation, and since gays found little refuge in the Christian church at large, a new fellowship was needed to welcome them and affirm their total personhood, homosexuality included.

They were right in many ways. God indeed loves gays as

---

[2] Ibid.

[3] *Penpoint Journal*, June 1991, vol. 2, no. 3, p. 1.

much as anyone else, the gospel invitation is certainly open to them, and the church's response to them has generally been very poor and often hostile. Their interpretation of Scripture, however, causes many Christians, myself included, to take serious issue with their position. Their testimonies seem to show a pattern of placing personal experience above biblical standards. "If I'm still gay after trying not to be," they seem to say, "then God must have made me this way and so there must be a better way of looking at the Bible."

What lies behind such cavalier use of the Scriptures? Some would say rebellion, others would say a reprobate mind. I say it's deception.

Deception is an element of the end times which is seldom stressed, usually because turmoil in the Mideast or ecumenical trends steal the spotlight during discussions of Bible prophecy. Yet deception is a recurring theme in both Christ's and Paul's descriptions of the last days.

> The disciples came to Him privately, saying . . . "What will be the sign of Your coming, and of the end of the age?" And Jesus answered . . . "Take heed that no one deceives you" (Matthew 24:3, 4).
>
> Many false prophets will rise up and deceive many (Matthew 24:11).
>
> So as to deceive, if possible, even the elect (Matthew 24:24).
>
> God will send them strong delusion, that they should believe a lie (2 Thessalonians 2:11).
>
> Evil men and imposters will grow worse and worse, deceiving and being deceived (2 Timothy 3:13).

The deception of the end times, which for many reasons I believe we're living in, has an easy target in those of us indoctrinated by the self-love philosophy promoted in the 1970's and solidified recently even in the church. This philosophy expresses itself through a variety of modern heresies, including the "Name it and claim it" teachings, the Positive Confession Movement, and the Pro-Gay Theology. Particularly vulnerable is the Christian with homosexual desires, who is often seduced into thinking that seemingly natural inclinations are in and of themselves justification for violating biblical standards.

When I was being interviewed by comedienne Joan Rivers on her talk show, this philosophy came through to me with new clarity. Regarding my stance on homosexuality, she asked me, "But if God gave us these feelings, how can it be wrong to express them?" She was sincere. Like many people, she assumed the very presence of a feeling indicates its divine origins. "If it feels good, do it," we used to say. Today's version goes several steps further. "If it feels good, sanctify it!"

Deception usually expresses itself in a challenge to God's Word. "Has God indeed said?" the serpent intoned in Genesis 3. "Does the Bible really say?" the liberal theorist asks. Same song, second verse. And the appeal of deception is usually to the area of life we are the least willing to yield to God's authority.

That, as I see it, is why we are in the midst of this debate. Below I've listed the most common points of pro-gay theology as "Objections," because they represent objections to common views on homosexuality and Christianity. "Responses" are also included. They will, I hope, be of help to you when your biblical position is challenged. As always, you'll need to include your own insights and observations.

General Objections

Objection 1. Jesus said, "Come to me, *all* you who are weary and burdened," not just "Come unto me all you that are heterosexual." The gospel is for everyone, including gays.

Response. True, Christ's invitation is to everyone. Most Christians who believe homosexuality is unnatural do not believe that homosexuals cannot be saved – only that they, like all of us, are called on to repent of all aspects of life that are contrary to God's standards. (Remember that the first word of Christ's public ministry recorded in Matthew 4:17 is "Repent.") We are *all* called to repent just as surely as we are all called to salvation. Further, to say that no change in behavior or heart is necessary *after* conversion is to deny the very need for conversion in the first place. The Scriptures teach that Christ takes us as we are, then begins to bring all areas of our life, sexuality included, into subjection to Him, as modeled in His conversation with a woman taken in adultery:

> Jesus said to her, "Neither do I condemn you [I take you as you are]; go and sin no more"[repent] (John 8:11).

Objection 2. If gays didn't ask for their orientation, then God must have created it, so how could He condemn it?

Response. There is nothing in Scripture to suggest that if a thing seems natural it is inevitably God-given. But there is *much* in Scripture which condemns many "natural" states and desires:

> The natural man does not receive the things of . . . God (1 Corinthians 2:14).
>
> [You] were [before conversion] by nature children of wrath (Ephesians 2:3).
>
> The carnal mind is enmity against God, for it is not subject to the law of God, nor indeed can it be (Romans 8:7).
>
> Behold, I was brought forth in iniquity (Psalm 51:5).
>
> The heart is deceitful above all things, and desperately wicked; who can know it? (Jeremiah 17:9).

Objection 3. The church has shown condemnation, not love, to gays.

Response. True, in many respects. The problem here is not the church's *adherence to biblical principles*, but the harsh way that many Christians have promoted those principles (The Bible condemns homosexual acts, so gays are horrible people) and the church-sanctioned actions that have been taken against homosexuals. This once held true for other areas of behavior as well. For example, in Puritan times if a woman was found to have gossiped, she was tied to a stool, dunked in a lake, and held underwater for as long as a minute. Likewise, if a man neglected his attendance at church, he was put into wooden stocks for public humiliation. The problem was not the fact that the church denounced gossip or lack of fellowship, but the cruel treatment that people guilty of these things received. The answer is a balanced, compassionate method of promoting biblical truth, not a negating of that truth.

Objection 4. People use Bible verses to justify violence against gays, so it's potentially harmful to quote the Bible when criticizing homosexual behavior.

Response. The perverse use of certain Scriptures to justify violence is nothing new, and is remedied by proper use, not banishment, of those Scriptures. We wouldn't consider (I hope) neglecting to teach the Scriptures in which Jesus claims to be the only way to salvation because certain groups have used that claim to persecute people of other faiths! If a book, like the Bible, is misused, the problem is the *misuse* and not the tool itself.

Objection 5. People are saved on the basis of their faith in Christ, not their sexuality, be it homo or heterosexual.

Response. Affirming heterosexuality as the biblical norm is not an implication that heterosexuality saves people, any more than affirming the biblical injunctions against stealing does not imply that honesty saves people. Salvation through Christ and sexual morality are two distinct issues that should be kept separate.

Objection 6. There are many openly gay Christians who love God, experience spiritual realities, and have specific gifts and callings just like other Christians.

Response. The presence of spiritual gifts, whether preaching, evangelism, or any other gifts, is never an indication that the person in whom those gifts are manifest is justified in all other areas of life. Nor is the presence of God's Spirit in a believer proof that the lifestyle of that believer is pleasing to God. A quick glance at the experience of Christians from New Testament times to the present shows that Christians can be subject to serious error in belief or behavior and still manifest a Christian testimony. The Galatian church had fallen into legalism, the Ephesian church had lost its primary love for Christ, and the Corinthian church had suffered schisms and disorder in its assembly. Yet when these disorders were addressed by Paul and by Christ Himself, there was no implication that these churches were filled with unregenerate people. Just as their error in no way nullified their salvation, so their salvation in no way nullified their error.

Objection 7. Jesus said, "Do not judge, or you too will be judged," so when you say that homosexuality is wrong, you're guilty of being judgmental.

Response. Then we had better do away with huge chunks of the Old and New Testaments, because they're both full of statements about right and wrong. Jesus *did* teach that we cannot accurately address someone else's sin without first addressing our own (Matthew 7:1-4). But then He turns right around in Matthew 7:5 and tells us that, having examined ourselves, we *are* to address their sin! Additional commandments that He gave His disciples could hardly be fulfilled without first discerning whether a person's behavior was right or wrong (Luke 9:5; Mark 8:15; Matthew 18:15-19), and statements by other New Testament writers require judgment on our part when dealing with church discipline, doctrinal error, and social contacts (Romans 16:17, 1 Corinthians 5:3-5; Galatians 6:1; Ephesians 5:11; 1 Thessalonians 5:14; 2 Thessalonians 3:11-15; 1 John 4:1).

Objection 8. The Bible teaches us that the main duty of man is to love God first and then to love his neighbor as himself. That's got nothing to do with our sex life.

Response. On the contrary, that has everything to do with our sex life, as it has everything to do with every other part of our life. The command to love God is not fulfilled just by feeling love and reverence for Him, but by expressing our love in very practical ways: "Thou shalt love the Lord thy God with all thy heart, and with all thy soul, and with all thy mind, and with all thy strength" (Mark 12:30 KJV). Body and soul, mind and strength – nothing less. If we are unwilling to conform to God's will in any of these areas, then we have no business saying that we love Him. The question isn't whether or not we *claim* to love God, but whether or not *our actions are in harmony with His expressed will.*

Objection 9. The church used to believe that the Bible justified slavery, subjugation of women, and other heinous practices. If Christians were wrong about those issues, who's to say they aren't also wrong about homosexuality?

Response A. Using that same logic, we'll have to abandon all absolute views on anything for fear of being wrong.

Response B. Those who justified slavery by biblical passages misread the passages, quite likely to suit their own prejudice. Nowhere does the Bible *commend* slavery; rather, it acknowledges its existence. Additionally, not all passages translated "servants" mean literal "slaves," but often mean "house servants" or "employees."

Objection 10. Writers of the Bible knew nothing about loving, committed relationships between homosexuals. All they knew of homosexuality was the kind that was practiced in temple prostitution or idolatrous ceremonies, so of course they condemned it in that context.

Response A. If the Bible was just another book of theories and allegories this argument might stand. But if it is indeed God-inspired, intended as a guide for belief and conduct, then it is unthinkable that God – who is no respecter of persons – would be so careless as to offer no guidance in His revealed Word to the thousands of homosexuals He knew would exist throughout time, if indeed their relationships were legitimate in His sight.

Response B. Even if it could be proven that there was no such thing as a "committed homosexual relationship" in biblical times, biblical authors such as David, Daniel, Ezekiel, and John were prophetically inspired to write about things that were to exist in the future as well as things that did exist at the time of their writings. Surely, if homosexuality was legitimate and natural, there would have been some reference to homosexual relationships in the future, if not the present.

Specific Scriptural Objections

> But if I were a Christian homosexual, I think this one question would disturb me most: am I trying to interpret Scripture in the light of my proclivity, or should I interpret my proclivity in the light of Scripture? – Paul Mooris,
> *Shadow of Sodom*, 1978

> You shall not lie with a male as with a woman. It is an abomination. . . . If a man lies with a male as he lies with a woman, both of them have committed an abomination (Leviticus 18:22; 20:13).

Objection 1. Prohibitions against homosexuality in the Levitical code have no relevance to us today because Christians are not under the law (Romans 6:14).

Response. The fact that anything is forbidden in Mosaic law (which covers issues as diverse as ceremony, diet, sex, and clothing) does not make for a compelling argument for prohibiting it today if it is forbidden *only* under the law and nowhere else in Scripture. We are indeed under grace and not the law. But it is notable that God's commandments to abstain from homosexual acts are contained in chapters 18 and 20 of Leviticus, which deal primarily with behaviors that are condemned in both the Old and New Testaments (incest, idolatry, homosexuality, adultery, witchcraft).

Objection 2. Jesus said nothing about homosexuality in any of the Gospels. We should base our beliefs on the teachings of Christ, not Paul or the other New Testament writers.

Response A. First, that doesn't mean He said nothing about homosexuals during His earthly ministry – only that we have no record of His doing so. John said that all the books in the world couldn't contain a full account of Christ's works (John 21:25).

Response B. There are several serious offenses Christ doesn't mention in the Gospels – child molestation, rape, spouse abuse – yet we wouldn't assume that any of these were acceptable simply because of their omission from Christ's teaching!

Response C. As important as they are, the teachings of Christ are not the only focus of the Gospels. His life, work, death, and resurrection are also accounted for in these books, with the Acts, Epistles, and Revelation giving more detailed instructions in areas of conduct and belief.

> For this reason God gave them up to vile passions. For even their women exchanged the natural use for what is against nature. Likewise also the men, leaving the natural use of the woman, burned in their lust for one another, men with men committing what is shameful (Romans 1:26, 27).

Objection 3. The people committing homosexual acts in Romans chapter 1 were idolaters who worshiped images, not God; therefore that passage does not condemn homosexuality, but only idolatry and the subsequent excesses that often go along with it.

Response A. The chapter condemns both idolatry and a variety of practices (not just homosexual) that *sometimes* stem from it, but which are condemned apart from idolatry. For instance, covetousness and fornication, listed in verse 29 of the same passage, may have also stemmed from the reprobate nature of the people described herein, but they are also named as sins in and of themselves throughout Scripture, as is homosexuality, whatever the origins.

Response B. Homosexual desires and actions are described in this passage, independent of idolatry, as being "vile affections," "against nature," and "unseemly," again, *in and of themselves.*

Objection 4. Chapter 1 of Romans does not condemn homosexuality, but homosexual acts committed by people who are really *heterosexual.* They "changed their nature." Since homosexuality was not "natural" to them, they should not have indulged in it, but the passage does not condemn homosexual acts between people who are *genuinely* homosexual.

Response A. Paul's wording here is not nearly that vague. Had he meant to imply that homosexual attractions were unnatural only to *heterosexuals,* he could clearly have said so (as in "the men who were basically *heterosexual* became basically *homosexual,* thus changing their true nature"). Instead Paul uses wording that appears even stronger in the original Greek.

The Greek words he uses for "men" and "women" here are rare in the New Testament, being used only when the writer wishes to emphasize the gender of the subject. When we see the word "man" in the Gospels and Epistles, we are usually seeing a translation of *anthropos* which carries a more general meaning (much the way we use "men" or "fellows" to refer to men in general, and "male" when we want to emphasize gender status). Only when New Testament writers similarly wished to emphasize gender did they resort to the term for man Paul uses here in Romans 1: *arseen,* a word used only here and in Matthew 19:4; Mark 10:6; Luke 2:23; and Galatians 3:28, all of which are Scriptures wanting to emphasize gender to make their point. The same is true of the term he uses here for "women," which is *gune* in lieu of more common *theleia*, which is usually used to refer to women. *Gune*, like *arseen*, emphasizes the gender of the subject and, like *arseen*, appears in the New Testament only in verses emphasizing "female."

These terms are crucial to the argument. Paul especially emphasizes in Romans 1 that homosexuality is unnatural to the man *as a male (arseen)* and to the woman *as a female (gune)*, not because of what may or may not be natural to their personality, but because of what is unnatural to their *gender*.

Response B. If Paul in this chapter only criticizes homosexual acts committed by people to whom they did not come "naturally," shall we then assume that the rest of the sins listed in Romans 1 also are sins only if they are committed by those to whom they do not come "naturally"?

Response C. These people do not appear to have been heterosexual men and women committing homosexual acts, since Paul describes them as "burning in lust" for each other. "Burning in lust" is an intense phrase which hardly describes predominantly heterosexual people indulging in homosexual acts for convenience's sake (as often occurs in prisons).

Response D. If these people *had* truly been heterosexual and were now truly homosexual, thus changing their nature, the homosexuality itself is still described in clearly derogatory terms, with no clause stating that it would have been normal if they had *always* been homosexual.

Pro-gay apologists are prone to say that, if a person is truly homosexual, he can never become truly heterosexual, yet they often quote this passage as an example of truly *heterosexual* people committing a sin by becoming truly *homosexual*. Are we then to assume that a person who is heterosexual can become homosexual, but a person who is homosexual cannot become heterosexual? Something's wrong here.

Objection 5. The activity described in Romans 1 is excessive, impersonal sex – pure lust without love. That, not homosexuality, is the problem here.

Response A. Romans 1 is not a description of a Roman orgy. Paul in no way indicates that the sexual activity here between men and men or women and women is highly promiscuous. It is *the very nature of the sexual conduct itself* that he considers unnatural.

Response B. When other Scriptures condemn heterosexual lust and indiscriminate heterosexual wantonness, this also provides clear guidelines for heterosexual behavior. No such guidelines exist for homosexual behavior.

> Do not be deceived. Neither fornicators, nor idolaters, nor adulterers, nor homosexuals, nor sodomites . . . will inherit the kingdom of God.
>
> . . . knowing this: that the law is not made for a righteous person, but for the lawless and insubordinate . . . for fornicators, for sodomites (1 Corinthians 6:9; 1 Timothy 1:9, 10).

Objection 6. The Greek word *arsenokoites*, commonly translated "abusers of themselves with mankind" or "homosexuals," did not mean that at all, but meant "male prostitute."

Response A. The Greek word *pornos*, used by Paul and translated "fornicator" in the passages above and numerous other places, technically means "male prostitute" and would certainly be used by Paul when referring to one. (Although it is sometimes interchangeable with "fornicator," the meaning is clearly male prostitution, as the word *pornos* is the masculine counterpart to *porne*, which is without exception translated as "harlot" in the New Testament (e.g., Matthew 21:31; Luke 15:30; 1 Corinthians 6:15; Hebrews 11:31; James 2:25).

Response B. *Arsenokoite* is derived from two Greek words – *arseen*, meaning "male," and *koite*, meaning "couch" or "bed," usually with a sexual connotation, as in Hebrews 13:4: "Marriage is honorable in all, and the bed (*koite*) is undefiled" (KJV). The combination of the two terms does not even suggest prostitution – only sexual contact between two men.

"If people want to accept homosexuality as normal, that is their option, but they do so against the indisputable teaching of the Bible." So say Doctors Glenn Wood and John Dietrich in *The AIDS Epidemic: Balancing Compassion and Justice*.[4] I agree. To disregard traditional teaching is risky – it's even more foolish to disregard the obvious facts: Homosexuality is *never* mentioned in Scripture in anything but negative terms, both Old and New Testament writings contain prohibitions against not only homosexuality but sexual relations of all kinds outside heterosexual marriage, and there is nothing in the entire Bible offering any commendation of or instruction for homosexual relationships. The pro-gay theology is laid on a very shaky foundation indeed.

[4] Glenn Wood and John Dietrich, *The AIDS Epidemic: Balancing Compassion and Justice* (Portland, OR: Multnomah Press, 1990), p. 237.

Part Five

MINISTRY TO HOMOSEXUALS

CHAPTER TEN

THE DYNAMICS OF CHANGE*

Bob Davies and Lori Rentzel

In their book, "Coming Out of Homosexuality," Bob Davies, executive Director of Exodus International, and Lori Rentzel, author and former counselor with the ex-gay ministry group, "Love in Action," describe their spiritual journey in coming out of the homosexual lifestyle.

Our deliverance from homosexuality comes from a Person, rather than a method," says Frank Worthen, who spent more than twenty years in homosexuality before leaving that lifestyle and starting Love In Action in 1973.

As Frank discovered, the interesting thing about the change process is that change itself is not our goal. Change is what *results* as we pursue a far more important and compelling goal: knowing, loving and "beholding" Jesus.

"And we, who with unveiled faces all reflect the Lord's glory, are being transformed into his likeness with ever-in-

*Taken from *Coming Out of Homosexuality* by Bob Davies and Lori Rentzel. ©1993 by Bob Davies and Lori Rentzel. Used by permission of InterVarsity Press, P.O. Box 1400, Downers Grove, IL 60515.

creasing glory, which comes from the Lord, who is the Spirit" (2 Cor 3:18).

In coming out of homosexuality, we sometimes focus *too* intensely on our inner hang-ups, misbeliefs, past hurts and sinful tendencies. Looking inward, we may feel as if we're gazing into an ever-deepening pool of confusion and despair.

Release and healing come as we look upward – to Jesus – and enter more deeply into fellowship with him. The cry of our heart becomes, *God, I want to know you. I want to love and worship you. I want to be a man or a woman who reflects your image. Cleanse me from everything that stands between you and me.*

God delights to answer such a prayer. He alone understands the complex combination of choices and circumstances that have shaped us to make us who we are today. He is fully aware of our pain and our weaknesses, yet his vision of "who we are in Christ" far exceeds our powers of imagination. His desire for us surpasses – and, in fact, inspires – our desire for him.

Change is a cooperative venture between God and ourselves through the power of the Holy Spirit. His grace woos and empowers us to make the choices that lead to freedom in our sexuality and in every other area of life. We seek him and he reveals to us not only who he is but who we are as well.

Some of us struggle with a distorted view of God that makes it difficult for us to trust him, especially in such sensitive areas as sexuality and identity. We may not be able to separate our image of God from that of an abusive or disappointing authority figure in our past. When this is true, we can confess this to God and ask him to heal us of this misperception. He is faithful to do this in ways that personally speak to us and reassure us.

Surrender and Change

Why do some people make it out of homosexuality while others don't? We have thought a lot about this question, reflecting on the many people we know who have made a firm and lasting break from homosexuality and on others who have not.

One common denominator among those men and women experiencing significant change involves the issue of *control* in their lives. These individuals have decided to follow Christ and do his will at any cost.

Perhaps you have heard sermons about "surrendering" or "yielding" to Christ and wonder what this implies about your struggles. Some feel revolted at the whole idea of surrender, fearing they will lose their autonomy to the control of a celestial dictator. Others welcome the thought, hoping to be released from the constant challenge of making difficult choices and decisions.

Basically, surrender is an act of faith. It is a step of deep commitment, which involves: (1) giving God permission to work in our life as he pleases, and (2) making a decision to trust him in the midst of our life circumstances, believing he is working through them for our ultimate good.

When I (Lori) first accepted Christ in 1973, my commitment was at best reluctant. Mentally I was convinced that Christianity was true, that "Jesus was the Way." But I remember attending a prayer meeting where everyone was singing "The cross before me, the world behind me . . ." Looking around at this circle of believers, their eyes closed in reverent worship, I wanted to run out of the room. The cross did seem to loom before me. But the world sure wasn't behind me. In fact, it looked pretty good to me that night.

For the next year and a half I was miserable. Every day was a battle just to remain interested in God. I felt more at home at a keg party than at a Bible study, yet I felt like a hypocrite in both places. I knew too much of God to deny his reality, but my efforts to peacefully coexist with him were producing unbearable strain and tension.

Finally I was able to see that *having Christ in my life* was not going to work. What God actually was requiring of me was that I *have my life in Christ* (Rom 6:11).

Author C.S. Lewis said, "Fallen man is not simply an imperfect creature who needs improvement: he is a rebel who must lay down his arms."[1] I made a decision to come to God on his terms – unconditional surrender. *God, I want your way,* I prayed. *I want Jesus to be Lord of my life.* And I meant it.

The relief that came over me was exhilarating. While I still encountered difficult challenges and painful choices, the Christian life became a joy and a strength to me rather than a burden to be endured. God and I were on the same team now, facing the battle together. He was my rock, my ally, rather than my enemy.

All Christians face the decision of accepting or rejecting Christ's lordship. However, the former homosexual faces it sooner than most.

Coming out of homosexuality into wholeness requires deep emotional healing and a restructuring of our whole identity. As our Creator, God is the only one who knows exactly how to restore our personality. For him to complete this healing work he calls for our cooperation.

Our natural tendencies are to squirm off the operating table, run when we should rest, and quit taking our antibiotics as soon as we feel better. The grace and power to resist these tendencies come as we get to know the Lord better, learning to trust in his care for us.

There are times when life's pressures seem intolerable and its rewards nonexistent. But these are the times when God remains faithful to the commitment we have made to him. In the midst of heartache and extreme difficulties, he shows us his infinite ability to resolve impossible situations.

The Choice to Surrender

For some former homosexuals, coming face-to-face with this decision of a deeper surrender to Christ can happen at

[1] C.S. Lewis, *Mere Christianity* (New York: Macmillan, 1952), p. 44.

unexpected times in unexpected ways.

At church one Sunday morning in September 1978, I (Bob) learned that a well-known evangelist would be speaking in the evening service. I spent the rest of the day reading his autobiography, which told stories of his adventures sharing Christ around the globe. That evening I went to church filled with expectation, ready to hear a challenging testimony.

Things didn't go as I had expected. During the service, I could sense the speaker's deep commitment to Jesus Christ. I heard about the thousands of lives he had impacted, and I felt convicted about my own shallow commitment.

Lord, I prayed, *I want my life to count like that man's life is counting for your kingdom.* In my spirit I sensed an unexpected question: *Are you willing to pay the price?*

I pondered that question for the next three days.

I sensed God challenging me to give him every part of my life in a much deeper way than I ever had before. I felt his spotlight shining on one dark area of my life – my homosexuality – that I had kept carefully hidden from everyone. For years, I had offered many prayers: *God, please take this problem away* and *Lord, if you will heal my homosexuality, I will be an on-fire Christian. Then my life will* really *count for your kingdom.*

None of my past prayers seemed to make much difference.

Now I knew God was calling me to a deeper commitment than anything I'd experienced, and I didn't like it. I wanted to hang on to . . . what? My homosexuality? Not really. But there was something in the way, some unseen barrier preventing me from total surrender.

Perhaps it was pride. And fear? Yes, I was terrified of what God would ask. Maybe someday I would have to tell others about my homosexual struggles. My heart pounded at such a horrifying possibility.

Over the next several days I fought and kicked, firmly resisting God's challenge. Finally, exhausted, in the early hours of a late summer night, I yielded. *OK, God. I will give this area of my life to you.* This simple statement marked a major turning point in my life.

My decision did not instantly release me from homosexuality; rather, it opened me up for God to begin working in a deeper way. Since that day in 1978 God has gradually overhauled my life, a transformation that has affected my career, my personality and my sexuality.

Submitting Our Homosexuality

Now let's look at specific applications of this principle to the issue of recovery from homosexuality and lesbianism.

• *Surrendering to Christ means learning to obey him a step at a time in the process of recovery.* For some this step may mean opening up for the first time to another individual regarding their homosexuality.

Jim said, "I've prayed for years against these feelings, but nothing has worked." But Jim had never confessed his struggles to anyone except God. Like Jim, many people will not consider this option. They discount it as impossible because of their position in church, their prominence in a small community, or their fear of losing a job, a marriage, a family.

These are legitimate concerns, but all of us need the support and encouragement of others. There is power in mutual confession. "But if we walk in the light, as he is in the light, we have fellowship with one another, and the blood of Jesus, his Son, purifies us from every sin" (1 John 1:7).

• *Acknowledging Christ's lordship means trusting in his timing for recovery.* The God-do-this-now-or-else mindset is a deadly pitfall in the healing process. Think about a doctor's response if a cancer patient said, "I'll give you two months to fix me. If your treatments don't eradicate every symptom of cancer, I'll quit." Similarly, we cannot put time limits on our healing process. God has a unique timetable for each of us.

• *Yielding to Christ means persevering despite painful emotions or powerful attractions.* We may experience intense rage, sorrow or jealousy, and yet be progressing wonderfully in our healing process. Sometimes God waits until we have developed a solid level of trust with him before allowing such emotions to surface. Likewise, we may find ourselves overwhelmed with feelings of homosexual or lesbian desire. These may come from any number of sources, including satanic attack and fatigue. Or they may be surfacing along with many other repressed feelings. When these emotions occur, we can acknowledge them, pray for God's strength to deal with them, then seek understanding and healing for the underlying issues.

Avenues of Change

Christians throughout the ages have had sinful habits to overcome and misbeliefs to replace with truth. The same Christian disciplines that have helped them will help you too.

• *Practicing God's presence.* A powerful discipline and channel of healing is learning to practice God's presence: quieting ourselves before God, resting in him, enjoying his fellowship. "Be still, and know that I am God" (Psa. 46:10).

We can practice God's presence as we do our work, visit with a friend, take a shower or cut up vegetables for dinner. I (Lori) like to quiet myself before God to prepare for times of prayer and intercession. Sometimes I get so relaxed in God's presence that I never do get around to putting my prayers into words, yet I come away assured that my heart's petitions have been heard.

Another wonderful aspect of practicing God's presence is what author and lecturer Leanne Payne describes as "Listening for the healing word." Her book, *The Broken Image*, is a great resource on the effectiveness of healing prayer in overcoming homosexuality and lesbianism.

On listening to God, she says: "Thus, in the Presence, listening to the word the Spirit sends, spiritual and psychological healing takes place. Our Lord sends a word – of joy, judgment, instruction, guidance. And that word, if hidden away in an obedient heart, will work toward the integration of that personality. As I listen and obey, I *become.*"[2]

As we listen to God, spending time in his presence, we discover our true identity in Christ.

• *Praying for ourselves.* In our personal prayer times, we need to be honest with God about our homosexual or lesbian thoughts, desires and struggles. He is not shocked by confessions of involvement in masturbation, pornography or other sexual sins. Nothing we do or say comes as a surprise to him. Confessing our sins and shortcomings to God is the only means to forgiveness (1 John 1:9), and each of us needs a clean start every day, free from the weight of condemnation from our past.

Most of us go through times when prayer feels like a dry habit. We can help alleviate this by being as specific as possible in our prayers, letting God know our deepest heart's desires, our hopes for how he will work in our lives. Many people record their prayers, leaving a blank space to write in the date when God answered that prayer and how. (Don't forget to go back in your list and record answers!)

Others have found encouragement from visual aids which remind that God answers prayer. Jane, for example, keeps a large jar near her bed. When God answers a specific prayer, she drops a colored marble into the jar. As the weeks have come and gone, Jane has been amazed at the number of marbles that now sit in her bedroom as a colorful reminder of God's interest in her life.

• *Praying for others.* We may be burdened for our old friends who are still actively involved in homosexuality. Sometimes they are not interested in hearing about our decision to seek change. Prayer is a powerful way of reaching out to them, whether they are aware of it or not. Here are some

---

[2] Leanne Payne, *The Broken Image: Restoring Personal Wholeness Through Healing Prayer* (Westchester, IL: Good News, Crossway Books, 1981), p. 150.

specific ideas on praying for old friends. Write down the names of friends you think about who are still pursuing homosexuality. Ask God to open their eyes to the truth about where their sexual choices are leading. Pray that God will prolong the lives of your friends who have AIDS, and ask that he bring Christians into their lives who can love them and share the truths of eternity with them in a noncondemning way. *If you have just left the gay lifestyle, you are not strong enough to go back and witness to your friends. But you can be very effective in prayer.* Turn your concerns into prayer requests.

• *Praising and worshiping.* "The individuals most likely to leave homosexuality behind," says Frank Worthen, "are those who have an excitement about God, and anticipation of what he will do next in their lives. They see him at work even in small details, and their hearts are full of praise."

The psalms, particularly the songs of David, illustrate the powerful effect of releasing deep emotions to the Lord through music. Here is how music played a healing role in helping one woman come out of the lesbian lifestyle.

Deborah's childhood was marked by trauma, including repeated episodes of sexual abuse. She grew up "emotionally frozen," with little sense of boundaries or security. Even after becoming a Christian, Deborah stumbled from one sinful relationship to another. Then, after experiencing God's presence in a new way at a women's retreat, the Lord gave her a key to unlock her emotions: singing.

"God showed me that if I would sing out my hurts and feelings, they would come to the surface and be healed." One day while singing songs of praise, Deborah recalls, "God's praise broke into my heart as never before. I had a wonderful sense of being a newborn baby, cradled in her daddy's arms. I felt warm and secure, and looked up to see God's eyes of love for the very first time."

Later, Deborah raced across a field with outstretched arms, shouting and laughing in her newfound discovery of God the Father's love. "Daddy loves me! My daddy loves me!" she yelled over and over again, her heart bursting with joy. God had revealed himself to her in a new direct and profound way.[3]

• *Studying the Bible.* Jack was an avid Bible reader, but he found that he had trouble remembering specific verses. Someone suggested he begin a "personal concordance." Jack bought a lined notebook, then began watching for special verses that applied to his struggles. These he wrote in his notebook under different headings. Jack struggled with homosexual fantasies, so he watched for verses he could write under his "Thought Life" heading. He also struggled with pornography, so he recorded such verses as "I will set before my eyes no vile thing" (Psa. 101:3) in another section. Jack also adapted verses slightly to apply them directly to his situation: "I have made a covenant with my eyes not to look lustfully at a [man]" (Job 31:1). Jack found that there were *many* verses that did not specifically mention homosexuality but which were applicable to his everyday struggles.

Other possible headings for a personal concordance include the root issues of homosexuality and the emotions you are dealing with during this time in your life (feeling inferior, afraid of other Christians, loneliness, sexual frustration, masturbation, fear, healthy relationships, femininity, dealing with parents.)

The main point here is to personalize the Scriptures to your own life and struggles. Although it is helpful to read and even memorize the Bible, the key is *application.* Biblical principles and insights must be worked into the fabric of your life before you will begin to see effective change.[4]

• *Journaling.* Recording our thoughts in a journal is an excellent way of tracking our forward progress. We all tend to feel that we are stagnating at times. If we can go back and read

---

[3] Adapted from Jeanette Howard, *Out of Egypt* (Speldhurst, Kent, England: Monarch, 1991), p. 232.

[4] There are excellent study Bibles available which will help you with this principle of application. We especially recommend the Life Application Bible and the Life Recovery Bible.

through old journals, we will immediately see our growth. "A journal is a good road map to see how far you've come," says Deborah, who has kept a journal since high school.

Journaling is different from keeping a diary. Instead of writing day-to-day events, in a journal you record your emotions and impressions of what God is doing in your life. Some people write in their journals daily, others weekly or several times a month. You can include poems and prayers to God, as well as spiritual goals for the next week, month or year. Several excellent Christian books are available on journal techniques.[5]

This activity is especially recommended for those of you who don't have someone right now to whom you can "spill your guts." Writing down your thoughts and prayers is an excellent method of self-therapy. "You will find depths of healing that you will not find in the presence of another person," says one former lesbian. "Journaling offers a tremendous opportunity for us to enter into intimacy with the Lord."

"You'll discover that as you write down your problems, many times you'll find the answers right in front of you, " says Jeff Konrad, a former homosexual and author of *You Don't Have to Be Gay.* "I can't begin to tell you how many times I went to my journal and reread sections of it for encouragement. There were depressing days when I wasn't doing well and I was thinking, *What's the use, I've failed again.* But after reading parts of my journal, I could see just how far I'd come. A lot had changed; I had grown in many ways."[6]

A Christian Support Network

In examining the question of why some people make it out of homosexuality while others don't, we have noticed two

---

[5] For example, Ronald Klug, *How to Keep a Spiritual Journal* (Minneapolis: Augsburg, 1993).

[6] Jeff Konrad, *You Don't Have to Be Gay* (Hilo, HI: Pacific House, 1992), pp. 57-59; available from Regeneration Books, P.O. Box 9830, Baltimore, MD 21284.

interrelated characteristics common among those who are successful: (1) the extent of their separation from their gay support network, and (2) the quality of their involvement with a local church.

God has made us social creatures. Most people, even introverts, do not exist happily in complete isolation from others. We all desire to spend time with others who share our interests, whether it's through joining the local health club, attending AA meetings, supporting a certain political candidate, or joining a local drama or music group. Through group involvement, our social needs are met and our interests and skills are reinforced.

When you come away from homosexuality, there may be a huge vacuum left in your social life. Some other group of people must replace your gay social circles, or you will be drawn back in. Few, if any, people leave homosexuality on their own. Nearly all the ex-gays we know have made this difficult transition with the strong support of Christian friends. Most of these significant friendships have formed through local church involvement. *Unless your relationships with other Christians become (and remain) stronger than your relationships with gay friends, you will probably return to homosexual involvement.* That's a strong statement, but we have found it true in almost all of the ex-gays we've known over the years. The gay community doesn't want defectors. Neither does Christ. Whom do you desire to serve?

For you, as a Christian, the church is the natural place to find a new network of supportive friends for your healing journey. Homosexual behavior, like any sin, is overcome by God's power. God uses people in this process, and he has established the local church as a place for healing and interpersonal support. In Hebrews 10:25 this principle is clearly stated: "Let us not give up meeting together, as some are in the habit of doing, but let us encourage one another." The Bible exhorts us to link ourselves with other Christians. This is especially vital for the man or woman coming out of homosexuality.

Church Involvement

Perhaps you have not been in church for years. Or maybe you attend a church, but nobody knows about your homosexual struggles. You may already have a group of supportive friends but wonder if more people in your church need to know about your sexual struggles.

You may find yourself in the same situation as Tim, the man who wrote this letter: "I'm at the point of total despair. Homosexuality has been a silent struggle in my life. During the past three years, I have succumbed to a double life – playing church on one hand and living as a practicing homosexual on the other. My situation is both overwhelming and futile to me. There is no one in my church that I feel free to confide in about my situation."

If you are like Tim and the thousands of men and women like him, you have four options:

• *Keep silent and remain in your church.* Your sexual struggles will probably not change. You will not overcome your homosexuality and eventually will probably drop out of church altogether in discouragement.

• *Remain in your church and confide in a church leader.* Over the years, I (Bob) have talked to dozens of pastors and other church leaders who are eager to help members of their congregation who struggle with homosexuality. Often these pastors have not had much experience in dealing with this issue, but they are anxious to learn. Opening up to a pastor, elder or adult Sunday-school teacher may be the best move you ever make in seeking answers.

• *Remain in your church and find help outside the church.* For the sake of family (spouse, children) or many other reasons, some ex-gay men and women decide that leaving a church that is not able to help them is not an option, at least for now. For these people the best solution is to find counseling or peer support outside their church. For example, they remain part of a home church for Sunday services but attend a weekly support group for ex-gays or they see a professional counselor at a local Christian agency.

• *Look for a new church.* This option should be the last one you consider. Looking for a new church home can be an exhausting, frustrating and time-consuming experience. But if overcoming homosexuality is a major goal during this season of your life, it is worth the investment of time to seek a healthy church home where you can make significant strides forward in your spiritual walk.

Disclosure Issues

Some ex-gays and former lesbians have been surprised by the positive reaction when they told their pastor about their homosexual struggles. Janice joined a local church and became active in ministering to the elderly, which brought her great joy. But as time went by, she felt as if a major part of her life was being carefully hidden from others. This secrecy bothered her.

"I began to experience greater and greater temptations in the area of homosexuality," Janice remembers. "For so long, I had hoped that the Lord would just let me off the hook and I wouldn't have to tell anyone."

Then one night Janice received an unexpected phone call that changed her life. On the other end was a man whom she didn't know. He accused Janice of being a lesbian and threatened physical violence. Janice told the man, "I'm a Christian now," and hung up.

But she was terrified – not so much of what the man might do to her but of her church finding out about her past. All that week the voice on the phone haunted her. Finally in desperation she decided to go and tell her pastor.

She got an unexpected reaction.

"My pastor was very encouraged by my testimony," Janice recalls, "and thought that I should share it with the whole church. I wasn't too excited about that idea."

But, although the pastor's words made her nervous, the more Janice thought and prayed about his proposal, the more she felt convinced that his suggestion was exactly what God wanted her to do.

The day of the service came and Janice felt a deep peace inside. "I knew Jesus was with me. The Holy Spirit gave me the boldness to share my story and the majority of people received it with love. And I felt a freedom in that area of my life that I had wanted for so long."

Janice says that, through the experience of sharing with her church, she discovered the truth of the Scripture, "They overcame him [Satan] by the blood of the Lamb and by the word of their testimony" (Rev. 12:11).

John Smid also had many positive experiences when he began telling his church in Omaha, Nebraska, about his homosexual past. John recalls, however, that he also had some fears. "As part of my church's singles' group, I was invited to weekend conferences where I had to share a room and even the same bed with another man in the group.

"I will never forget the first night I slept in the same bed with another guy from church. I lay perfectly still, making sure I didn't cross an imaginary line down the middle. *I don't want Dan to think anything weird is going on,* I thought. *If he knows of my past, he won't want to share a room with me – much less a bed.*"

At first John was cautious about who he told of his past because he was afraid that he would not be invited to events like men's retreats. But he discovered that his fears were groundless. "I found that those who really cared for me as a brother in Christ said my past homosexuality didn't bother them in the least. They were still willing to be my friends."

John felt a great release when he let other men know about his struggles. His friends became his prayer partners as he continued to work through the underlying issues which had led him into homosexuality in the first place.[7]

---

[7] Adapted from the article "Overcoming Fears of Relating to Men" by John Smid (Love In Action, P.O. Box 2655, San Rafael, CA 94912). Used by permission.

CHAPTER ELEVEN

MINISTERING TO PEOPLE WITH AIDS

Mike Hawkins

Mike Hawkins was diagnosed with AIDS in December of 1991. He founded Christian Aids Network and has served as its director since 1992. In this chapter, he shares the story of "Johnny," a young AIDS victim, as well as his own journey through this dark disease.

How do you minister to people with AIDS? You minister to people with AIDS the same as you would minister to anyone else who is facing a chronic or terminal disease. The needs are much the same with the only difference being the stigma attached to this disease. This stigma will play a minor role in ministering to the AIDS patient, however, it creates some special needs unique to AIDS.

Johnny came to my office just a few weeks after he had been diagnosed with AIDS. He had seen an article in the local newspaper about my own journey through AIDS and the ministry it had spawned. He was reaching out to get answers to many of his questions about this disease and what it meant to him. He also needed to identify with someone else who was also infected by the deadly virus. Mostly he was seeking hope.

The marching band Johnny played in during college gave each of its members a nickname. Johnny's was "Chuckles," which suited him perfectly. Johnny could face the most challenging struggles and still find a way to laugh. Beneath the laughter was a young man with some very real hurts, and over the next year he experienced much pain and challenge from his disease.

Johnny was a brand new Christian. Having strayed from the faith of his childhood, Johnny became involved in a lifestyle of homosexuality and drug abuse. It was in this lifestyle that he was infected by HIV (Human Immunodeficiency Virus), the virus which causes AIDS. He abandoned this lifestyle when he received the news that he had tested positive to the antibodies of HIV commonly known as HIV Positive (HIV+).

Johnny was fortunate to have two wonderful, loving parents who welcomed him into their home once again, being fully aware of his lifestyle. Their desire was to be there for their son regardless of the risks and fears they had. They hoped and prayed that he would straighten out his life but the most important thing was to walk with him in facing the trauma of living with AIDS.

Many people with AIDS face this disease alone. They don't have friends, family, or anyone who will walk with them, who will love them unconditionally and remain consistent in their care. As you minister to the person with AIDS remember that your non-judgmental attitude and your consistent devoted compassion are so vitally important in their lives.

About a week after Johnny moved back into his parents' home, his parents had a pre-planned trip to go on retreat with their church. Johnny knew that if he didn't go with them, they would cancel their plans so, grudgingly, he went along.

While on retreat, Johnny realized he had never truly surrendered his life to God. He didn't know what a relationship with Jesus really was all about. He made a public commitment of his life to Christ and came home a new creation. Johnny cried out to God as David had in Psalm 51:10-13 (NIV) "Create in me a pure heart, O God, and renew a steadfast spirit within me. Do not cast me from your presence or take your Holy Spirit from me. Restore to me the joy of your salvation and grant me a willing spirit, to sustain me. Then I will teach transgressors your ways, and sinners will turn back to you." Johnny finally found the peace and hope that comes from knowing that God's grace and love were his, even with all the bad he had done in his life.

The most important thing you can do for the PWA (Person With AIDS) is to share your faith. Introduce them to a loving God who will look beyond their faults and love them, a God who promises eternal life through faith. The same God that saves you from your sin can also set them free from whatever they are facing in their life. How do you do that?

Most people facing death ask the questions: "What's next?" "Is there more?" "Am I ready?" "Is there a heaven or hell?" As you develop a friendship with the PWA, you will have opportunities to discuss many of these things with them. In sharing your personal faith, remember that while sin separates us from God, His grace redeems us from that sin. Talk frankly about your own relationship to Christ.

Attitude is so important. Your motivation and attitude should be to share the blessings of being God's child, not to condemn the sin(s) in someone's life. It is God's Holy Spirit who convicts, not you. The most important thing is to lead them to a relationship with Jesus and allow Him to work in their life. Don't single out a specific sin. For instance, if you know that a PWA was infected through promiscuous sexual activity outside of marriage, don't say "God can save you from your adulterous behavior." Say, "God can save you from your sin no matter what that sin may be." Let them know that Romans 3:23 says "For all have sinned and fall short of the glory of God." You're on the same level as they are. Share also that Romans 6:23 says "For the wages of sin is death, *but* the gift of God is eternal life in Christ Jesus our Lord." They don't have to be worthy of that gift, rather God's grace provides it freely to all who call on the name of the Lord. Ephesians 2:8-9 "For it is by grace you have been saved, through faith – and this not from yourselves, it is the gift of God, not by works, so that no one can boast." Romans 10:13 "Everyone who calls on the name of the Lord will be saved."

Sharing your faith is easy. Your relationship with Jesus and the hope, peace and joy that it brings should be easy to talk about especially with someone who may really be interested in your views on life and death.

Don't forget to listen to what the PWA says. So many times we know we have the answers to their problems and we get so busy trying to convince them, we fail to listen to their response. Sometimes people need time to digest things in their minds. They need time to understand and fully believe that God could really love them individually. Be patient and LISTEN! They will tell you what they need from you.

If they reject your message of faith or even discussion of God, don't abandon them and count them as loss. They may not be ready to face the issues of their own mortality. They may need to see the consistency in your life and that you are who you say you are. I have known several young men who were angry at God and didn't want to share their feelings. I have seen each of them come to a place of peace because of the patience of those who ministered in their lives.

PWA's are grieving their own approaching death so they may be angry at God for "allowing" this to happen. They may be angry at God for "punishing" them. God is big enough to handle their anger. It is a *normal* phase of grief to be angry at God, yourself, and those around you. The answer is patience. Allow the PWA the chance to experience their grief at their own pace and pray that God will grant them the peace they are desperately seeking.

The PWA feels very vulnerable and doesn't always have a lot of control over many areas of their life. They will need you to be constant and unfailing in your love and care before they can deal with sharing in issues which may cause a great deal of turmoil in their life.

How do you share your faith? With your consistent love, with your constant care, with patience, remembering it's God's grace and His Holy Spirit that save, not you. In other words, you share your faith with a PWA just like you would share it with anyone else.

I met Johnny a week after he committed his life to Christ. Johnny still had not shared with all of his immediate family that he had AIDS and confidentiality was extremely important. Living in a small community outside of the big city, he knew that the "gossip mill" would have news of his illness all over town in a matter of days, which was a terrifying thought to him and his parents. They had read all the horror stories of homes being burned down, people losing their jobs and total isolation. They were adamant that no one needed to know.

When someone is diagnosed with the dreaded news that they have AIDS many things flood their minds and lives. Their first instinct is to withdraw and tell no one. When someone is diagnosed with terminal cancer they reach out to others for much needed support in facing their last days. The AIDS patient, most of the time, does not feel the same freedom to reach out for support. They fear rejection; they fear retaliation; they fear exposure of a lifestyle; they fear being asked how they got the disease; they fear being alone. The PWA believes it's better just not to tell anyone and then they won't have to face those fears. The truth is that in most cases they must face them anyway in order to find peace of mind.

If an AIDS patient has trusted you with the news of their AIDS diagnosis, it is an honor. It means they are willing to share the most vulnerable part of their lives with you and to take the risk that you might possibly reject them or expose them. Confidentiality is extremely important. Repeated reassurance that you will be there for them and that anything said in confidence will be kept in confidence is especially important early in your ministry. It will greatly ease their mind.

A PWA needs time to determine whom they can trust with an issue they themselves are so uncertain about dealing with. They will need time to learn and understand their illness themselves before being ready to deal with the questions, fears and emotions of others in facing AIDS. Again, consistency and patience are key elements.

Johnny and his family wanted the opportunity to tell family members themselves about the news of Johnny's infection rather than have them find out through word of mouth. Yet, they weren't ready to do that. They felt ill equipped with answers about the disease and the way Johnny had become infected. They were ashamed and embarrassed. They also felt that the more people who knew Johnny had AIDS, the more idle gossip and misinformation would be given.

I had found, in my own pilgrimage, that sharing my disease with family and friends was a great release and brought untold peace for me and my family. I didn't always feel that way.

Like Johnny, my parents had been there for me from day one. They were always supportive and loving. Together, we decided not to let everyone else in our extended family know I was HIV positive. After all, I had not developed the syndrome of illnesses or conditions that are known of as AIDS so it was easy to hide.

When someone is infected with HIV, it takes many years for the virus to destroy the vast immune system. Unless they are tested, they will show no signs of infection for 5 to 15 years and sometimes longer. Therefore a person can live with this virus for long periods of time, undetected by anyone else. Many live with the hope that they will never progress into AIDS.

This causes confusion for many. When does a person

have AIDS? A person is diagnosed with "full blown AIDS" when their immune system becomes weakened enough that their body can no longer fight common infectious germs in their environment. Each one of us comes into contact with enough germs each day to kill us. The immune system is what keeps those germs from causing illness.

As the immune system becomes weaker, the person infected by HIV begins getting sick from these diseases. They are no longer able to naturally fight them off. Because people rarely, if ever, get sick from these infections, doctors can determine that a person has AIDS when they start appearing in the HIV positive individual.

Because of this, it was easy for me to hide my infection from others since my immune system was not weakened to the point I would show any signs of illness. However, in December of 1991, I was diagnosed with full blown AIDS. I had become infected with a disease, histoplasmosis, that people with healthy immune systems could easily fight, but my immune system was no longer strong enough. This infection ravaged my body and within days had begun to destroy every major organ in my body.

Finally the doctor told my parents that she didn't think that I would recover and that it was time to call the family to come say their last good-bye. Now, my parents and I were faced with a burden we could no longer hide and we needed to have the support of our friends and loved ones. We began to reach out and tell others that I had AIDS and was not expected to live. Instead of the rejection we expected, we found that our church, our friends and our family rallied around us and gave us the support we so desperately needed.

People began to pray. They began to pray that God would heal and preserve my life. All across the nation prayers began going up to God that He would step in and do what the doctors couldn't. God answered those prayers and a few days later I was well enough to go home from the hospital. God healed me of histoplasmosis and has preserved my health since. I still have AIDS. I have almost no immune system at all, yet God's grace continues to keep me healthy and active most of the time.

I wanted to share this same peace with Johnny and his parents but I knew that they needed time just like I did. I began by sharing my own story. They needed to grasp onto the hope that the same could happen in their lives.

Step by step, we began finding ways for them to build a support system around themselves. We began with their minister. They were so uncertain. When the day came that they had scheduled to meet with their minister, Johnny's mom literally became ill and they almost canceled their meeting. Johnny believed that what they were doing was good and necessary. He had a real peace about it and urged his parents to go ahead and face their fears.

Their minister was stunned and saddened to learn of Johnny's illness. He cried as they shared with him the news that Johnny had been diagnosed with AIDS. He assured them that it would be kept confidential and that he loved them. He would support them through their journey. He also made himself available if they had any needs.

As a family, they were incredulous that their minister would have so much compassion and love. They said to me, "I don't know what I expected him to say, but his tears said so much." He grieved with them. He loved them and pledged to be a part of the support that they were building around themselves.

The next step was to include their family. As they began sharing with grandparents, cousins, aunts and uncles, they found the same love and willingness to stand behind and beside them. From these positive experiences they were then able to focus on reaching out further. Knowing that they had a measurable amount of support, it became less fearful to reach out to others.

About a month later I was scheduled to speak at a church in a small country town to share my testimony. I asked

Johnny if he would go with me since the trip was going to be a long one. He agreed to go. As we visited on the way, I asked Johnny if he wanted to say something to the church about his own testimony. He agreed and felt that he would like to do that. As Johnny and I shared our personal testimonies of faith, many in the church were moved with compassion. The encouragement they gave Johnny and me was incredible. Johnny had his first glimpse that God can use AIDS as a tool for good in building His kingdom. He was beginning to understand the realities of Romans 8:28, "And we know that in all things God works for the good of those who love him, who have been called according to his purpose."

In 2 Corinthians 12:7-9 it says ". . . there was given me a thorn in the flesh, the messenger of Satan to buffet me lest I should be exalted above measure. Concerning this I entreated the Lord three times that it might depart from me. And He has said to me, 'My grace is sufficient for you, for power is perfected in weakness.' Most gladly, therefore, I will rather boast about my sickness, that the power of Christ may dwell in me" (KJV). God has provided many opportunities for me to share my experience with others. He has taken the tragedy and despair of AIDS and turned it into a powerful tool of his grace and mercy.

In sharing my story with others I have seen many come to a deeper relationship with God. I have seen young people commit their lives to waiting until they are married to have sex and avoiding the risks of also becoming infected with this virus. I have seen my own relationship with God take on a new intimacy I might never have experienced without AIDS. While AIDS is a disease of death, it also teaches us how to really live! AIDS has brought me closer to my family and has been a catalyst to repair so many relationships. That is what Paul means about power perfected in weakness. That is why he says "I will rather boast about my sickness . . . ."

I have learned that God is bigger than all life's problems and troubles. He is bigger than AIDS. When I thought my life was over he taught me how to live and continues to protect my body from death.

AIDS has become more than just . . .

Acquired
Immune
Deficiency
Syndrome.

In my life it now is an . . .

Adventure
In
Divine
Submission.

AIDS has taught me that if I will just submit my life, my frustrations, my problems, my worries and fears to God on a daily basis, He is faithful to meet all my needs and I am able to "boast about my sickness that the power of Christ may dwell in me."

One of the best pieces of advice I received from a minister was this. "What are you doing for Jesus?" I needed to be active in building God's kingdom. But I have AIDS, what can I do? AIDS does not limit God. He loved me in spite of my faults and wanted to use me for His glory because I had surrendered my life to him. I had all the same opportunities to serve God as all His other children.

As long as I was caught up in myself, my own pain, my own fears and my self pity, I experienced the despair so often associated with AIDS. When I put my eyes on Jesus and began serving him and others, then I found the "peace which passes understanding." Johnny was beginning to grasp onto the idea that he was a worthy servant in God's kingdom.

Johnny and I traveled with our families and shared our testimonies in different churches where we found encouragement and saw God mightily move amongst His people. Johnny was glad to be able to use his testimony for good and for God's glory. One of his favorite verses was Isaiah 40:30-31, "Even youths grow tired and weary, and young men stumble and fall; but those who hope in the LORD will renew their strength. They will soar on wings like eagles; they will run and not grow weary, they will walk and not be faint." Johnny was now able to walk and not be faint.

Johnny died from AIDS related lymphoma, July 14, 1994. His last days were filled with love and peace. He used every opportunity to share his faith with others and had such a sweet peaceful spirit that the hospital workers knew his life was different. They had seen many AIDS patients come and go but none like Johnny. The love, the support and the overwhelming sense of peace were unique to them. Even in his death God used him to bring hope to others.

I have seen many other families over the past three years who were able to move beyond their fears and develop the support system they desperately needed. As each of them has begun to reach out they have found love and acceptance. Our monthly support group has also been a lifeline to many who need time before sharing with others the burdens facing their family. Check in your area to see if there are any Christian support groups. CASA, Christian AIDS Services Alliance has been established to provide referral information of the ministries across the U.S. which provide support, care and information from a Christian perspective. If there is no established ministry in your area, pray about beginning one. Encourage the PWA to reach out to others with this disease and learn all they can about the experiences of others. Their doctor may be a good source.

For PWAs and their families learning about the disease process and "how, what, and why" the virus destroys the immune system is extremely helpful in giving a measure of security and a sense of control. As they learn that they are *living* with AIDS and that all aspects of the disease are not beyond their control, they find some peace. Helpful resources are listed at the end of this chapter.

Some practical advice for ministering to the AIDS patient and their family is helpful. These are some tips I have found useful in my ministry.

- Visit — If hospitalized, short visits but frequent. If not hospitalized have a weekly time that you get together for a meal or just sit and talk. (Or whatever you deem adequate).
- Minister to the family or "partner" — It gives the patient peace of mind to know their family is cared for.
- Offer to stay with the patient at night when they are hospitalized. It gives the loved ones a chance to rest if they are keeping a bedside vigil.
- Offer to stay with patient while loved ones go out to eat, do grocery shopping, do laundry, etc.
- When you visit call ahead to see if there are any needs.
- Help the PWA discover all they can about their disease.
- Be a good listener. Listen without offering advice or trying to fix the frustration or pain. Listen for subtle clues about the patient's emotions. Ask questions which promote conversation or prod the PWA to express their feelings.
- Don't be judgmental.
- Bring reading materials or music when you visit.
- Pray with the AIDS patient. They will appreciate it in most cases.
- Look for opportunities to talk about spiritual matters.
- Tell the PWA when you will return and then be there.
- Consistency and patience are vital.
- Make sure they have your phone number easily accessible and make yourself available anytime they just need to talk.
- Encourage a PWA to do as much for themselves as they can.
- Offer help that relates to the situation of a person preparing to die. Things like composing final letters, planning funerals, wills, and other things that are difficult for the AIDS patient to initiate.

Ministering to the AIDS patient and their families is a joyous opportunity to share in the comfort that Christ has given to all of us. It says in 2 Corinthians 1:3-5, "Praise be to the God and Father of our Lord Jesus Christ, the Father of compassion and the God of all comfort, who comforts us in all our troubles, so that we can comfort those in any trouble with the comfort we ourselves have received from God. For just as the sufferings of Christ flow over into our lives, so also through Christ our comfort overflows."

Other Resources:

The AIDS Epidemic; A Balance Between Compassion and Justice by Glenn Woods, MD, and John Dietrich, MD. An excellent book with disease information and helpful advice on issues surrounding AIDS.

Christians in the Age of AIDS by Shepherd and Anita Smith: A book which offers AIDS information and instructs Christians for response.

CASA, Christian AIDS Services Alliance
PO BOX 3612
San Rafael, CA 94912-3612
Phone referrals: (410) 268-3442

Christian AIDS Network
1411 N Classen Blvd. #111
Oklahoma City, OK 73106
Phone: (405) 525-3733

AIDS Resource Hotline
Churches of Christ
Phone: (214) 669-AIDS

CHAPTER TWELVE

TO THE CHURCH: CONFLICT, CONVICTION, & COMPASSION*

Joe Dallas

In this final chapter, Joe Dallas makes a call to all Christians to stand firm on biblical teaching concerning the sin of homosexuality but to extend the open arms of love to the sinner.

> In this regard gay activists mirrored the passage of confrontation politics – the purpose of protest was no longer to make public a point of view, but rather to halt unacceptable practices – the traditional willingness to tolerate the views of one's opponents was discarded. – Ronald Bayer, 1981

We stepped out of the auditorium single file, facing a crowd of gay activists holding candles, waving signs, and blowing whistles. Security guards had formed a narrow aisle for us to walk through, but there were still less than five feet between us and the protestors. Their banner identified them as "Queer Nation," their signs exhorted us to "Heal Ourselves," "Stop the Violence," and a few other things unmen-

*Taken from *Desires in Conflict, Answering the Struggle for Sexual Identity* by Joe Dallas, Harvest House Publishers, 1991. Used by permission.

tionable in this writing. Their faces were even more expressive than the slogans they repeated: "Stop the violence, stop the hate"; "Once queer, always queer"; "Sexist, racist, anti-gay, born-again bigots go away!"

Their hatred was louder than their shouting, more colorful than the expletives they were hurling at us. We were a sorry lot, we bigots; certainly we were no credit to the tradition of fascism that they accused us of carrying on. No self-respecting hatemongers would have conducted themselves the way we did. Few of us shouted back, none of us threw punches. Instead, without cue or prompting, we linked arms, faced the crowd, and began singing hymns. Some knelt and prayed on the spot, others tried vainly to engage the protestors in some reasonable dialogue. Most of us watched, refusing to avoid the ugly scene but also determined not to contribute to its ugliness. It was quite a way to cap off an evening of worship and teaching.

It was the 16th Annual Conference of Exodus International at the University of Toronto in Canada. This conference, held in a different location each year, provides Exodus leaders with a chance to meet and network with other ministry leaders; teach workshops on sexuality, relationships, and recovery; and meet with parties interested in our work. Most of us look forward to the week-long gathering. It is usually peaceful and provides a much-needed boost to our morale.

We'd already heard some rumblings of protest before the confrontation with Queer Nation. From the time we arrived in Canada, newspaper reports had carried quotes from gay leaders denouncing us and our view on homosexuality. That's nothing new — the quickest way to be the Bad Guy these days is to question the legitimacy of homosexuality and hold a traditional view on moral issues. But we were surprised at the lengths to which they had gone this year to harass and intimidate us.

So yes, we expected a little trouble. And no, nothing terrible happened. Intense and enlightening, but not terrible. As the confrontation continued that night, I spoke with a few of the activists. "Your presence here is oppressive to us," one of them informed me.

"But how," I asked, "is it oppressive to hold a different viewpoint? We're not forcing it on you; in fact, the way you live your life is your own business and I wouldn't interfere. But don't we have a right to offer whatever help we can to people who aren't satisfied being gay?"

"Well," he said, "we think your ideas are crazy and homophobic."

End of discussion; he walked away.

My ideas? Did I write the Bible? It occurred to me and several other people with whom I later spoke that our viewpoint, which is held by the majority of Christians, was what prompted the outrage. The protestors weren't reviling us; they were reviling the notion that homosexuality is abnormal, immoral, and a perversion of God's intention for sexual experience. As long as we – or anyone – hold such a view, there will be controversy. Our confrontation was a microcosm of what the church at large is about to face.

There are basically two ways we can respond to the confrontation: We can modify our beliefs or stand our ground. Many congregations are opting for the former, sacrificing biblical integrity in the name of compassion. That's tragic, and, as Chuck Smith of Calvary Chapel stated recently, "a sign of weakness within the church that it [the issue of whether homosexuality and Christianity are compatible] is even a topic of debate. It should not even be a question because the Bible is very clear on the subject."[1]

The second option is to stand our ground, refusing to be intimated by the growing number of voices clamoring for a revision of clear biblical teaching. But how we stand our ground is equally important. There we are faced with a seem-

---

[1] "Non-Traditional Churches Welcome Gays to Flock," the *Los Angeles Times*, June 21, 1991, section B, p. 12.

ingly impossible challenge: to express our convictions with reason and compassion. "To be really Bible-believing and true to our living Christ, each issue demands a balance which says 'no' to two opposite errors," says Francis Schaeffer. "We can neither compromise love in the name of holiness; nor can we compromise holiness in the name of love. Or to say it another way: the devil never gives us the luxury of fighting the battle on just one front."[2]

We can't duck the issue of homosexuality, but neither can we effectively address it unless our response is balanced. To take it a step further, not only will our response need to be balanced; it will need to recognize the individuality of the homosexually oriented person we're dealing with. Not all gays are activists. Some are activists, others are more moderate, and others are dissatisfied with their sexuality and want our help. Obviously our approach to these groups will have to vary. I'd like to look briefly, then, at the gay activist, the moderate, and the Fighter and offer some thoughts on a balanced, effective response to each.

The Church and the Activist

In a *Tale of Two Cities* Dickens described an uprising of people who had been pushed too far, oppressed for too long, victimized too horribly. The citizens of France had been ground underfoot by the Aristocrats, treated inhumanly and taxed without mercy by the upper-class tyrants. They brooded for years, planning the day they would take over and reverse the power structure. When the revolution came and their position of power over the Aristocrats was secured, they exacted vengeance without reason, blindly striking down anyone who opposed them and establishing a new form of terrorism that, to them, was really justice. They went into overkill, and though their initial grievances against their ene-

---

[2] Francis Schaeffer, *The Great Evangelical Disaster* (Westchester, NY: Good News Publishers, 1984).

mies were legitimate, their newly established system was every bit as tyrannical as the one they had overthrown. The oppressed were now the oppressors, lopping the heads off anyone who questioned them.

You can't look at the tactics and goals of gay activists without seeing the correlation. To begin with, they, too, have been frequently mistreated. And many of their complaints against the church and society are legitimate. Try to understand a bit of their background.

A Genesis of Rage

They never asked for their homosexual orientation. They had no control over whatever influences in early life contributed to it. They never chose to be attracted to their own sex; they only became aware, at some point, that those attractions existed.

Usually their awareness of their sexual feelings came as a vague realization that they were "different." That difference may have been noticeable to others (when boys are effeminate or girls "boyish"), or it may have been a private sense of feelings that other kids didn't seem to have. Most kids in this position are aware of homosexual feelings before they even know what homosexuality is. Sooner or later they hear the jokes about "queers." Not sure what a "queer" is, they assume only that, whatever it is, it's not a very popular thing to be. When it occurs to them that the definition of a "queer" or "fag" matches their sexual feelings, they are aware of their homosexuality, but they're also aware of the reaction they'd get from almost anyone they would disclose their orientation to. Their friends would ostracize them; their parents would be shocked, or devastated, or rejecting (or so they assume, and often they're absolutely right). And so begin the years of secrecy, hiding, self-loathing.

At first they assume or at least hope that, as time passes, they will outgrow their homosexuality. Often they pray hard and concentrate even harder, trying to change. And, sadly, they often assume that the problem is them – that something is fundamentally sick or evil about them to have these feelings. Their environment doesn't help much. By the time they've entered adolescence they know that to be gay is, in most teenage circles, one of the worst things one can be. This drives them further inward, more determined than ever to let no one in on their secret.

Of course, in some cases it's no secret at all. God help the teenage boy who's effeminate, the teenage girl with masculine traits. They are the objects of senseless cruelty, harassed and ridiculed at every turn by their peers. Yet even in the cases of adolescents whose homosexuality isn't obvious (they're the majority, by the way) there's an understanding that they, too, would be openly persecuted if their peers knew the whole truth.

Can you imagine, on top of the inward turmoil these kids experience, the rage that starts to build inside of them? They are isolated, lonely, and often abused by others who fear them or loathe them or both. The church tells them they're sinning and society (in general) tells them they're oddballs, yet no one tells them what to do about it! They're in pain, to be sure, but someday that pain will translate into anger.

At some point they consider the gay community – a community that will accept them as they are, made up of people like them who have experienced a similar emotional journey. They make a decision to "come out," to quit fighting their inclinations and accept them, and in many cases to advise friends and loved ones of their decision. The coming-out experience is exhilarating. Finally the secret's out; no more hiding, fearing, pretending. For most, it feels wonderful. And for those who are activists today, the decision to come out was probably accompanied by a commitment: "I will never allow anyone or any group to ever put me down, humiliate me, or oppress me in any way ever again!"

. . . .

> Most of the repenting that needs to be done on this issue of homosexuality needs to be done by straight people, including straight Christians. By far the greater sin in our church is the sin of neglect, fear, hatred, just wanting to brush these people under the rug. — Richard Lovelace, 1981[3]

Add to these personal experiences the animosity that's been growing between conservative Christians and gays these past few decades. The burgeoning Gay Rights movement of the late sixties and early seventies begged some sort of Christian response. A natural result of the sexual revolution of the sixties, the Gay Rights movement began to force itself on American consciousness as gays began identifying themselves without apology in larger numbers. No longer were they asking for tolerance; they were demanding acceptance for themselves and their sexuality. Unbeknownst to most of us, they made tremendous political, educational, and even religious inroads. (As early as 1969 some denominations were quietly reconsidering their stand on homosexuality.) Yet by and large, the church offered little in the way of comment. Worse yet, virtually no efforts were made to extend the gospel to these people. Maybe we were afraid of the subject, or perhaps we were intimidated by our own ignorance of it. At any rate, our lack of compassion was marked by our failure to respond to a huge, growing need in America.

Our response accelerated from silence to a deafening roar in the mid to late seventies, beginning with what is now considered a watershed event in the Gay Rights movement – the Anita Bryant Crusade in Dade County, Florida. In 1976, when Dade County passed an anti-discrimination bill prohibiting discrimination in housing or employment based on sexual orientation, Miss Bryant took action. With the encouragement of her pastor and supporters, she spearheaded a

---

[3] Richard Lovelace, professor at Gordon-Conwell Theological Seminary, from "Homosexuals Can Change," *Christianity Today*, Feb.6, 1981, p. 37.

referendum which gained national attention. Believing that legislation such as that of Dade County was in fact highly discriminatory toward those holding traditional moral values, she successfully campaigned to have the law repealed. Although the outcome of the Bryant campaign was favorable, the events occurring during the campaign itself would once and forever change the church's response toward homosexuality, a change that was, in many ways, not for the better.

Essentially, we seemed to rise up in unanimous protest against the notions that homosexuality should ever be considered normal and that homosexuals should be granted the same minority status afforded to race, sex, and religion. That protest was good in and of itself, but the way it was expressed was actually damaging in many cases. Remember, these were the early days of Christian television, when ministers were finding new avenues of influence through the airwaves. And so over the air our leaders began expressing strong views not only on homosexuality but on homosexuals themselves. And that is precisely where we erred.

Extravagant, ill-informed remarks about gays were hurled from the televangelists' studios. It wasn't enough to preach against the sin of homosexuality, we needed to underscore our point by degrading, in the public's eye, anyone who practiced it. With little concern for accuracy, we exploited the stereotype most Americans had of homosexuals – they were all promiscuous, they were all effeminate, they all practiced their vile deeds in public places and posed a serious threat to the safety of our children. We weren't always wrong, of course. Some homosexuals fit that description quite well. But far too many of them didn't, a fact we refused to realize. It was politically expedient to cast them all in the same mold, as if to allow that some of them were rather moderate citizens would have somehow weakened our argument against their habits and lifestyles.

Not only were irresponsible generalizations becoming commonplace, they were also being made with a certain degree of relish. We wanted, it seems, to believe the very worst about these people and encourage others to do the same. Even more disturbing was the lack of gospel invitation extended to the gays. At the very least, one would think that having spent time and energy denouncing them, we would have ended our rebukes with an explanation of the grace of God manifest in the cross. Instead, like Jonah preaching to the Ninevites, we really seemed to hate these people and care little for their salvation. We wanted them stopped, but we didn't want them saved. Or so it appeared.

We sent a strong message to the gay community in those days: "We'll fight you every step of the way, and although we claim to "love" souls as Christ loves them, we don't care much for yours. What we do care about is your defeat, and that will be the focus of our efforts when we deal with you."

That is a message they will never forget.[4]

. . . .

> Jesus did not see disease as God's judgment but as an opportunity to show God's glory and mercy.
>
> – Glenn Wood, M.D. and John Dietrich, M.D., 1990[5]

If irresponsibility marked our public stance toward homosexuality in the seventies, we outdid ourselves in the eighties during the advent of the AIDS epidemic. Our hearts were unmoved when we saw pictures of emaciated young men crying

---

[4] Rev. Troy Perry, founder of the Universal Fellowship of Metropolitan Community Churches (MCC), the largest pro-gay church in existence, adds an interesting point here. "If the Church had really done their missionary work – I don't think that MCC would ever have existed" [from Paul Morris, *Shadow of Sodom* (Wheaton, IL: Tyndale House, 1989), p. 29]. Though Perry doubtless means that the church should have both evangelized homosexuals *and* accepted their homosexuality, his words hold true nonetheless. If the church had concentrated more on reaching souls regardless of background or orientation it is entirely possible that, as Perry states, there would be no "gay churches."

[5] Glenn Wood and John Dietrich, *The AIDS Epidemic: Balancing Compassion and Justice* (Portland, OR: Multnomah Press, 1990), p. 279.

in agonized confusion. They were beneath our compassion; instead, we pronounced (with smug satisfaction) the judgment of God upon the perverts of America. We seemed to feel they'd gotten what was coming to them and one would almost think we rejoiced in it. Preacher after preacher reminded his congregation that homosexuals were tasting God's wrath, and it was about time. We judged, we pontificated, we rambled.

But where was our compassion? We'd become adept at hard truth, but couldn't see that AIDS was affording us the greatest opportunity we'd ever had to finally reach the gay community with the gospel. Didn't it sink in that people were dying, alone and desperate, waiting to be harvested right before our eyes? Where were our missions, our visitation programs, our calls to action? *Did we really feel that the soul of a homosexual was of less value to God than the soul of a heterosexual?*

The greatest chance of a decade went up in smoke before our eyes. Our pronouncements of judgment did little good for these people. Doing good and showing mercy to them was relegated to the liberals, the New Agers, and the gays themselves. They filled the gap we should have bridged from the beginning. They stepped in with service programs, hospital visitation, and human comfort. While we pointed our fingers, the non-believers and the cults extended their hands. If the message we'd sent to the homosexual in the seventies was one of contempt, the message of the eighties was one of indifference, even in the face of death.

And so they perceived our response, accurately so in many instances, and they reciprocated. They returned our contempt twentyfold, considering us to be a community of cruel, twisted people. The hatred we felt from the Queer Nation protestors was, I believe, the fruit of our own mishandling of the homosexual issue.

You might well say, "But all Christians didn't blow it! Many of us really *did* care about AIDS patients and gays, and never meant them any harm." You may be right, but remember that the church, for better or worse, is represented by its most visible spokespersons. When they speak, those to whom they speak assume that they represent all of us. And so the anger many of them felt during their early years was fueled all the more by their perception of us, a perception that was not always inaccurate.

Maximum Overkill

But our errors will never justify the antics of the homosexual militants. Like the French citizens in Dickens' story, they've gone into overkill. In *Tale of Two Cities* the citizens forbade anyone to speak against their new order under threat of the guillotine. And gay activists, not content to allow anyone to speak against them or their goals, are equally open about their intolerance:

> Articles in *Outweek* [a gay publication] have backed taking away free speech from anyone alleged to be homophobic and have urged the use of violence against straight oppressors.[6]

The French citizens railed against the violence the Aristocrats had committed against them, yet they advocated mass violence against their former oppressors (and anyone they deemed an enemy of the republic) without apology or exceptions. So gay activists consider terrorism an acceptable method of achieving their ends and silencing their enemies:

> A recent cover [of *Outweek*] featured a lesbian pointing a gun at the reader, with the headline: "Taking aim at bashers!" [Presumably "gay bashers," which often means anyone who opposes homosexuality.] Another proclaimed, "We hate straights."[7]

---

[6] "Gay Life, Gay Death," *The New Republic*, Dec. 17, 1990, vol. 203, no. 256, p. 24.

[7] Ibid., p. 24.

The double standard here is nearly unbearable. Activists unanimously decry the violence committed against gays. In some cases they cite violent acts of gay bashing in which clearly disturbed people physically, randomly attack gays. This type of violence should be decried by all of us, and its perpetrators punished to full extent of the law. At other times, though, they consider verbal slurs to be acts of violence, acts which they themselves commit boldly and openly (and not against the people who directly attack them, by the way, but against those of us they've targeted as "homophobes"). And in some cases, they encourage the very sort of violence they condemn when it is directed against them.

By the way of example, one of the best know AIDS activists in America is Larry Kramer, founder of the militant group ACT UP (AIDS Coalition to Unleash Power) which is the forerunner of other such groups. Kramer is on record as advocating violence and even murder:

> He [Kramer] then began the meeting with a soft spoken announcement that he wanted to set up a group to do target practice, to learn how to use guns against the police and gay-bashers.[8]
>
> Asked to be more precise, Kramer looks grim and says that "the new phase is terrorism...I don't know whether it means burning buildings, or killing people or setting fire to yourselves."[9]
>
> "I think, when I am ready to go," [referring to his health after learning he'd been exposed to the AIDS virus], "I'll take somebody with me."[10]

Many in the gay community disagree strongly with Kramer, and many would not back his call to violence. But think for a minute: If a Christian leader ever made such state-

---

[8] Ibid., p. 25.

[9] "Kramer Vs. Kramer," the *Los Angeles Times*, June 20, 1990, section E.

[10] Ibid.

ments, would there be a major newspaper in America that wouldn't splash his words on the front page? If Randall Terry, Jerry Falwell, or Phyllis Schlafly (all of whom are considered bigots and homophobes by the gay community) advocated any form of violence against gays, wouldn't there be a national outcry, and rightfully so? Yet somehow a nationally recognized leader in the gay community can publicly encourage murder without impunity. Something's very, very wrong here.

As the French citizens had a common name for a common foe, "an enemy of the Republic," so the gay activists have a name they slap on anyone they're at odds with, "the homophobe."

Few modern words have been so inaccurately and unfairly utilized as has the word "homophobia." A phobia is an unreasonable fear or dread of an object, causing a person to avoid the object and provoking a panicked response in its presence. Now, there may be people who are terrified of homosexuals and homosexuality, unable to tolerate its presence, and thrown into panic when confronted by it. But in most cases, the term simply doesn't apply. There are bigots, of course, who unreasonably hate and mistreat gays. The term "prejudice," "bigotry," or "stupidity" might better apply to them. But the misapplication of "homophobia" doesn't stop with them. It is slapped without hesitation on anyone who states that homosexuality is wrong, unnatural, whatever. How convenient to simply dismiss the arguments of anyone who opposes gays by saying, "He's homophobic – end of discussion." And in more and more circles, the label "homophobe" carries a stigma as great as the label "white supremacist" or "neo-Nazi."[11]

So a clever system has been set up here. The homophobe is the enemy that has to be stopped. The homophobe is

---

[11] A good argument against such misuse of terms is found in an editorial entitled "Is Homophobia the Equivalent of Racism?" in *Newsweek*, Mar. 12, 1990, vol. CXV, no. 11, p. 27.

anyone expressing views on homosexuality contrary to the pro-gay viewpoint, whether his views are founded in religion, personal conviction, or prejudice. The "damage" the homophobe does warrants a removal of his freedom of speech and religion through any means, and, of course, the church is the major promoter of homophobic viewpoints.

In short, the church must either change its views or be silenced.

How can we respond to the militants? First, through repentance. We can, and must, admit our wrongs. Yes, their tactics are deplorable and unwarranted, and no, there's no justification for the terrorism they're inflicting on us. But we have to admit our part, however large or small, in the animosity, and so perhaps we are reaping, in part, the very hatred we've sown.

Second, we cannot allow ourselves to become what they say we already are: Hateful, mean-spirited bigots. It would be easy to respond to their hatred with a bit of our own, but – and this is vital – *that's exactly what they want us to do*! It will only validate their accusations against us. Evil cannot be overcome with evil; it can only be overcome with good.

But good doesn't mean weak, which is my third point. We cannot afford to be coerced into silence. The Christian church is perhaps the last organization that continues to promote values which forbid homosexual practices. The militants know that, and that makes us an important target.

In a way, this is a continuation of the controversy of the gospel. Whenever Christianity is preached in its fullness it challenges prevailing viewpoints and inconveniences somebody. Christ Himself is a case in point. He gained popularity through His teachings and miracles, which made Him a distinct threat to the position of power held by the chief priests and Pharisees. They openly admitted that if people continued to follow Him, Rome would sense an insurrection, step in and take over the local government, and thus remove the Pharisees and priests from their position of power (John

11:47,48). Paul found himself in a similar position when he preached in Ephesus. His preaching caused many Ephesians to abandon their idolatry, which put a noticeable damper on the sales of idols and infuriated the local "idol manufacturers" (Acts 19:25-27). In both cases, a concern for the people who might benefit from the gospel had nothing to do with the actions taken against Christ and Paul; rather, these actions were taken because the promotion of Christian belief was undermining the political and social agendas of certain people who demanded that its promoters be silenced.

There is the possibility, then, of nothing less than full-scale terrorism in the near future, terrorism intended to frighten us into either changing our views or never expressing them. If we allow ourselves to be so intimidated, we will deserve the contempt of society, the displeasure of God, and the place of spiritual impotence we will surely find ourselves in.

Who knows? Persecution has traditionally strengthened the church. Perhaps the onslaught of gay militancy will unite us in ways unthinkable until now.[12]

The Church and the Moderate

Not all homosexually oriented adults are radicals. Most, in fact, probably don't approve of radical tactics, although they rarely speak out against them. In my opinion, the majority of homosexually oriented adults are moderates. They live and work among us, make major and significant contributions to our culture, pay their taxes, and want simply to live their lives as they see fit.

There are the people we wouldn't normally envision

---

[12] It looks as though we're finally beginning to fight back. A Christian who was sharing his faith in the West Hollywood section of Southern California, which has a large openly gay population, is suing the city officials of West Hollywood for failing to intervene when he was assaulted, spat on, threatened, and intimidated by gay activists. According to his suit, city officials took no action on his behalf though they were aware of the incident(s) (*Christian Times* newspaper, Aug. 1991, vol. 12, no. 8, p. 5).

when we think of "gay." Whether or not they're open about their sexuality, there is nothing in their demeanor or behavior that is offensive. Many of them are likable, responsible citizens.

We seldom identify them because they seldom identify themselves to us. When they do, our response to them should be no different than to any other person: one of respect, consideration, and the normal concern we express for anyone's soul.

Remember, the goal of the church is not to make "straights out of gays." It is to preach the gospel, and there's no reason an exception should be made for the gay moderates. They are not forcing a political agenda on us, as their radical brethren do. So our first priority, as with anyone else, is to share Christ and treat our fellow humans with courtesy and honor.

Often people ask, "How do you witness to a gay?" The question itself shows a certain misunderstanding. Why should witnessing to gays be any different than witnessing to anyone else? Their homosexuality is not our main concern. The state of their souls is. And if the gospel is something they're not interested in, we should respect their free choice as we should anyone else's. We needn't feel obligated to argue over sexual matters with people who have no interest in such an argument. I see no reason why a Christian should automatically target a gay friend or co-worker as an object of reformation. "As much as possible," Paul said, "Live at peace with all men." That's a good Scripture to keep in mind when responding to moderates.

Actually, I feel the best way to witness, at times, is to listen. And when witnessing to a gay friend, listening may be your most effective tool. It may also be educational for you.

Glenn Wood refers to a friendship he struck up with a gay university professor. The professor is someone Dr. Wood obviously admires; he describes him as an outstanding teacher and an intelligent, likable individual. He didn't know the man was gay until they'd had several conversations together. Once he acknowledged his homosexuality, he began telling Dr. Wood what his life was like – how it felt to have watched 32 of his friends die of AIDS, how being a victim of gay bashing had affected him, how cruel he felt some Christians had been to gays in general. Dr. Wood, who apparently did more listening than talking, describes his reaction:

> I had been transformed in that thirty-minute conversation. I had vicariously experienced the pain of another human being . . . by the grace of God and the openness of a fellow mortal, I gained new insight into the anguish of this world.[13]

The Church and the Fighter

> We are all playing Christian club games while men and women around us are tormented by sin, too timid to bare their bosoms, too ashamed to ask our help. —John White, *Eros Defiled*

The church's response to the Fighter largely determines whether or not he'll keep fighting. All the counseling offered to him in this book is still in vain if he doesn't have a church to love him, support him, and relate to him.

So first off, we need to recognize the existence of homosexually oriented believers in our churches. I hope by now you will agree that they exist, and if they exist, a need for ministry exists with them.

There's no reason ministries to such people can't be developed in our churches. After all, when we preach against the evil of a lifestyle or activity, we should also be seeking alternatives to offer in place of the thing we're condemning.

Our response to abortion is a good example of alternative action. For years we've railed against the crime of murdering the unborn, yet to the woman in crisis pregnancy we offered little in the way of alternatives. Naturally, telling

---

[13] Glenn Wood and John Dietrich, *The AIDS Epidemic: Balancing Compassion and Justice*, p. 114.

people they were doing the wrong thing without helping them do the right thing was unsatisfactory. Finally we realized we had something other than condemnation to offer. Christian ministries to women in crises began to appear. Halfway houses for single mothers gave women a safe place to complete their pregnancies without financial burden. Christian adoption networks took some of the administrative burden off women who opted for adoption instead of abortion. Crisis pregnancy counseling became a common outreach activity of many churches. We had cursed the darkness long enough; it was time to light a candle.

To this day few such candles exist for the Fighter. Yet we can't deny the prevalence of homosexuality and so, as we did with the abortion issue, we've got to establish ministries that will meet the special needs of the Fighter.

Support group ministries are one good alternative. We see such groups in many churches for believers dealing with substance abuse, divorce, relationship difficulties, smoking, and eating disorders. Why is homosexuality, clearly a major problem, so often neglected? Forming a group to address the issue is no major undertaking. I'd like to offer a few ideas on establishing such a group.

Specialized ministry groups should never take the place of church fellowship or a normal social life. They should, rather, supplement it. That should be made clear from the start.

The function of such a group is to provide a safe, godly environment where people can openly discuss their homosexual struggles; learn from the experiences of others who've gone through similar struggles; be accountable to a group of Christians who are genuinely concerned; and know they have friends who are regularly praying for them, available to them, and rooting for them.

Mature leadership is mandatory for a group like this. And the leadership does *not* have to be made up of people who've experienced homosexuality. (That's a common misnomer –

only "ex-gays" can minister to gays, only "former drug addicts" can minister to drug addicts, etc.) It would be far better, in fact, if more people who've never been involved with homosexuality would involve themselves in these ministries. All parties could learn from each other, and come to realize how much they really do have in common.

It doesn't take a lot of expertise to develop these ministries. Some basic knowledge about homosexuality is helpful, of course, and groups like Exodus International can provide useful information. But a willingness to be involved in the lives of Fighters is the starting point from which solid, successful ministry to them can develop.

Which brings us to the larger issue of discipleship and intimacy in the church. When we function as a body – a group of believers who acknowledge their need for each other, who take time to know each other, and who commit themselves to each other's welfare – we create a godly environment where healing of all kinds can take place. That is the most effective way to address the needs not only of the Fighter but of all Christians. Solid, bonded relations in the church are a more noble goal than large congregations, fancy programs, and bigger buildings. That is the essence, the form of Christianity that expresses Christ's intention for His people.

> Love, and the unity it attests to, is the mark Christ gave Christians to wear before the world. Only with this mark may the world know that Christians are indeed Christians and that Jesus was sent by the Father. —Francis Schaeffer

APPENDIXES

RESOURCES

APPENDIX A

READING LIST

This book has tried to offer a sampling of various authors who have either personally dealt with homosexuality or have ministered to them in a professional way. The following reading list includes the most recent works on the subject. These books, as well as a more complete list of books dealing with the entire range of sexual issues from a Christian perspective, can be obtained from:

Regeneration Books
P.O. Box 9830
Baltimore, MD 21284-9830
(410)661-0284

HELPING PEOPLE STEP OUT OF HOMOSEXUALITY

Frank Worthen

This book, formerly titled *Steps Out Of Homosexuality*, offers a realistic and compassionate approach to overcoming homosexuality.

DESIRES IN CONFLICT

Joe Dallas

The author addresses the needs of the Christian who deals with homosexual temptations. It is written directly to the person struggling with homosexuality, but it is also a very helpful resource for friends, families and church members who seek to understand how they can assist the struggler.

SODOM'S SECOND COMING
F. LaGard Smith
A review of the history and politics of the Gay rights movement along with a response to Gay theology.

YOU DON'T HAVE TO BE GAY
Jeff Konrad
Recently revised, this popular book is written as a series of letters from the author, a former homosexual, to a friend who is struggling with whether or not to try to leave the gay life.

PURSUING SEXUAL WHOLENESS
Andrew Comiskey
The author, founder of Desert Stream ministry and developer of the Living Waters Sexual Redemption in Christ program, imparts an extraordinary depth and breadth of understanding to sexual brokenness.

HOMOSEXUALITY: A NEW CHRISTIAN ETHIC
Elizabeth R. Moberly
The author, a research psychologist, formerly at Cambridge, presents a theory of homosexual root causes that has gained widespread acceptance among Christians ministering to homosexuals.

EMOTIONAL DEPENDENCY
A Threat to Close Friendships
Lori Thorkelson-Rentzel
With understanding and compassion, the reader is helped to identify unhealthy dependencies and idolatrous relationships.

THE BROKEN IMAGE
Leanne Payne
This is a classic that anyone who struggles with homosexuality, or who wishes to minister to the homosexual, needs to read.

REPARATIVE THERAPY OF MALE HOMOSEXUALITY
Joseph Nicolosi, PhD.
This book provides new insights and practical means for offering help to homosexuals.

DEADLY SECRETS
Karen Linamen and Keith Wall
A great book for ministers, parents and teenagers, this is the story of a committed Christian who became deeply involved in compulsive homosexuality.

THE HEALING OF THE HOMOSEXUAL
Leanne Payne
The author shares her years of ministry in healing prayer to men and women bound in homosexuality.

FACTORS IN FREEDOM
The Struggle with Life Dominating Sin
Ed Hurst
This is a practical handbook for those struggling with any life-dominating sinful lifestyle or habit; substance abuse, overeating, smoking, etc.

HOMOSEXUALITY: LAYING THE AXE TO THE ROOTS
Ed Hurst
Overcoming homosexuality requires more than abstinence; it requires dealing with those root issues that give birth to and sustain the homosexual orientation.

CHALLENGE TO THE CHURCH
Ed Hurst
This is a collection of writings that is an excellent resource for ministers, teachers, church members in general, and for those who struggle with homosexuality.

SHATTERING THE SILENCE
Ed Hurst
This is a very useful book for anyone either struggling with homo-

sexuality or seeking to help a loved one who is struggling.

HEALING FOR THE HOMOSEXUAL

For a number of years, this booklet has been the standard for presenting a biblical view of homosexuality for ministers, for people struggling with homosexuality, and for their families and loved ones. Offering case histories, principles for counseling homosexuals, and help in the form of questions and answers, this book is an excellent introduction to ministry to homosexuals.

HOMOSEXUAL NO MORE

William Consiglio

Addressed to both male strugglers and to counselors, this book has much to offer that is beneficial to both.

COUNSELING THE HOMOSEXUAL

Michael R. Saia

The author combines this practical experience in helping Christians overcome homosexuality with psychological understanding and sound Biblical principles to provide a guide for any Christian called to counsel, on either a lay or professional basis, people struggling with homosexuality.

MICHELLE DANIELLE IS DEAD

Marie S. Rice

This unique, privately published book tells the true story of Mike and the road he travelled from homosexual and female impersonator to Christian husband and father.

HOMOSEXUAL PARTNERSHIPS

Why Same-Sex Relationships Are Not a Christian Option

John Stott

Taken from John Stott's *Social and Sexual Relationships in the Modern World, Volume II*, this small booklet presents, in a compassionate but powerful way, the reasons why even monogamous same-sex partnerships are not an option for the Christian.

Appendix A

COUNSELING AND HOMOSEXUALITY

Earl D. Wilson

Part of the publisher's "Resources for Christian Counseling" series, this book is especially suited for the experienced counselor who needs a deeper understanding of homosexuality.

STRANGERS IN A CHRISTIAN LAND

Darlene Bogle

This book offers help and encouragement to loved ones of and those who minister to homosexuals, showing the way to healing and restoration through love and understanding.

ON THE ORIGINS AND TREATMENT OF HOMOSEXUALITY

Gerard van den Aardweg

This book is written for the professional counselor. It is an excellent resource, providing insights into characteristics of parents of homosexuals, and is also useful in providing information on bisexuality, transsexualism, transvestitism, pedophilia, sadomasochism, and other conditions not readily dealt with.

ESTABLISHING GROUP MEETINGS

Frank Worthen

A valuable book for leaders of ex-gay ministries, it discusses group philosophy as well as how to set up a group, group size, the role of the group leader and other practical issues.

THE FRIENDSHIPS OF WOMEN

Dee Brestin

Through God's Word, Dee Brestin reveals a pattern for friendship that can direct a woman's gift for intimacy and help her be the redemptive agent God planned her to be. Homosexuality is treated in the context of friendship with the hope for change and deliverance.

FALSE INTIMACY

Harry W. Scampers

Finally, a book that deals with sexual addiction from a truly Christian perspective.

KINSEY, SEX AND FRAUD

Judith A. Reisman and Edward W. Eichel

Any Christian addressing homosexuality or sexuality needs to know the false premises that underlie these reports and most public understanding of sexuality today.

Appendix B

MINISTRY NETWORK

There is real help that is available for those who are struggling with homosexuality. The problem is that much of it is not well publicized and many times people don't know what to look for. ***Exodus International*** *is an umbrella group that includes a variety of ministries that specialize in helping people overcome homosexuality through the power of Jesus Christ. This chapter contains their history and locations throughout the country.*

A. THE HISTORY OF EXODUS INTERNATIONAL

Bob Davies

When God first gave me a glimpse of my future ministry with homosexuals, I was horrified.

It was an early summer day in 1976, and I'd been praying about my future for weeks. My six-month evangelism school at Youth With a Mission's outreach center in southern Germany was coming to an end. What did God have for me next?

I was outside working – pulling weeds from between the cobblestones on the driveway – when a very clear picture came into my mind: I was back home in Vancouver, Canada, standing outside a well-known gay bar, handing out tracts to homosexual men going in and out the front door.

An evangelistic ministry to homosexuals? You've got to be kidding, I thought. *Lord, I'll do ANYTHING but that!*

The idea of such a ministry terrified me – but not because I was afraid of gays. On the contrary, I understood them very well. I'd struggled myself with homosexual feelings for years, although I'd never acted on them. Still, the same-sex attractions caused me much guilt and shame, and I was determined that no one would ever find out about "that part" of me.

I was confronted several more times that year with the idea of homosexual ministry. One day in a magazine I read the testimony of a former gay activist who had converted to Christianity.

Then, back home in Canada, I saw a book called *Gay Liberation* in a local Christian bookstore. Authored by a woman only identified as "Roberta," the book told her autobiography of years in lesbian activities, and how God had freed her from that lifestyle.

I'd never read such a book before, and I promptly sent a letter to the author by way of her publisher, telling her some of my own experiences.

Roberta wrote me right back. She had started a small outreach to homosexuals, she told me, and asked if I could help her put together a cassette tape of testimonies. "I believe you could be a very important part of this," she said. "We could do it together."

I wrote her back, telling her that I wasn't interested at all in helping with her ministry to homosexuals. *That's the last thing I want to do*, I thought.

I had no idea that, for years, Roberta Laurila had been praying for me – and for hundreds of others like me who would eventually be raised up around the world to work in the field of ex-gay ministry.

Appendix B

An Early Pioneer

May 1973 — San Rafael, California

One of the first ex-gay ministries was founded in 1973 in the San Francisco Bay Area. "Love in Action" began when God dramatically intervened in the life of a highly-successful businessman named Frank Worthen.

It all started on May 24, 1973. Frank had just locked his inside office door and was heading for the back entrance of his import store, car keys in hand. He was going to drive 15 miles south into San Francisco and visit a new homosexual hang-out that had just opened.

Suddenly Frank's mind flashed back to the time of his father's death when he was fourteen. "God, please be my Father for the rest of my life," he'd prayed. Frank had committed his life to the Lord as a young teen, but had subsequently left the church to pursue homosexual activities. Despite his life of immorality, he felt that the Lord had been watching over him.

But now Frank sensed that God was giving him an ultimatum: *If you continue in rebellion, I will remove My hand of protection from your life.*

Frank paused in the hallway, and suddenly turned to one of his employees whom he knew was a Christian.

"Michael, can you take me to your church . . . right now?"

They drove to the little chapel several miles away. The smell of spring blossoms hung in the air. As Frank and his young employee knelt in front of the altar, the colors from the stained-glass window formed a collage of color on the rug behind them.

Frank wept as he began confessing his sins. Over the next twenty minutes, he sensed a growing release from twenty-five years of rebellion.

Frank began attending church several times a week with his young employee from work. Despite his homosexual background, men and women in the small fellowship embraced him warmly, and soon formed a tight web of support around him.

"They would come visit me during the week and ask how I was doing," recalls Frank. Many of them shopped at his popular import store, and they never failed to offer encouragement to the newest member of their church.

Frank says now that his survival as a Christian depended on the emotional and prayer support he got in those early days.

"I was 44 by this time, and sex was increasingly hard to come by," he says. "Yet, after my recommitment to Christ, young men who ignored me in the lifestyle became [sexually] available to me. Satan brought all sorts of tempting situations to me.

"One night I picked up a hitchhiker, a fine-looking young man, who let me know he was interested in going home with me. I began witnessing to him about Christ, and couldn't believe that I was actually saying no to his overtures. The Lord was strengthening me."

Although there were times like this when Frank was severely tempted, he never once fell back into his old immoral lifestyle.

It soon become apparent that the Lord had His hand on Frank in a special way. Within a week of his conversion, other Christians began coming to him, men and women who were seeking to overcome homosexuality.

After six months, at the encouragement of his employee, Frank recorded his testimony on a cassette tape and began advertising it in a local underground paper, *The Berkeley Bard.* In the first year, over 60 men wrote for the tape.

Two years later, six men and women involved in Frank's growing ministry had their stories published in a book called *The Third Sex?*, and letters begging for help began pouring in from around the world. Soon the ministry demanded so much time that Frank sold his business and launched into full time Christian outreach.

Even by mid-1975, however, Frank still thought his ministry was unique. To his knowledge, he was the only Christian who had ever come out of the gay lifestyle and started an outreach to other homosexuals.

But that was soon to change in a dramatic way.

The Summit Conference
September, 1976 – Los Angeles

"Ann, I think we've got plenty of potato salad!" Joan DeGennaro joked. She and another EXIT staff member were standing next to a long table laden with food. They had spent hours the previous night peeling and cooking dozens of potatoes for this luncheon. Other containers were generously filled with bean salad, rolls, and delicate slices of cold meat.

Joan looked around the Fellowship Center. A group of sixty-two delegates – mostly male – sat around small circular tables. A small vase of yellow daisies provided a splash of color against the blue tablecloths covering each table. The animated buzz of conversation was frequently broken by loud laughter.

Frank Worthen was sitting at one table with Barbara Johnson. Barbara had discovered in the summer of 1975 that her youngest son was involved in the homosexual lifestyle. Devastated, she'd gone to Melodyland Hotline Center for counseling, then contacted Frank in February, 1976, after reading *The Third Sex?*

"Your ministry isn't the only outreach to homosexuals," she told him. "Did you know there's a similar ministry down here in Anaheim?" Frank was so excited that he flew to Los Angeles at the next opportunity to meet the staff of EXIT, the "Ex-gay Intervention Team" at Melodyland. That afternoon, Frank and the EXIT staff decided to put together a weekend seminar for anyone else around the country who was involved in helping homosexuals find freedom.

The EXIT staff had a toll-free WATS line, and they began calling well-known churches around the country. "Do you know of anyone in your area who is counseling homosexuals?" they asked, and soon learned that over a dozen ex-gay ministries had been established around the country.

After invitations went out, sixty-two delegates gathered at Melodyland for a three-day weekend conference during September 10-12, 1976. Right from the opening session, the air sparkled with excitement. "The atmosphere was electric," said one woman who attended. Everyone sensed that God was doing something special.

Until that weekend, ex-gay ministries had felt isolated, and were largely unsupported by the church at large. Many Christians were embarrassed to discuss heterosexual issues, let alone homosexuality. The "gay world" was still hidden, mysterious, threatening. Openly testifying of deliverance from such an abhorrent lifestyle was taboo. As one person said, "You can talk about overcoming drugs, alcohol – even adultery or murder. But don't talk about being gay."

Some Christians also had other irrational fears, such as fear of their children being seduced by former homosexuals at their church. So the ministries had little financial or emotional support from the church at large.

But now, for the first time, a roomful of people sensed their common calling from God: helping men and women find freedom from homosexuality. This gathering was later dubbed the "EXIT Summit Conference" and became an annual occurrence, with attendance increasing tenfold in the years ahead.

One woman who attended the first conference was Robbi Kenney, a friend of Roberta Laurila. During the final session, there was discussion on one important subject: "Where do we go from here?" The idea of loosely affiliating as a ministry network met everyone's approval, and then a discussion began on what to call the fledgling work.

"How about the name 'Exodus?'" suggested Robbi. "Homosexuals finding freedom reminds me of the children of Israel leaving the bondage of Egypt and moving towards the Promised Land." There was a unanimous agreement on

Robbi's suggestion, and the name "Exodus" was born.

Before leaving the gathering, delegates adopted a statement of intent:

"EXODUS is an international Christian effort to reach homosexuals and lesbians. EXODUS upholds God's standard of righteousness and holiness, which declares that homosexuality is sin and affirms His love and redemptive power to recreate the individual.

"It is the goal of EXODUS International to communicate this message to the Church, to the gay community, and to society."

A brand-new network of ministries reaching out to homosexuals was officially underway.

The Opposition Begins
June 1977 – Oakland, California

During the following year, Exodus ministries flourished in a euphoria of mutual fellowship and youthful zeal. The second conference, held in Oakland, California, during June, 1977, attracted over 100 eager participants.

Then the opposition began.

Reporters from local gay and secular newspapers invaded the opening session of the conference. In the next day's *San Francisco Examiner*, Exodus was branded a "fundamentalist, anti-gay organization that uses deprogramming techniques." The local gay press lamented, "Many of the people present were pathetic messes." Frank Worthen was labeled "a happy celibate." Most of the media linked Exodus with the Anita Bryant Crusade making national headlines at that time.

Unfortunately, numerous ministries did not survive the next two years. The reasons are varied. Outreaches which had begun in isolation from the Body of Christ were particularly vulnerable. Without proper spiritual and emotional support, the leaders quit when discouragement hit.

In some cases, the naiveté of local church leaders contributed to a ministry's demise. A few churches began to enthusiastically endorse the idea of ex-gay ministry, but showed a serious lack of judgment in choosing a leader for their outreach. Having "a testimony" was seen as the only qualification necessary, even if the ex-gay leader had only been a Christian for several months.

Some leaders featured in national Christian magazines had a moral relapse soon after their stories were published. Sadly enough, most of these catastrophes could have been avoided. People's stories were often written up prematurely. Back then, an ex-gay testimony was unique; publishers didn't look too closely at how long someone had been out of homosexual behavior before pushing them into the public eye.

So the early days of the ex-gay movement were like the early days of flight: some pioneers soared to new and unknown heights, but there were also some spectacular, and highly-publicized, crashes. A few churches, and even whole denominations, were so burned that it took them years to once again look at healing ministry for homosexuals.

Spiritual warfare also began in earnest. The homosexual world was Satan's domain and, until now, few Christians had publicly testified of a homosexual past. Indeed, many churches were dubious as to whether such a change was even possible. The enemy wanted to hide the possibility of healing from homosexuality. Those who came forward with such claims were hit with increased temptations when their testimonies were publicized.

The ex-gay movement also attracted ridicule from various religious pro-gay groups. One leader of a national pro-gay ministry began publishing booklets "exposing" the Exodus movement. His newsletter publicized the news whenever any ex-gay leader fell back into sin.

Exodus leaders also faced opposition at the local level. One ministry director, speaking at a local Presbyterian seminary, had faculty members stand up and openly ridicule his position during an evening presentation. Other ministries found it nearly impossible to get bookings in local churches when their subject matter became known.

The press, the church, the spiritual warfare – all provided a challenge to the ex-gay movement. But perhaps the most difficult test was just ahead: internal strife within Exodus itself.

Friction From Within

June, 1979 – San Rafael, California

It was a sunny Sunday morning, and I couldn't wait to get to church. One of my pastors, Frank Worthen, was due back from the annual Exodus conference and I was anxious to hear all the details.

I spotted Frank almost as soon as I walked into church. "How was the conference?" I asked eagerly. Frank looked past me. "I don't even want to talk about it," he groaned, and walked away.

I was stunned.

Recently relocated from Vancouver, Canada, I'd only been at Love In Action for three weeks. In the following months, I overheard bits and pieces about what had transpired at the Exodus IV conference. What I heard wasn't too encouraging.

The gathering, held at a retreat center near Johnstown, PA., had been a fiasco. Only ex-gay ministry leaders were invited, and it was anticipated as a week of intense prayer and seeking the Lord about unresolved questions related to overcoming homosexuality.

But as the week progressed, a crisis developed. It soon became apparent that there were two groups of people at the conference, both with a very different opinion on a crucial issue. One group insisted that the term "ex-gay" implied heterosexuality and the possibility of marriage; another group thought that sexual orientation could not be changed and they were ready to settle for "homosexual celibacy."

Each side was adamant; during the week, there were some flaring tempers, harsh words and hurt feelings. A deep feeling of disunity engulfed the group. Discouragement was rife; one leader suggested buying T-shirts for all delegates bearing the slogan, "I survived the Johnstown disaster."

By the end of the week, there was one main question on the hearts of many leaders: would Exodus survive?

Actually, these controversies were not new. Brewing under the surface since the inception of Exodus, they came to a full boil the week of Exodus IV in 1979. But they had been prodded along by a speaker at the previous year's conference.

"Our acceptance of gay people, both orientation and behavior, must be greater" he told delegates. "God may never enable me to lose my gay orientation, no matter how hard I try. But I'm glad that I'm still part of a body of believers who will take me as I am."

The speaker's suggestion that his same-sex orientation might never change startled Exodus board members, who immediately held an impromptu meeting in the hallway outside the classroom. They decided to finish the session with discussion by the whole group.

"It sounds like you're offering no way out," a ministry leader challenged the speaker. By the time others had expressed other opinions, it was clear that a Pandora's box of controversy had opened.

This controversy was not easily resolved for several reasons. The ex-gay movement was still young, and some ministry directors were not yet solidly grounded in the Scriptures. A lot of their opinions were based on personal experience – and they were still in the process of being healed from their homosexual past.

When it came to answering questions on the nature of redemption and sanctification – specifically applied to the homosexual issue – few of these leaders were sufficiently informed to give in-depth answers.

Exodus was also undergoing the painful growth process

of encompassing many different denominational belief systems and approaches to ministry. Although some differences were obvious – demonic deliverance versus discipleship, instant change versus long-term healing – others were much more subtle, such as the nature of sanctification of the role of women in leadership.

It was becoming increasingly obvious that there was a variety of opinions within Exodus on a fundamental question: "What does it really mean to be healed from homosexuality?"

New Understanding
1979-1980 – San Rafael, California

In July of 1979, a new series of teachings began appearing monthly in the *Outpost* newsletter, an ex-gay ministry in Minneapolis. Written by Ed Hurst, the material presented a startling new truth to me: homosexuality was just the surface symptom of deeper "root" issues which needed healing. I'd probably heard this concept before, but it had never hit me with such power.

Over the next year, I eagerly watched each month for a new "root" to be discussed. As the months passed, Ed covered such topics as self-pity, rejection, fear, envy, deception, rebellion and bitterness. He related them all to the specific issue of homosexuality and I was amazed at the depth of his insights.

"If I could just get rid of this one problem in my life [homosexuality], then I'd really have it together as a Christian," had always been my attitude. Now, for the first time, I began to recognize how extensive a healing God needed to do in my life.

I realized that as these underlying issues were resolved, the issue of homosexuality would be changed in my life. Just as poison applied to the roots of a tree eventually brings the whole structure crashing down, so I had to allow the Lord to deal with the hidden "roots" of my sexual identity struggles.

In one sense, the "tap root" of my struggle had ended

when I said "yes" to the Lord in moving to Love In Action. At that time, I had handed over my sexuality to Him in a new way, extending His Lordship into that area of my life. (I've come to realize that the Lordship of Christ can be an ongoing decision, as God brings new areas of our life to light, areas which still need to be surrendered to Him.)

In the ministry, I came to see the importance of "walking in the light" with other believers, being willing to open the deepest parts of my life to those who could offer loving support. Because I had never acted on my homosexual desires, I did not have to struggle with such issues as achieving celibacy or leaving a lover. But the "roots" that prompted the same-sex attractions were just as deep in me as in others who came to Love in Action seeking help.

In fact, I discovered that, after others had been at the ministry for some months or even several years, they came to the same point where I had begun when I first arrived: dealing with the deeper issues or "roots." As sexual purity began to come forth, they no longer worried about sexual involvement with another person; they began to wrestle with issues like pornography, masturbation, and a disciplined thought life.

As the healing process continued, deeper and deeper levels of one's life were touched. Freedom was a process, occurring step by step over a period of time.

I also came to appreciate the church's role in healing. My home church in San Rafael was a perfect example. Church of the Open Door is an interdenominational fellowship which is very open to the ministry of Love In Action. All the staff attend that church; Frank Worthen is one of the pastoral staff. The ministry has been intimately involved in the church for over fifteen years. During a typical Sunday morning service, up to half the people leading the service are graduates of the LIA program – from organist to pianist to soloist to sound technician. Members are involved in the church structure at every level.

In this church, I experienced something new: honest communication and fellowship with men who had never been gay. In previous churches, I fit well into the singles' groups, but I'd always carefully hidden my sexual struggles. At Open Door, such anonymity was impossible. As soon as people found out why you'd come to San Rafael, you were known as a participant in "the program."

But, to most people at Open Door, it didn't matter.

Men in the church were friendly and affectionate to all of us Love In Action members. Their support was very affirming. And I learned about the struggles of non-gays, too. I was amazed at their private confessions: straight men would tell me that they, too, had struggled with the homosexual issue in some way in their past, although not to the same depth I had. They may have experienced a certain curiosity, or had an experience with another boy during early adolescence, or had some doubt or question about their own sexual identity somewhere along the line. Or maybe they had also struggled with pornography or masturbation. Sexual purity was an issue for *all* of us.

My relationships took on a whole new depth that I'd never experienced before. For years, I'd lived behind walls of fear and isolation, keeping the truth of my homosexual struggles carefully hidden. Now I was living "outside the walls" for the first time in my life. And in ways I did not even know at the time, I was being healed at a deeper level of my identity as a male than I'd ever known.

Outside Input

June, 1980 – Seattle, Washington

By June 1980, the uproar from Exodus IV had subsided and the conference was a resounding success. Keynote speaker for the week was Art Katz, a Messianic Jew with a prophetic ministry, who presented a challenging call to personal holiness to the 51 conferees.

Katz' message was "something a lot of us needed," recalls

Robbi Kenney, a member of the Exodus board during that time. "Art was instrumental in bringing some new understanding of what God was requiring of us all in the area of personal holiness."

At one memorable session, Katz told delegates about the first time his Christian community in rural Minnesota had to slaughter a pig, which had put up a horrible fight before it dies. "That's what the sin nature is like," he told us. "It kicks and squirms and squeals until it's totally dead."

Then Katz explained. Our sinful past would fight to survive, but we had to daily put it to death through the power of Christ working in us. His story was a graphic illustration not soon forgotten. After that conference, one delegate had some new stationery printed with the bold heading in gold script: "There is a dead pig reality." And Exodus president Frank Worthen collected pig memorabilia for years after that gathering.

Despite the jokes, Exodus leaders realized an important lesson: The church at large had important input to offer our small group of ex-gay members. Any group in isolation can head off into a doctrinal wasteland; with the help of the whole Body of Christ, hopefully Exodus could stay on track.

Arthur Katz had another significant contribution to Exodus that week. With his prodding, the board took an unequivocable stand against the idea that a homosexual orientation was somehow acceptable or even neutral. The general consensus among Exodus leaders from that point on: temptation is not sin (Hebrews 4:15), but the homosexual orientation is an expression of humanity's sinfulness – and cannot comfortably coexist within the context of a total commitment to Jesus Christ.

That same year, the Exodus policy statement on homosexuality was published. Drawn up by several members of the Exodus board, it took a firm stand: "liberation from homosexuality includes repentance from homosexual behavior, identity and lifestyle."

Frank Worthen left no doubt where he stood when his ministry, Love In Action, published a newsletter that September:

"At a recent conference, I took issue with some brothers who were calling themselves 'homosexual Christians.' In our discussion, which lasted several hours, I used the word 'anathema' to describe how I regarded the use of the term. . . . I utterly reject the joining of two words that are so diametrically opposed to one another."

Frank said this position denied one of the major themes of the New Testament: "We have a new identity in Christ." A few people quietly left Exodus at this point, but most stayed and embraced the position that Frank, as Exodus president, had forcefully affirmed.

Relocation to San Rafael
January 1983

"Exodus has tended to be an inward-looking group," said Alan Medinger to the rest of the Exodus board during their mid-winter meeting in Denver. "Our vision has been too narrow. We've not been on the offensive in proclaiming Christ's power to deliver people from homosexuality."

The other board members agreed with Alan's challenge and met for special prayer the next day. During their final session together, they offered suggestions on how to implement a solution to the problems Alan had expressed.

The board decided to permanently locate the Exodus office in San Rafael, California, where mail would be overseen by staff from Love In Action, the largest and best-established of the ex-gay ministries. The Exodus office would also give assistance and advice to new ministries, plus publish books, tapes and other materials to aid ministries and churches desiring help in reaching homosexuals.

Public exposure for the annual conference was increased. Exodus VIII that year was advertised in several national publications. The board decided to form an overseeing board of reference, drawing well-known people from several denominations, who could "watch over" the board of directors. During the next year, a ten-person board of reference was formed, consisting of Christian leaders from numerous denominations.

Increasing publicity came to Exodus ministries during the next several years. National publications like *Charisma* and *Christianity Today* began reporting on our activities, prompting a flood of mail to the San Rafael office.

These magazines affirmed the legitimacy of the Exodus movement. For example, Beth Spring wrote the following statements in the September 21, 1984, issue of *Christianity Today*: "Until more churches learn to address the acute spiritual and emotional needs of homosexuals, groups that are part of the Exodus coalition intend to fill the gap. Staffed by people who have endured the pain of passage out of homosexual behavior, these ministries offer authentic models of change for men and women still struggling with a misplaced sexual identity."

An increasing number of new books coming out on sexual issues began referring readers to the Exodus address and phone number. The largest Christian radio and television ministries around the nation began using Exodus as a referral for their listeners seeking help with homosexuality. Exodus was rapidly gaining a new level of credibility in Christian circles.

A New Urgency

June 1987 – St. Paul, Minnesota

"We are in a spiritual battle of staggering proportions," said Alan Medinger in his closing address at the Exodus XII conference. Over 200 men and women from 45 different ex-gay ministries around the nation listened attentively as Alan continued.

"Until now, widespread church support for redemptive ministry to homosexuals has been lacking, but AIDS is changing that. Voices in the church previously speaking out in defense of the homosexual lifestyle are now strangely silent."

During the early 1980s, Exodus ministries had noticed a growing disinterest in the church over the issue of homosexuality. Multiple books on the subject had poured off the evangelical presses in the late '70s, then there was silence. During the same time period, the theology of homosexual behavior had been fervently debated in mainline denominations, then most of the committees had turned their attention to other "urgent" issues of the day.

Then came AIDS.

Suddenly, the topic of homosexuality was of crucial concern again. Pastors around the nation were shocked to discover that members of their church had been infected with the AIDS virus, mostly through homosexual activities. The problem of homosexuality – even within evangelical churches – could no longer be ignored.

So the AIDS issue created a new wave of interest in ex-gay ministry. Attendance at the annual Exodus conference climbed to 125, then 200, then soared to 350 people.

There was a new spurt in the formation of ex-gay ministries, and most of them sought affiliation with Exodus. Drawing on the lessons of the past, the Exodus board drew up a list of strict qualifications for these new ministries seeking Exodus endorsement.

The most important qualification concerned local accountability. In the early days, too many ministries had operated as "lone rangers," without any supervision from the local church community. Now, Exodus ministries were required to have local spiritual accountability by a local pastor or board.

Exodus leaders were also cautious about endorsing ministries begun by new converts. So ministry directors were required to be free from homosexual activity for at least one year before their application for endorsement would be considered. All ministry directors were also required to be active participants in a local church, so that Exodus leaders would be thoroughly integrated into their local church congregations.

These changes in ministry standards during the mid-1980s produced increased stability and maturity in the ex-gay movement. The recidivism rate among ministry leaders declined drastically, compared to the early days of Exodus. As ministry directors matured, an increasing number entered into marriage and parenthood (Frank Worthen was married in November, 1984). These men and women became leaders in their local church fellowships *apart from* their homosexual background, rather than their "testimony" being the basis of leadership.

The Exodus conferences attracted an increasing number of pastors and lay counselors who did not have a homosexual past, but who realized the urgent need of addressing the homosexual issue in their local community.

Outstanding pastors, denominational leaders, psychologists and other Christian leaders spoke at the annual conferences, which grew to include over 400 participants. Theological imbalances were hammered out as these speakers addressed many issues from a wide spectrum of denominational viewpoints.

International Growth

Exodus also saw a significant growth internationally during the early 1980s. Five participants came to the 1981 Exodus conference from the Netherlands. One of them, Johan van de Sluis, had been out of homosexuality for over ten years and was directing a street ministry in Amsterdam.

Johan returned home after the conference, determined to help launch a European coalition of ex-gay ministries. He wrote letters to many Christian organizations in Europe, and the response was so positive that Johan began planning a European Exodus conference.

In May 1982, about 75 men and women gathered at "De Burght," a Christian conference center on the south coast of

Holland. Participants came from the Netherlands, Great Britain, West Germany, Denmark, France, Switzerland and the USA. The Europeans expressed a desire to be an autonomous group with their own board, functioning equally with the Exodus North American coalition. Soon Exodus Europe was off and running.

Meanwhile, similar activities were occurring in the South Pacific. Peter Lane, a former worker for Teen Challenge in Queensland, Australia, had been street witnessing to homosexuals for over six years when he visited Love In Action in San Rafael during the summer of 1983.

Peter returned home with a new determination to help develop ex-gay ministries around Australia and New Zealand. Over the next five years, several ministries did begin, or were strengthened through Peter's enthusiastic support. Interestingly, most were directed by men who – like Peter – had never struggled with the homosexual issue in their own lives.

The resulting coalition joined the growing international network as "Exodus South Pacific" in January 1988. Ministries in Australia and New Zealand now gather for their own annual conference.

Today, Exodus International encompasses 65 ministries in 40 different U.S. states, two Canadian outreaches, ten ministries in six European countries, seven ministries in Australia and three in New Zealand.

Plans are underway for ex-gay ministries to be established in other world regions, primarily South America and the Far East. An increasing number of North American workers are being sent overseas to establish new works, or to strengthen already-existing foreign outreaches.

And no one is more thrilled about the growth of Exodus than Roberta Laurila, whose prayers through the years have continued unabated since her vision back in 1967.

"Much happened since that time," she agrees. "While I continued to intercede, God began calling forth former gays to minister. I have been blessed beyond measure. What a wonderful God He is!"

All around the world, former homosexuals share her excitement about a life-changing God. And they're grateful for the prayers of one faithful woman who led the way.

B. MINISTRY REFERRAL LIST

This list is updated regularly. Please inform Exodus of any information changes. Applications for referral membership are available from our headquarters office. *Qualifications for Referral Ministries*: Agreement with Exodus doctrine and policy, in existence at least two years; has a policy-making board or governing body with the power to remove or change leadership. The ministry director has been free from immoral sexual behavior for at least two years; has attended a national Exodus conference; is active in a local church and has spiritual accountability there.

Each entry includes a list of whom the ministry is equipped to help, and may include any of the following: men and women overcoming homosexuality, family/friends, spouses, adolescent females and males, children of gay parents, HIV+ persons, pedophiles, female and male survivors of sexual abuse, heterosexual and homosexual sexual addicts, transsexuals, and transvestites. Each entry also lists services available in three categories: support, resources, and other. Contact ministries directly for further details on services they offer.

Abbreviations and terms: "men" stands for men overcoming homosexuality; "women" stands for women overcoming lesbianism. "Lic./prof." stands for "licensed/professional" counseling. "Living Waters" is a structured, small group program for addressing issues surrounding sexual brokenness. "Library" indicates a lending and/or reference library is available. If a ministry is listed as offering several kinds of groups in several locations, not necessarily each type of group is offered in each location.

Most ministries have phone message machines, and some ministries will *only* return long-distance phone calls if you specify they may call you back collect. Also, phone support may require your making an appointment, and letter support may be for a limited time only.

ALABAMA

Nikon, PO Box 19631, Birmingham, AL 35219. 205/967-7273. Tom Nelson. *Serves* men, women, family/friends, spouses, sexual abuse survivors (female, male). *Support*: individual lay consultation. *Other*: seminars, speaking engagements.

ALASKA

Kerusso Ministries, PO Box 210909, Anchorage, AK 99521. 907/333-4673 (M-Th/10-4). Michael Johnston. *Serves*: men, women, family/friends, spouses, adolescents (female, male), children of gay parents, HIV+ persons, pedophiles, sexual abuse survivors (female, male), sexual addicts (heterosexual, homosexual), transsexuals, transvestites. *Support*: group (integrated Bible study and support within established adolescent, single adult, young married, single mother, and older adult groups within the church body), individual lay consultation, letter, phone (24 hours daily). *Resources*: literature, newsletter. *Other*: evangelism, HIV/AIDS ministry, seminars, speaking engagements.

CALIFORNIA

Los Angeles, Orange County, and San Diego Area

Desert Stream Ministries, 12488 Venice Blvd., Los Angeles, CA 90066-3804. 310/572-0140 (M-F/1-5). Andy Comiskey. *Serves*: men, women, family/friends of HIV patients, HIV+ persons, sexual abuse survivors (female, male), sexual addicts (heterosexual, homosexual). *Support*: groups – Los Angeles area and Orange County (HIV/AIDS, family/friends of people with HIV), individual lay consultation, Living Waters (men, women), phone (M-F/1-5), referrals to lic./prof. counseling. *Resources*: audiotapes, literature, newsletter, videotapes. *Other*: HIV/AIDS ministry and training, Living Waters Leadership Training, seminars, speaking engagements.

Genesis Counseling, 2745 E. Chapman Ave. #202, Orange, CA 92669. 714/744-3326 (M-F/10-3). Joe Dallas. *Serves*: men, women, family/friends, spouses, HIV+ persons, pedophiles, sexual addicts (heterosexual, homosexual), transsexuals, transvestites. *Support*: groups (men, wives, parents/family), individual lay consultation, lic./prof. counseling. *Resources*: audiotapes, newsletter, videotapes. *Other*: educational resources, seminars, speaking engagements.

Thomas Aquinas Psychological Clinic, 16542 Ventura Blvd. #416, Encino, CA 91436. 818/789-4440 (24-hour answering service). Joseph Nicolosi. *Serves*: men, family/friends, adolescent males, children of gay parents, sexual abuse survivors (male), sexual addicts (homosexual). *Support*: group (men), lic./prof. counseling, phone (by appointment). *Resources*: audiotapes, library, literature, videotapes. *Others*: seminars, speaking engagements.

Sacramento Area

HIS Ministry, c/o Sunrise Baptist Church, 8321 Greenback Ln., Fair Oaks, CA 95628-2699 (Sacramento area). 916/969-3929 (M-Th/8-5; F/8-4). Carl Conli. *Serves*: men, family/friends, spouses, adolescent males. *Support*: groups (men, parents/family), individual lay consultation.

San Francisco Bay Area

Agapao, 501 Cambridge St., San Francisco, CA 94134. 415/586-9495 (Tu-F/9-noon; New Life Vineyard). Jim Brooks. *Serves*: men, women, family/friends, spouses, sexual addicts (heterosexual, homosexual). *Support*: group (men, women), individual lay consultations.

Love In Action, PO Box 2655, San Rafael, CA 94912. 415/454-0960 (M-F/9:30-12;1-5). John Smid. *Serves*: men, women, family/friends, spouses, adolescents (female, male), children of gay parents, HIV+ persons, pedophiles, sexual abuse survivors (female, male), sexual addicts (heterosexual, homosexual), transsexuals, transvestites. *Support*: groups (women), individual lay consultation, letter, phone. *Resources*: literature, newsletter. *Other*: men's live-in program, seminars, speaking engagements.

New Beginnings, 175 Nortech Parkway, San Jose, CA 95134. 408/262-0900 extension 412. Jakii Edwards. *Serves*: men, women, children of gay parents, sexual addicts (heterosexual, homosexual). *Support*: group (multi-cultural, co-ed group), individual lay consultation, phone. *Other*: Bible studies, evangelism, seminars, speaking engagements.

Transformed Image, PO Box 51411, San Jose, CA 95151. 408/496-9888 (Tu-F). Michael Dismore. *Serves*: men, women, family/friends, spouses, HIV+ persons, sexual addicts (homosexual), others (we have a sign language interpreter for the deaf at our support group meeting on a bi-weekly basis). *Support*: groups (men, women, other – occasional group meetings for family members), individual lay consultation (one time only), letter, phone (by appointment, evening hours preferably). *Resources*: library, literature. *Other*: networking with churches, speaking engagements to youth groups and Bible studies.

Words of Life, 1608 Claycord Ave., Concord, CA 94521. 510/685-4343 or 510/825-7138. Michael Duarte. *Serves*: men, family/friends, spouses, adolescent males, children of gay parents, HIV+ persons, pedophiles, sexual abuse survivors (male), sexual addicts (heterosexual, homosexual). *Support*: groups (men, parents/family, HIV/AIDS), individual lay consultation, letter, Living Waters (men), phone. *Other*: speaking engagements.

Other Areas

The David Project, 42 Broadmoor Plaza #3, Santa Barbara, CA 93105. 805/569-2486. Herb Davids. *Serves*: men, family/friends, spouses, children of gay parents, pedophiles, sexual abuse survivors (male), sexual addicts (heterosexual, homosexual). *Support*: individual lay consultation, phone. *Resources*: audiotapes, library. *Other*: seminars, speaking engagements.

Liberty, PO Box 2652, Lompoc, CA 93438. 805/735-8143. Carol Norrander. *Serves*: women, family/friends. *Support*: individual lay consultation, letter, phone. *Resources*: audiotapes, library, literature, videotapes.

New Creation Ministries, 2513 W. Shaw Ave. #102-A, Fresno, CA 93711. 209/227-1066(M/1-4; Tu-F/9-noon, 1-4). Bud Searcy. *Serves*: men, women, family/friends, spouses, adolescents (female, male), HIV+ persons, sexual addicts (heterosexual, homosexual), other (Christian leaders struggling with sexual issues). *Support*: groups — Fresno, Visalia (men — combined ex-gay and sexual addiction, women, parents/family, wives, TLC series on sexual addiction), individual lay consultation, letter, phone. *Resources*: audiotapes, library, literature, newsletter. *Other*: consultations with pastors/leaders on Transforming Congregations, evangelism, seminars, speaking engagements.

COLORADO

Where Grace Abounds, PO Box 18871, Denver, CO 80218. 303/322-2027 (Tu-F/9-5). Mary Heathman. *Serves*: men, women, family/friends, spouses, sexual abuse survivors (female, male), sexual addicts (heterosexual, homosexual), transsexuals, transvestites. *Support*: groups – Boulder, Colorado Springs, Denver; individual lay consultation; letter; lic./prof. counseling; phone. *Resources*: audiotapes, literature, newsletter. *Other*: seminars, speaking engagements.

CONNECTICUT

HOPE Ministries, BOX 604, 60 Skiff St., Hamden, CT 06517. 203/248-5274 (M-F/11 AM-6 PM). Bill Consiglio. *Serves*: men, women, family/friends, spouses, sexual abuse survivors (male), sexual addicts (homosexual). *Support*: groups – Hamden, CT; Northampton, MA; New York, NY; Providence, RI (men, women, parents/family, wives), lic./prof. counseling, letter, phone. *Other*: seminars, speaking engagements.

Shoreline Christian Ministries, 17 Water St., Guilford, CT 06437. 203/453-2390 (M-Th, Sat/9-5). Tom Ruotolo. *Serves*: men, women, family/friends, spouses, adolescents (female, male), pedophiles, sexual abuse survivors (female, male), sexual addicts (heterosexual, homosexual), other (willing to help transsexuals and transvestites). *Support*: individual lay consultation, lic./prof. counseling, phone. *Resources*: audiotapes, library, literature, newsletter. *Other*: seminars, speaking engagements.

DELAWARE

See also Pennsylvania – Harvest for a group in Wilmington, DE. (Harvest: 215/985-4031.)

FLORIDA

Eleutheros, 1298 Minnesota Ave. Ste. D, Winter Park, FL 32789 (Orlando area). 407/629-5770 (M-Th/10 AM-4:30 PM). Rick and Gwen Hughes. *Serves*: men, women, family/friends, spouses, HIV+ persons, sexual abuse survivors (female, male), sexual addicts (heterosexual, homosexual). *Support*: groups (men, women, parents/family, wives, adult survivors of childhood abuse [men, women], Search for Significance [men]), individual lay consultation, lic./prof. counseling, phone. *Resources*: audiotapes, literature, newsletter, videotapes. *Other*: HIV/AIDS ministry, seminars, speaking engagements.

Eleutheros – Gainesville, 2631 NW 41st St. Suite C-2, Gainesville, FL 32606. 904/371-2466. Dean Schultz. Contact for details of services available.

Eleutheros – Jacksonville, 5640 Timuquana Rd. Suite 6, Jacksonville, FL 32210. 904/778-0638. Myra Noyes. Contact for details of services available.

Straight Ahead, c/o Calvary Temple, PO Box 16889, Temple Terrace, FL 33687 (Tampa area). 813/988-3557. David Steege. *Serves*: men, women, family/friends, spouses, sexual abuse survivors (female, male), sexual addicts (homosexual). *Support*: groups – Clearwater, Tampa (men, women, other), Living Waters (men, women). *Resources*: audiotapes, library. *Other*: seminars, speaking engagements.

Worthy Creations, 3601 Davie Blvd., Ft. Lauderdale, FL 33312. 305/680-3538 (M-F/noon-5). Richard Culbertson. *Serves*: men, women, family/friends, spouses, children of gay parents, HIV+ persons, sexual abuse survivors (female, male), sexual addicts(homosexual), transsexuals, transvestites. *Support*: groups – Davie, Ft. Lauderdale, Ft. Myers, Hollywood, Miami, Pompano, West Palm Beach (men, women, parents/family, HIV/AIDS), individual lay consultation, Living Waters (men, women), phone, referral to lic./prof. counseling. *Resources*: audiotapes, literature, videotapes. *Other*: Bible studies, HIV/AIDS ministry, seminars, speaking engagements.

GEORGIA

Living Stones Fellowship, c/o Mt. Paran Church of God, 2055 Mt. Paran Rd. NW, Atlanta, GA 30327. 404/261-0720, extension 280. John Barber. *Support*: group. *Resources*: literature.

Pneumatikos, PO Box 6808, Macon, GA 31208. 912/825-1158 (M-Th/5:45 PM-10 PM; F-Sun/all day). Randy Hortman. *Serves*: men, women, family/friends, spouses, adolescents (female, male), HIV+ persons. *Support*: group (men, women), individual lay consultation, letter, phone. *Resources*: audiotapes, library, literature, newsletter, videotapes. *Other*: evangelism, speaking engagements.

Resurrection Ministries (formerly called Katapauo), PO Box 95205, Atlanta, GA 30347. 404/636-5924. (M-F/9-5). Mike Caven. *Serves*: men, women, family/friends, spouses, adolescents (female, male), pedophiles, sexual abuse survivors (female, male), sexual addicts (heterosexual, homosexual), transvestites. *Support*: groups (men, parents/family), individual lay consultation, Living Waters (men, women). *Resources*: literature, newsletter. *Other*: seminars; speaking engagements; Friday evening praise, worship, and Bible study.

IDAHO

Bellwether Ministries, PO Box 15766, Boise, ID 83715. 208/376-2559 (M-F/9-4:30). Sharon Slocum. *Serves*: men, women, family/friends, spouses, HIV+ persons, adolescents (female, male), children of gay parents, sexual addicts (homosexual). *Support*: group (wives), individual lay consultation, letter (limited), lic./prof. counseling, Living Waters (men, women), phone. *Resources*: audiotapes, library, literature, videotapes. *Other*: evangelism, HIV/AIDS ministry, seminars, speaking engagements.

ILLINOIS

Nehemiah Ministries and Fellowship, PO Box 773, Urbana, IL 61801. 217/344-4636 (M-F/8-5). Kent Paris. *Serves*: men, family/friends, spouses, adolescent males, children of gay parents. *Support*: group – Champaign (men), individual lay consultation, letter, phone. *Resources*: newsletter. *Other*: seminars, speaking engagements.

Reconstruction Ministries, 3457 N. University #200, Peoria, IL 61604. 309/679-1347. Contact for details of services available.

IOWA

Freedom Ministries, PO Box 12189, Des Moines, IA 50312-9404. 515/244-8073. Jack Morlan. *Serves*: men. *Support*: group (men). *Resources*: audiotapes, library, literature. *Other*: seminars, speaking engagements.

KANSAS

Freedom At Last, PO Box 13314, Wichita, KS 67213. 316/267-8779 (M,Tu,Th). Michael Babb. *Serves*: men, women, family/friends, spouses, adolescents (female, male), children of gay parents, HIV+ persons, sexual abuse survivors (female, male), sexual addicts (heterosexual, homosexual), transsexuals, transvestites. *Support*: groups – Hutchinson, Wichita (men, women, parents/family, wives, HIV/AIDS), individual lay consultation, letter, Living Waters (men, women), phone. *Resources*: audiotapes, library, literature, newsletter. *Other*: evangelism, HIV/AIDS ministry, live-in program (men), seminars, speaking engagements, other (in process of organizing a hospice).

Second Chance Ministries, PO Box 12265, Overland Park, KS 66282-2265 (Kansas City area). 913/541-1044 (M-F/1-5). Pat Smith. *Serves*: men, women, family/friends, spouses, sexual abuse survivors (female, male), sexual addicts (homosexual), transsexuals, transvestites. *Support*: groups – Overland Park, KS, and Kansas City, MO (parents/family; female and male sexual abuse survivors), individual lay consultation, Living Waters (men, women), phone. *Resources*: audiotapes, library, newsletter. *Other*: Bible studies, seminars, speaking engagements.

KENTUCKY

CrossOver Ministries, PO Box 23744, Lexington, KY 40523. 606/277-4941. Jerry Leach. *Serves*: men, women, family/friends, spouses, HIV+ persons, sexual abuse survivors (female, male), sexual addicts (heterosexual, homosexual), transsexuals, transvestites. *Support*: groups (men, women, parents/family, wives, HIV/AIDS), individual lay consultation, letter, Living Waters (men, women), phone (Wednesday; every evening). *Resources*: audiotapes, library, literature, newsletter, videotapes. *Other*: HIV/AIDS ministry, seminars, speaking engagements.

Pathway Ministries, PO Box 9404, Louisville, KY 40209-0404. 502/361-2106. Martin Ward. *Support*: group, individual lay consultation. *Resources*: literature, newsletter. *Other*: speaking engagements.

MAINE

Amazing Grace Ministries, PO Box 8234, Portland, ME 04104. 207/879-2554. Jane Boyer. *Serves*: men, women, family/friends, spouses, sexual addicts (heterosexual, homosexual), transsexuals, transvestites. *Support*: groups (parents/family, wives), individual lay consultation, letter, Living Waters (men, women), phone. *Resources*: audiotapes, library, literature, newsletter. *Other*: seminars, speaking engagements.

Crown of Life Ministry, PO Box 11404, Portland, ME 04104. 207/828-1025. Rev. Edgar Bailey. *Serves*: men, family/friends, spouses, sexual abuse survivors (male), sexual addicts (homosexual), transsexuals, transvestites. *Support*: group – South Portland (men), individual lay consultation, phone. *Resources*: audiotapes, library, literature. *Other*: seminars, speaking engagements.

MARYLAND

Regeneration, PO Box 9830, Baltimore, MD 21284. 410/661-0284 (M-F). Regeneration Books information line: 410/661-4337. Alan Medinger. *Serves*: men, women, spouses, pedophiles, sexual addicts (heterosexual, homosexual). *Support*: groups (men, women, sexual addiction [heterosexual men]), individual lay consultation, lic./prof. counseling, letter, phone. *Resources*: literature, newsletter. *Other*: catalog of books on homosexuality, inner healing prayer, prison ministry to sex offenders, seminars, speaking engagements.

MASSACHUSETTS

Transformation Ministries of Boston, PO Box 1313 Back Bay Annex, Boston, MA 02117. 617/445-1787. Peter Robicheau. *Serves*: men, family/friends, spouses, adolescent males, sexual abuse survivors (male), sexual addicts (heterosexual, homosexual), transsexuals. *Support*: group (men), individual lay consultation, letter, phone. *Resources*: audiotapes, literature, newsletter. *Other*: evangelism, seminars, speaking engagements.

White Stone Ministries, c/o Ruggles Baptist Church, 874 Beacon St., Boston, MA 02215. 617/266-3633 (Tu-F/9-4). Bob Boudrow. *Serves*: men, women, family/friends, spouses, adolescent males, children of gay parents, HIV+ persons, sexual abuse survivors (female, male), sexual addicts (heterosexual, homosexual), transsexuals, transvestites. *Support*: groups (parents/family, wives), lic./prof. counseling, Living Waters (men, women), phone (Tu-Th/12-4 PM). *Resources*: literature, newsletter. *Other*: seminars, speaking engagements.

HOPE Ministries, College Church, PO Box 203, Northampton, MA 01061. 413/586-0057. Pastor Dave McDowell. Contact for details of services available.

MICHIGAN

Hyperniken Counseling Services, 2020 Raybrook SE #206, Grand Rapids, MI 49546. 616/942-2063 (M-F/9-5). Vern Dunmire. *Serves*: men, women, family/friends, spouses, adolescents (female, male), children of gay parents, HIV+ persons, pedophiles, sexual abuse survivors (female, male), sexual addicts (heterosexual, homosexual), other (child sexual abuse, family, couple/marriage). Also general Christian counseling. *Support*: groups (men), individual lay consultation, lic./prof. counseling. *Other*: seminars, speaking engagements.

Reconciliation Ministries, PO Box 10237, Detroit, MI 48210-0237. 313/730-8111 (M-F/9-5). Greg Tousignant. *Serves*: men, women, family/friends, spouses, adolescents (female, male), children of gay parents, HIV+ persons, pedophiles, sexual abuse survivors (female, male), sexual addicts (heterosexual, homosexual), transvestites. *Support*: groups – Detroit, Romulus, St. Clair Shores (men, parents/family, wives), individual lay consultation, letter, lic./prof. counseling, phone (M-Sat/9-5). *Resources*: audiotapes, literature, newsletter. *Other*: HIV/AIDS ministry, seminars, speaking engagements.

MINNESOTA

Eagle's Wings, c/o North Heights Lutheran Church, 1700 Hwy. 96, Arden Hills, MN 55112. 612/522-2782 (M-Th/1-4:30). Wendell and Nancy Anderson. *Serves*: men, women, family/friends, spouses, HIV+ persons, sexual abuse survivors (female, male). *Support*: groups – Minneapolis (men, women, parents/family, parents of HIV/AIDS, wives), individual lay consultation, letter, phone (M-Th/1-4:30). *Resources*: audiotapes, library, literature, newsletter, videotapes. *Other*: seminars, speaking engagements.

Outpost, PO Box 7067, Minneapolis, MN 55407. 612/827-1419. Joseph Hallett. *Serves*: men, family/friends, spouses, adolescent males, children of gay parents, HIV+ persons, sexual addicts (homosexual). *Support*: groups (men, wives, HIV/AIDS), individual lay consultation, letter, Living Waters (men), phone (Tu-F/11-3). *Resources*: audiotapes, literature, newsletter, videotapes, *Other*: HIV/AIDS ministry, seminars, speaking engagements.

MISSOURI

New Dawn West, 444 W. Grand, Springfield, MO 65807. 417/866-2361 (M-F/9-4). Wayne and Joan Doyle. *Serves*: men, women, family/friends, spouses, sexual abuse survivors (female, male), survivors of rape. *Support*: group (combined men, women, and family members), individual lay consultation, letter, lic./prof. counseling. *Other*: seminars, speaking engagements, witness team.

See also Kansas – Second Chance for a group in Kansas City, Missouri, area. (Second Chance: 913/345-0559.)

NEW HAMPSHIRE

ReCreation Ministries, PO Box 551, Manchester, NH 03105-0551. 603/625-9132. Chuck and Sue Therrien. *Serves*: men, women, family/friends, spouses, HIV+ persons, sexual abuse survivors (male), sexual addicts (homosexual). *Support*: group, individual lay consultation, letter, phone (by appointment only). *Resources*: audiotapes, library, literature, newsletter. *Other*: evangelism, HIV/AIDS ministry, seminars, speaking engagements.

NEW JERSEY

New Dawn Ministries East, PO Box 3689, Wayne, NJ 07474-3689. 201/694-2938 (This is our church office number. Please ask for New Dawn Ministries, leave a message/ number, and Sal will phone back.) Sal and Carol Latella.

Serves: men, women, family/friends, spouses, pedophiles, sexual abuse survivors (female, male), sexual addicts (homosexual). *Support*: group (men), individual lay consultation,, letter, phone (evenings by appointment only). *Other*: referrals to lic./prof. counseling, seminars, speaking engagements.

See also under Pennsylvania – Harvest for a group in Princeton, New Jersey. (Harvest: 215/985-4031.)

NEW MEXICO

Free Indeed Ministries, c/o God's People of Praise, 2417 Wyoming NE, Albuquerque, NM 87112. 505/275-9623 (M-F/9-noon). Barbara Swallow. *Serves*: men, women, family/friends, spouses, pedophiles, sexual abuse survivors (female, male), sexual addicts (homosexual), transvestites. *Support*: group (parents/family), individual lay consultation, letter, Living Waters (men, women) phone. *Resources*: audiotapes, library, literature, videotapes. *Other*: evangelism, seminars, speaking engagements.

NEW YORK

All In His Name Ministries, c/o New Life Assembly of God Church, 14 North Street, Buffalo, NY 14202. 716/881-5558 (church); 716/884-3227 (answering machine). Ralph Frick. *Serves*: men, women, family/friends, spouses, adolescents (female, male), children of gay parents, pedophiles, sexual abuse survivors (female, male), sexual addicts (homosexual), transsexuals, transvestites. *Support*: groups (men, women, parents/family), individual lay consultation, letter, phone (by appointment only). *Resources*: library, literature, newsletter. *Other*: Bible studies, seminars, speaking engagements.

HOPE Ministries of New York City, Calvary Baptist Church, 123 W. 57th St., New York, NY 10019. 212/246-4357. Pastor Ken Geis. Contact for details of services available.

Whosoever Will Ministry, PO Box 277, Middletown, NY 10940. 914/374-8128 (M-F/1-5). Penny Dalton and Elaine Sinnard. *Serves*: men, women, family/friends, spouses, HIV+ persons, sexual abuse survivors (female). *Support*: individual lay consultation, letter, phone (by appointment). *Resources*: library, literature, videotapes. *Other*: Bible studies, speaking engagements.

NORTH CAROLINA

Breaking Free, PO Box 225 DTS, Boone, NC 28607. 704/963-7772 or 919/877-5649. John Benson. *Serves*: men, women, family/friends, spouses, sexual abuse survivors (female, male), sexual addicts (heterosexual, homosexual), other (codependency, self-worth). *Support*: groups (codependency, Search for Significance, Pursuing Sexual Wholeness), individual lay consultation, letter, phone. *Resources*: audiotapes, library, literature, videotapes. *Other*: inner healing conferences, speaking engagements.

Crossroads, PO Box 10388, Charlotte, NC 28212. 704/536-6705. Rick Buchan. *Serves*: men, women, family/friends, spouses, adolescent males, HIV+ persons, sexual abuse survivors (male), sexual addicts (homosexual). *Support*: groups (men, parents/family, wives), individual lay consultation, letter, phone. *Resources*: audiotapes, library, videotapes. *Other*: seminars, speaking engagements.

Olive Branch Ministries, PO Box 20042, Raleigh, NC 27619-0042. 919/829-1489 (M, W-F/6 PM-10 PM). Tony Bishop. *Serves*: men, women, family/friends, spouses, sexual abuse survivors (female, male), sexual addicts (heterosexual, homosexual). *Support*: groups (men, women), individual lay consultation, phone (M, W, Th/6 PM-10 PM; occasionally Sat, Sun). *Resources*: audiotapes, library. *Other*: seminars, speaking engagements.

Recovery House, [formerly called Stepping Stones], 1524 E. Morehead St., Charlotte, NC 28212. 704/342-4433 (M-F/9-5). Linda Marshall. Recovery House is an ecumenical outreach ministry of Catholic Social Services. *Serves*: men, women, family/friends, spouses, sexual addicts (heterosexual, homosexual), transsexuals, transvestites. *Support*: groups (men, women, parents/family, wives), individual lay consultation, letter, Living Waters (men, women), phone. *Resources*: audiotapes, literature, videotapes. *Other*: Bible studies, seminars, social activities, speaking engagement.

OHIO

Healing Touch Ministry, PO Box 395, Dayton, OH 45459. 513/885-1051 (M-F/8-5). Charles Voelker. *Serves*: men, women, family/friends, spouses, adolescents (female, male), children of gay parents, HIV+ persons, pedophiles, sexual abuse survivors (female, male), sexual addicts (heterosexual, homosexual), transsexuals, transvestites. *Support*: groups (men, women, married men, parents/family, wives), individual lay consultation, letter, Living Waters (men, women), phone (M-F/8-5). *Resources*: audiotapes, library, literature, newsletter, videotapes. *Other*: evangelism, HIV/AIDS ministry, seminars, speaking engagements.

Prodigal Ministries, PO Box 19949, Cincinnati, OH 45219-0949. 513/861-0011 (Tu-F/9-5). Jerry Armelli. *Serves*: men, women, family/friends, spouses, adolescents (female, male), HIV+ persons, pedophiles, sexual abuse survivors (female, male), sexual addicts (homosexual), transsexuals, transvestites. *Support*: groups (men, women), individual lay consultation, letter, phone. *Resources*: library, literature, newsletter. *Other*: HIV/AIDS ministry, hospital visitation, seminars, speaking engagements.

OKLAHOMA

The First Stone, 1411 N. Classen Blvd. #111, Oklahoma City,

OK 73106-6619. 405/525-FREE [405/525-3733]. Jeff and Lezlie Janes. *Serves*: men, women, family/friends, spouses, adolescents (female, male), children of gay parents, HIV+ persons, pedophiles, sexual abuse survivors (female, male), sexual addicts (heterosexual, homosexual), transsexuals, transvestites. *Support*: groups – Oklahoma City and Lawton (newcomers, parents/family, wives), individual lay consultation, Living Waters (men, women). *Resources*: audiotapes, library, literature, newsletter, videotapes. *Other*: HIV/AIDS ministry, seminars, speaking engagements.

Restoration Outreach, PO Box 55236, Tulsa, OK 74155. 918/254-1175 (Tu-Sat/9-5). Jerold and Wanda Harris. *Serves*: men, women, family/friends, spouses, adolescents (female, male), children of gay parents, HIV+ persons, sexual abuse survivors (female, male), pedophiles, sexual addicts (heterosexual, homosexual), transsexuals, transvestites. *Support*: individual lay consultation, letter, lic./prof. counseling, phone. *Resources*: literature, newsletter, tapes, videos. *Other*: seminars, speaking engagements.

OREGON

The Portland Fellowship, PO Box 9205, Portland, OR 97207. 503/235-6364 (Tu-F/9-4). Phil Hobizal. *Serves*: men, women, family/friends, spouses, adolescents (female, male), HIV+ persons, *Support*: groups (women, parents/family, HIV/AIDS, other – mixed open meeting for men, women/strugglers, non-strugglers), individual lay consultation, Living Waters (men). *Resources*: audiotapes, library, literature, newsletter, videotapes. *Other*: seminars, speaking engagements.

PENNSYLVANIA

Day Seven Ministries, PO Box 265, Elizabethtown, PA 17022. 717/361-8414. Peter Lines. *Serves*: men, women, spouses, pedophiles, sexual addicts (heterosexual, homosexual). *Support*: groups (men, women, wives), individual lay consultation, letter, phone. *Resources*: library, newsletter. *Other*: seminars, speaking engagements.

Dunamis Ministries, 1111 Wood St., Pittsburgh, PA 15221. 412/731-3828 (M-F/1-6). Michael Lumberger. *Serves*: men, women, spouses, HIV+ persons, sexual abuse survivors (female, male), sexual addicts (heterosexual, homosexual), other (emotional dependency). *Support*: groups (HIV/AIDS, women's sexual abuse survivors), individual lay consultation, lic./prof. counseling, Living Waters (men, women), phone. *Resources*: audiotapes. *Other*: HIV/AIDS ministry, seminars, speaking engagements.

Free!, 321 Gettysburg Pike, Mechanicsburg, PA 17055. 717/766-7904. Gene Chase. *Serves*: men, women, family/friends, spouses, adolescent males, pedophiles, sexual addicts (homosexual). *Support*: groups – Hanover, Mechanicsburg (men, women), individual lay consultation, letter, phone (M-Su/9 PM-10 PM) other times by appointment). *Resources*: audiotapes, library, literature, videotapes. *Other*: seminars, speaking engagements.

Harvest, PO Box 53486, Philadelphia, PA 19105. 215/985-4031 (M-F/9-4:30). John Freeman. *Serves*: men, women, family/friends, spouses, adolescents (female, male), children of gay parents, sexual abuse survivors (female, male), transsexuals, transvestites. *Support*: groups – Philadelphia, PA; Wilmington, DE; Princeton, NJ (men, women, parents/family, wives), individual lay consultation, Living Waters (men), phone, referrals to lic./prof. counseling. *Resources*: audiotapes, literature, newsletter, videotapes. *Other*: seminars, speaking engagements.

RHODE ISLAND

See also Connecticut – HOPE Ministries for a group in Providence, RI. (HOPE Ministries: 203/248-5274).

TENNESSEE

Promise, c/o Christian Counseling Services, PO Box 60383, Nashville, TN 37206. 615/254-8341 (M-W/8 AM-8 PM; Th-F/8 AM-6 PM). Michael Malloy. *Serves*: men, women, family/friends, spouses, adolescents (female, male), HIV+ persons, sexual abuse survivors (female, male), sexual addicts (heterosexual, homosexual – local referral). *Support*: groups (men, women, parents/family), individual lay consultation, lic./prof. counseling. *Resources*: audiotapes, library, literature, newsletter. *Other*: HIV/AIDS ministry, seminars, speaking engagements.

Living Hope, PO Box 3352, Knoxville, TN 37927. 615/673-6552 (M-F/9-5). Jay Henderson. *Serves*: men, women, family/friends, spouses, sexual abuse survivors (male), sexual addicts (homosexual), transsexuals, transvestites. *Support*: groups (men, women), individual lay consultation, letter, Living Waters (men, women), phone. *Resources*: audiotapes, literature, newsletter. *Other*: seminars, speaking engagements, other (housing for homeless/transitional living, shelter for battered women and their children).

TEXAS

Christian Coalition for Reconciliation, PO Box 420437, Houston, TX 77242-0437. 713/465-7045 (M-F/12-5). Michael Newman. *Serves*: men, women, family/friends, spouses, adolescents (female, male), HIV+ persons, sexual abuse survivors (female, male), sexual addicts (heterosexual, homosexual). *Support*: groups (men, women, parents/family), individual lay consultation, Living Waters (men), phone (M-F/12-5). *Resources*: literature, newsletter. *Other*: seminars, speaking engagements.

Living Hope Ministries, PO Box 121012, Arlington, TX 76012. 817/640-4044 [Metro] (M, Th/1-4). Scott Musick. *Serves*: men, women, family/friends, spouses, children of gay parents, sexual abuse survivors (female, male), sexual addicts (homosexual). *Support*: groups (combined men and women, parents/family, wives), individual lay consultation, lic./prof. counseling. *Other*: speaking engagements.

Warrior! Ministries, 2611 Baltimore Ave., Wichita Falls, TX 76309-3705. 817/696-8114. Bradford Cosway. *Support*: group, individual lay consultation, letter, phone. *Resources*: newsletter. *Other*: HIV support group, evangelism, seminars, speaking engagements.

VIRGINIA

Set Free, PO Box 14835, Richmond, VA 23221. 804/358-8150 (M-F/9-4). Barry Anderson. *Serves*: men, women, family/friends, spouses, HIV+ persons (only men dealing with homosexuality), adolescent males. *Support*: groups (men, women, parents/family/ wives), individual lay consultation, letter, phone (M-F/9-4). *Resources*: audiotapes, library, literature, videotapes. *Other*: HIV/AIDS ministry (only men dealing with homosexuality), seminars, speaking engagements.

Sought Out, 168 Business Park Dr. #103, Virginia Beach, VA 23462. 804/631-0099. Katherine Allen. *Serves*: men, women, family/friends, spouses, children of gay parents, sexual abuse survivors (female, male), sexual addicts (heterosexual, homosexual), transsexuals. *Support*: Living Waters (men, women). *Resources*: audiotapes, literature, videotapes. *Other*: seminars, speaking engagements.

Regeneration – Northern Virginia, PO Box 1034, Fairfax, VA 22030-1034. 703/591-HOPE [703/591-4673]. Bob Ragan. *Serves*: men, women, family/friends, spouses. *Support*: groups – Fairfax, Falls Church, and Charlottesville, VA; individual lay consultation; phone. *Other*: literature, seminars, speaking engagements.

WASHINGTON

Metanoia Ministries, PO Box 33039, Seattle, WA 98133-0039. 206/783-3500 (M-F/9:30-5). Bob Brown. *Serves*: men, women, family/friends, spouses, adolescents (female, male), children of gay parents, sexual addicts (heterosexual, homosexual). *Support*: groups – Seattle, Tacoma (men, women, parents/family, wives, 12-Step/topical studies drop-in), letter, lic./prof. counseling, Living Waters (men, women), phone. *Resources*: audiotapes, library, literature, newsletter, videotapes. *Other*: seminars, speaking engagements.

Transformation Ministries, PO Box 55805, Seattle, WA 98155. 206/364-2306 (M-F/1-5). Carrie Wingfield. *Serves*: men, women, family/friends, adolescent females, sexual abuse survivors (female, male). *Support*: individual lay consultation, letter, phone (M-F/1-5). *Resources*: audiotapes, literature, newsletter, tapes, videotapes. *Other*: speaking engagements.

WASHINGTON, D.C.

Transformation Christian Ministries, 1017 12th St. NW, Washington, DC 20005. 202/371-0800 (M-F/9-5:30). Anthony Falzarano. *Serves*: men, women, family/friends, spouses, sexual addicts (homosexual), transsexuals, transvestites. *Support*: individual lay consultation. *Resources*: literature, newsletter. *Other*: men's live-in program, seminars, speaking engagements.

WISCONSIN

Broken Yoke Ministries, 25050 Bluemound Rd., Pewaukee, WI 53072 (Milwaukee area). 414/896-0841 (mornings; evenings). Bob Van Domelen. *Serves*: men, women, family/friends, spouses, pedophiles, sexual abuse survivors (female, male), sexual addicts (homosexual). *Support*: groups – Madison, Neenah, Pewaukee (men, women, parents/family), individual lay consultation, letter, lic./prof. counseling (on call), phone. *Resources*: audiotapes, literature, newsletter. *Other*: seminars, speaking engagements.

CANADA

BRITISH COLUMBIA

Another Chance Ministries, Burnaby Christian Fellowship, 7325 MacPherson Ave., Burnaby, BC, V5J 4N8. 604/430-4154 (M-F/9-5). Marjorie Hopper. *Serves*: men, women, family/friends, spouses, adolescents (female, male), HIV+ persons, pedophiles, sexual abuse survivors (female, male), sexual addicts (heterosexual, homosexual), transsexuals, transvestites. *Support*: groups (parents/family), individual lay consultation, lic./prof. counseling, letter, Living Waters (men, women), phone. *Resources*: audiotapes, library, literature, newsletter, videotapes. *Other*: evangelism, seminars, speaking engagements.

MANITOBA

New Direction for Life Ministries, PO Box 1493, Winnipeg, MB, R3C 2Z4. 204/943-6353 (M-F/9-5). Tye Gamey. *Serves*: men, women, family/friends, spouses, children of gay parents, HIV+ persons, pedophiles, sexual abuse survivors (female, male), sexual addicts (heterosexual, homosexual), transsexuals, transvestites. *Support*: groups (men, women), individual lay consultation, lic./prof. counseling. Living Waters (men). *Other*: seminars, speaking engagements.

ONTARIO

New Direction for Life Ministries, PO Box 1078, Stn. F., Toronto, ON M4Y 2T7. 416/921-6557 (M-Th/9-5). Patricia Allan. *Serves*: men, women, family/friends, spouses, adolescents (female, male), pedophiles, sexual addicts (homosexual), transsexuals, transvestites. *Support*: groups – Hamilton, Kitchener, Ottawa, Toronto (men, women, parents/family, wives), individual lay consultation, letter, lic./prof. counseling, phone. *Resources*: library, newsletter. *Other*: seminars, speaking engagements.

INTERNATIONAL CONNECTIONS

EXODUS EUROPE: True Freedom Trust, PO Box 592, London SE4 1EF, England. 081-314-5735. From USA/Canada: 011-44-81-314-5735. Chris Medcalf.

EXODUS SOUTH PACIFIC: Liberty, PO Box 308, Fortitude Valley, Queensland 4006, Australia. (07) 371-4705. From USA/Canada: 011-61-7-371-4705. Peter Lane.

Contributors

Michael Mazzalongo—Editor

Former Dean of Students at Oklahoma Christian University of Science and Arts. Served as missionary in French Canada, specializing in media evangelism. He was given a Religious Broadcasters Award in 1984 for his radio series "The Daily Gospel." He presently serves as the minister for the Choctaw Church of Christ in the Oklahoma City area.

Dr. J.R. Estep

Associate Professor of Christian Education at Great Lakes Christian College. Dr. Estep holds four graduate degrees in various fields of study including History, New Testament, and Christian Education. He is presently completing a second Doctorate in Education.

Dr. F. LaGard Smith

Dr. Smith is Professor of Law at Pepperdine University. He is the author of more than a dozen Christian books including the best selling *The Daily Bible*, *When Choice Becomes God*, *What You Need to Know About the New Age Movement*, and *Sodom's Second Coming*.

Dr. J.D. Robertson

Dr. Robertson is a licensed psychologist and serves in this capacity for the Campus Christian Fellowship at East Carolina University. He has also taught in this discipline as Professor of Counseling and Psychology at Johnson Bible College.

James Taylor

James Taylor is a nationally recognized speaker and advocate for the prevention of AIDS. His AIDS materials are listed with the Centers For Disease Control and Prevention. Mr. Taylor has specialized in presentations to high schools and colleges through his R.I.O.T. ministries based in Arizona.

Dr. Carl Bridges

Dr. Bridges holds his degree from Union Theological Seminary and has published over 30 articles dealing with religious subjects. He presently serves as Professor of Bible at Johnson Bible College in Knoxville, Tennessee.

Joe Dallas

Former Director of the International Ex-Gay Ministry Network, EXODUS. Mr. Dallas left the homosexual lifestyle to help others overcome this struggle. He presently directs Genesis Counseling, an ex-gay ministry center in Orange, California.

Bob Davies / Lori Rentzel

Bob Davies is the executive director of EXODUS International located in San Rafael, California. This is the largest ex-Gay ministry network in the world. Mr. Davies has written numerous articles featured in publications such as *Focus on the Family* and the *Moody Monthly*.

Lori Rentzel, formerly a counselor with Love in Action, an ex-Gay ministry. She is a freelance writer and editor based in California. Her most recent book is entitled *Emotional Dependence* (IVP).

Mike Hawkins

Mike Hawkins was diagnosed with AIDS in December of 1991. The disease has come close to taking his life several times but he has managed to establish the Christian AIDS Network which offers ministry to those who suffer with AIDS. Through C.A.N., Mike does work with AIDS victims as well as prevention education in schools and for community groups.